Mosque Jeddah

"Saudi Arabia: Travel Guide (Not Including Makkah)"

I hope you will find this book useful in planning your visit to Saudi Arabia

THANK YOU 🙏 FOR YOUR PURCHASE
Ibn Al Hamra

SAUDI ARABIA

EXCLUDING MAKKAH

IBN AL HAMRA

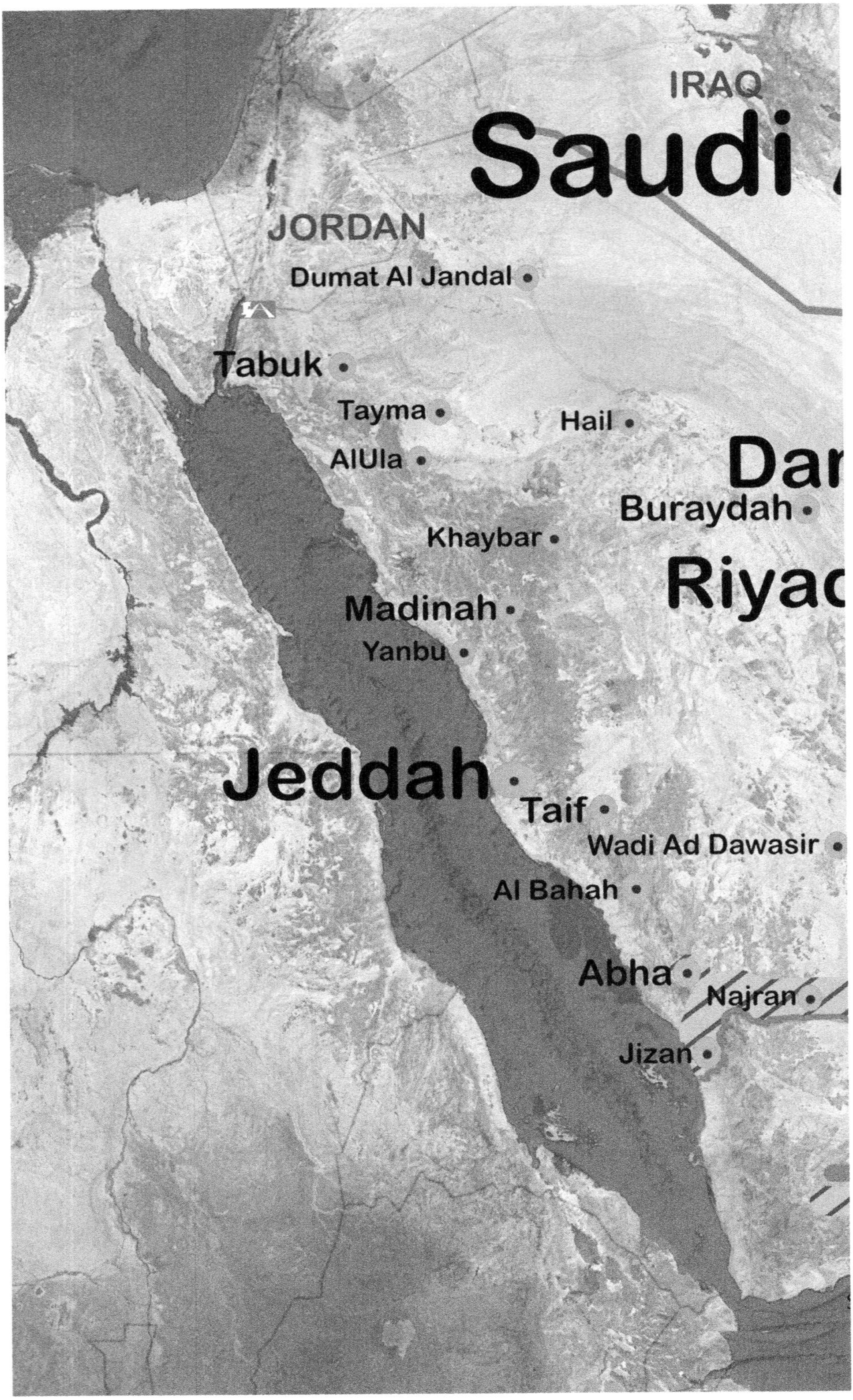
IRAQ
Saudi
JORDAN
Dumat Al Jandal
Tabuk
Tayma
Hail
AlUla
Buraydah
Khaybar
Riyad
Madinah
Yanbu
Jeddah
Taif
Wadi Ad Dawasir
Al Bahah
Abha
Najran
Jizan

Arabia

KUWAIT

mmam •

AlAhsa •

BAHRAIN
QATAR

dh •

U.A.E.

North

← 600 KM →

OMAN

YEMEN

Advise Against All Travel
Advise Against All But Essential Travel

🏔 international Border Crossing

SAUDI ARABIA – this map is not an authority on international borders

CONTENTS

INTRODUCTION

Saudi Arabia can be a fantastic country to visit, especially if you like to travel off the usual tourist routes - the country only issued Tourist Visas from 2019. Extraordinary scenery, remarkable historic sites and modern entertainment create an appealing destination. The book includes places of interest throughout the country, except Makkah. At some historic sites, you may be the only non-resident visiting a site – even the only visitor. The country is so large that this small book can only be an outline guide to Saudi Arabia. For some people, visiting only Jeddah and AlUla will be a great visit. For others, a more extensive, deep dive, exploration of the country may fit better.

In the book a brief overview of the geology of a site is given - so if you wish you will have an idea of what surrounds you. A quick history is also given. The maps are simple, far from the UKs Ordinance Survey - they give a broad overview rather than step-by-step options. Restaurant and Hotel listings are intentionally minimal - just to at least give a quick idea - and usually at the non-luxury end. There will be lots of hotels opening month after month - so a printed overview will be out of date even before its printed - and on-line booking sites will give innumerable reviews (hopefully real), rather than a one-person snap-shot.

Of course, this book is a limited glimpse of Saudi Arabia, so it cannot suggest if a visit to the country, or a specific place in Saudi Arabia is safe or right for you & your circumstances. Places to do some research on official opinions regarding visiting Saudi Arabia, include websites by your own government. Many government's foreign ministries give travel advice regarding Saudi Arabia Page22. These are broadly up-to-date and their advice also impacts personal travel insurance for a region. For instance, Najran Page181 is included within this book; however, all foreign governments absolutely advise against a visit to the town and surrounding areas. This advice against travel means many insurance companies will void claims made for incidents to visitors within the area. Your own insurance policy will give specific information about this.

For political and cultural views there might be coverage in your preferred media.

Options include The Guardian, Al Jazeera, Washington Post and Der Spiegal. There, of course, have been innumerable books published about Saudi Arabia. These will cover any topic a reader may be interested in.

Wide-ranging changes impacting visitors to Saudi Arabia might be made with no notice, and only become known when individual people become affected. These changes might include visa regulations & dress requirements. Opening times, costs and other issues will probably alter as tourism develops – so while effort has been made for the accuracy of the information in this book, no responsibility for any inconvenience, injury, or loss incurred by using this guide is assumed.

Some of the author's favourite places.

7/ **AlAhsa** – Souq Al Qaisariah in AlAhsa is a charmingly authentic market with a range of products aimed at the local population. I enjoy its proximity to other attractions and like the whitewashed Alamiriah School. The town has a relaxed atmosphere – adding to a holiday experience. For more see Page262

Souq Al Qaisariah

6/ **Jabal Fayfa** – this totally unexpected mountain rises up in a series of magnificent terraced agricultural fields. Looking down from the summit I found it extraordinary that each isolated minor-apex had a picturesque, whitewashed home – almost as if each were the castle for a ruler of their own mountain. A bonus, for me, is the different culture, if compared to the broad portrayal of Saudi. There is a drawback, that practically all governments warn against travel to this region of Saudi Arabia. For more see Page244

Fayfa

5/ **AlUla** is being heavily promoted as a destination, using the 3 core attractions of AlUla Old Town, Dedan and Hegra as marketing. Increasingly attached to these 3 are sports and cultural activities along with food-outlets. For me the biggest appeal of AlUla is none of these – it's the grand desolate scenery which towers over a river of Date Palms. For more see Page88

AlUla

4/ **Thee Ain & Rijal Al Maa** – are almost twin settlements, each of which climb up their own hill with a backdrop of wooded mountain slopes. I enjoyed both as each have their own distinct draw, a good information centre at Thee Ain & small museum at Rijal Al Maa - but for me the village ownership concept of Rijal Al Maa tips the balance. For more see Page217 & Page191

Rijal Al Maa

3/ **Najran** – beautifully located in a broad valley, with a ribbon of agriculture running though its heart, this a long way from the three massive cities which dominate the central band of Saudi Arabia. I enjoyed walking through its agricultural area - chatting with children and horse-men - with the scattering of mud-brick housing. Perhaps due to foreign governments issuing strong travel warnings against visiting the region, its places of interest are little visited by foreigners, despite their distinctive, attractive, local style. For more see Page181

Tower house Najran

2/ **Madinah** – the train journey from Jeddah to Madinah is excellent – matching some of the better trains in Europe. The Arabs might call my non-religious travel by it to Madinah a 'rahla'. The Prophet's Mosque is tremendous in scale and intimate in the emotions it creates. Tens of thousands of Muslims also arrived on the same day I did, as part of their journey of a lifetime. Many sat in the courtyards, some chatting with companions, others absorbing the experience. It demands a unique place in Saudi Arabia's places. For more see Page75

Prophet's Mosque

1/ **Al Balad** – with its ease of access, atmospheric streets and increasing number of cultural locations Al Balad is a must visit. I first visited it over 30 years ago, getting apprehended by the police for taking a video - fortunately I had asked the shopkeepers in the souq if they objected, all were very happy and as a result jumped in to rescue me from arrest. In essence its little changed physically since then – and possibly also little changed in a century - and far more open to tourism. The modern facilities of Jeddah in general, and its good international and regional communications simply add it its appeal. For more see Page44.

Bait Sharbatley

CHAPTER I
GETTING THERE

VISA

A visit visa (rather than resident or employment) for Saudi Arabia is available for citizens of 49 eligible countries (numbers probably will rise), including the **UK, USA, Germany** etc. Ensure your passport will be valid for at least 6 months from arrival – allow an extra period in case of travel delays.

There are 4 options to get a non-religious visit visa.

•An eVisa

•An on-arrival visa - either from a self-service machine at the immigration area - or a manned immigration counter.

•A 96-hour visa free of cost when flying with Saudia - or reduced cost with flynas - check their websites as this might change.

•A short-term pass if on a cruise-ship visit (say into Jeddah)

The cost of the **eVisa** is SAR535. At the moment this includes mandatory local insurance. The eVisa is valid for one year and allows multiple entries, with a maximum stay of 90 days per entry. This is valid for 1 year (with those multiple entry options) - check the terms on the website.

Visit the Ministry of Foreign Affairs Visa Portal: https://visa.mofa.gov.sa/Account/Loginindividuals - create an account using an email address and password. **A new dedicated Visa application site** https://ksavisa.sa/ is available - this is suggested by the https://visa.mofa.gov.sa so might become the official & only option. If you are one of the nationalities eligible for an eVisa there is no need to use any 3rd party's services.

Start a new visa application and select visa type as "Tourism Visa". Fill out the visa application with your personal and travel information - name, date of birth, passport details, anticipated date of arrival and departure. The passport-validity must be at least 6 months from actual arrival in Saudi. Don't expect that if there is a travel delay which pushes the validity on the wrong side the immigration person will waive this; so it's best to ensure there will be more than 6 months to cover any issues outside your control..

Scan your passport information page and a recent machine-readable passport-style photograph of yourself.

Select your tourist visa type and health insurance plan (insurance is mandatory as part of the application).

Pay the visa fee online using a credit or debit card.

Wait for the visa approval email – check the spam folder of your email, - it might take 5 days - or 5 minutes. Download your eVisa - have a printed copy available when you enter, and a version stored on your phone (you will then have 3 versions – the email, PDF on the phone & printout) so that at least something is available at immigration.

Though there is an **on-arrival visa** - it's entirely possible, especially on land borders, that an eVisa must be obtained in advance. For example, if crossing into Saudi by SAPTCO coach, the SAPTCO office may insist on seeing a visa approval before a person boards the coach. The government may fine bus companies and airlines for carrying passengers who do not meet the requirements to obtain an on-arrival visa, so transport companies always err on the side of caution and choose to refuse boarding. An eVisa is therefore highly recommended, irrespective of any tourism information through Saudi sites. On arrival cost SAR480 (incl. insurance): note the current difference in cost for an eVisa and an on-arrival visa.

For all visa types - ensure the passport is valid for 6+ months from date of arrival (ideally 6+ months from departure date). make certain your passport has enough blank pages when arriving – allow one empty page for the arrival stamp and one for the exit stamp.

VISA HAJJ & UMRAH For the Hajj, review the Saudi government site https://hajj.nusuk.sa/ and for Umrah www.nusuk.sa/

Insurance Included within your visa for Saudi Arabia is personal insurance, while in the Kingdom Page1. However, also having insurance from your own country when you visit Saudi Arabia is ideal. Third-party liability within Saudi Arabia is decided under a vastly different legal system to many Western countries. Therefore, any claims awarded in Saudi Arabia may attract a different compensation; usually, this will be less than in most Western countries. You will have to pay for medical treatment in Saudi Arabia. If appropriate, either through insurance or from your own pocket. Emergency evacuation in case of serious accidents needs to be considered. Review your own government's advice Page21

CUSTOMS

Importing goods and customs. https://zatca.gov.sa/en/RulesRegulations/Taxes/Pages/customs_individual/Prohibited-goods.aspx These regulations date from 2018 – that it before the opening of tourism. Expect there to have been unannounced changes based on several years of tourist arrivals.

Saudi law prohibits the importation of weapons, alcohol, narcotics, pork and pork products, and pornographic materials. Religious symbols, Crucifix, Hindu deities etc – these includes on Clothing or Jewellery. Personal videos, books, and magazines may be checked and be censored on arrival for Pornography – the definition of pornography is may be quite different from yours. In addition, customs officials might screen electronic devices for any material including things considered 'subversive' in nature. Consumer items like Binoculars, two-way Radio Transceiver are prohibited. Drones are in effect prohibited for visitors (https://uas.gaca.gov.sa/uas). Be circumspect regarding professional looking still Cameras and Video equipment as commercial permits for filming are required (review https://film.sa/ & https://misa.gov.sa/en/investor-journey-list/gcam/). There is zero tolerance for drug-related offences in Saudi Arabia. The penalties for the use of, trafficking, smuggling and possession of drugs (even residual amounts) are severe, up to the death penalty. Drugs include Codeine - because it contains an opioid. Similar issues cover alcohol. Your own government will have more information Page22.

Phones & SIM Cards If you intend to be in Saudi for more than a day or so - it's worth considering getting a local SIM Card (or eSIM) if your phone has a Dual SIM. They are easy to buy (Passport needed for ID) and available in many pre-paid options. Operators include STC, Mobily, Virgin, and Zain. STC probably has the most comprehensive network coverage - their visitor option is SAWA. SIM cards are available from phone company retail outlets (including at major International Airports) - or most mobile phone sellers. Talk through your needs & how long you will be in the country to ensure all the validities work for you - for example, do you need international calling? Having a VPN may be helpful. Recharge vouchers are available through mobile phone sellers and also supermarkets - large & small.

A local SIM will give you local internet access for app-based Taxi services, and if you will be driving, an option to use online map services without roaming charges - offline map options include Maps.me (download country) or Google offline maps. As in your own country, these mapping services may give incorrect driving instructions - use them cautiously.

Equally important, if you travel independently – a local SIM card will give you a local (disposable when you leave) number for WhatsApp messaging, which is relied on extensively in the country. This will mean you can communicate with service providers such as Car Hire, Hotels & so on – from a number they will know is a local Saudi one – and that they can call you, if needed.

Irrespective of the messaging service's claims regarding encryption security, online messaging services might be accessible by government officials in extremely security conscious Saudi Arabia.

INTERNATIONAL BORDERS

Saudi Arabia will soon (perhaps late 2024) have a Schengen style border agreement with the other GCC states (Gulf Cooperation Council – Bahrain, Kuwait, Oman, Qatar, UAE in addition to Saudi Arabia). This will have integrated systems that are likely to include the expected passport control and face recognition, vehicle registration, extraction of fines for traffic offences and criminal surveys.

Airports & Airlines

Saudi Arabia has many airports. There are three major international ones - Dammam - King Fahd International Airport; Jeddah - King AbdulAziz International Airport; and Riyadh - King Khalid International Airport.

Saudia www.saudia.com is the flag carrier for Saudi Arabia; there are other locally owned airlines, flyadeal www.flyadeal.com; Flynas www.flynas.com; Nesma www.nesmaairlines.com is an airline owned in Saudi but managed from Egypt; - and Riyadh Air www.riyadhair.com created in 2023.

Many other airlines fly into Saudi Arabia, including Air Arabia, British Airways, Emirates, KLM, Lufthansa, Qatar Airways, Turkish Airlines & Wizz Air. In general, transport from the airport into the city is reliant on taxi services. Jeddah has a train line which links the airport with Jeddah's Al Sulimaniyah Train Station - this is as far out of the city centre as the airport. Riyadh will have a Metro service, possibly open in 2024, which will link up to the city centre via an interchange at King Abdullah Financial District in the north of Riyadh. Secondary international airports include Abha International Airport, AlUla Prince Abdul Majeed bin Abdulaziz International Airport and Madinah Prince Mohammad bin Abdulaziz International Airport. Domestic airports serve most major cities.

Sea Ports

Ports that have ferry services include Jeddah and Duba Page69. Again, an eVisa is suggested along with complete original documentation for any vehicle, supported by suitable insurance and an international driving permit (Saudi Arabia requires the 1968 3-year version). If you are arriving with no car - and need to hire in Saudi - see Page32.

Cruise ports are Dammam, Jeddah, and Yanbu. For all visits, the cruise ship will handle entry requirements. The ports are in the town rather than kilometres from anywhere. There is a marina in Jeddah www.jeddahyachtclubandmarina.com that can handle private boats.

Land borders with neighbouring countries.

Jordan has the Durra/Aqaba border Page74 (on the west coast, and this border is advised in preference to the other Jordanian options) & less used for leisure (certainly not suggested) is Halat Ammar/Mudawara border (north of Tabuk), Al Haditha/Al-Omari. Iraq Arar (not readily useable for non-Saudi/Iraqi nationals as its newly opened). Kuwait - Al Khafji/Nuwaisib. Bahrain - King Fahd Causeway Page257. Qatar - Salwa/Abu Samra. UAE - Al Batha/Gheweifat. Oman - Umm Al Zamool/Ramlat Khaylah. Yemen (not useable by non-Saudi/Yemeni nationals). With all the land borders, there can be extreme delays - especially during holidays and religious pilgrimage times. Probably the only borders used by Tourists are the Aqaba, Al Khafji, King Fahd Causeway, Salwa, Al Batha – and the recently opened Umm Al Zamool.

SAPTCO https://saptco.com.sa coaches run between Saudi Arabia & Abu Dhabi, Ajman, Bahrain, Dubai & Sharjah. Dammam & Bahrain and Dammam & Abu Dhabi. Al Khanjry https://alkhanjrytransport.com/ offers a service between Riyadh and Muscat.

Obtaining a Visa in advance is suggested, and may be required by the bus management, irrespective of any other statements.

CHAPTER 2
GENERAL BACKGROUND

Weights & Measures Saudi Arabia uses the metric system - of weight, volume and speed/distance.

Time Local Time: Three hours + GMT (Greenwich Mean Time).

Telephone International telephone code +966 - there are area codes for fixed lines Riyadh - (0)11, Jeddah etc. (0)12, Dammam etc (0) 13 and so on. Mobile operators use (0)50 = STC (Saudi Telecommunication Company), (0)58 = Zain, (0)57 = Virgin – other codes are being added.

Internet domain .sa

Electricity Supply Electrical voltage 230 (rarely 127) AC 60Hz; British three-pin sockets are widely used and occasionally 2-pin European continental style. The UK is 230v and 50Hz, so Saudi power is usually compatible with UK standards, though you may need a socket adaptor.

The USA and Canada run on 120v and 60Hz; therefore, you need an adaptor for power and plug sockets. Australia runs on 230v and 50Hz so though you may not need a power adaptor but will need an adaptor for plug sockets. Adaptors may be available in a hotel - it certainly is in larger supermarkets and hypermarkets.

British style plug and socket.

Working Hours Work Hours: Government: From 08:00-14:00. Friday and Saturday are the weekend breaks. Companies: Office hours typically from 08:00-midday / 16:00-20:00 (or 08:00—17:00). Friday & Saturday is the weekend. Retail and services have longer hours. In major shopping malls, the working hours may be 10:00-22:00, with supermarkets working an hour on either side of this. Malls are typically open 7 days a week. Friday opening hours are after mid-day prayers – till late night.

Public Holidays in Saudi Arabia

Non-Islamic holidays in Saudi Arabia are based on a fixed date against the Gregorian calendar.

Feb 22 & 23 Foundation Day Government Holiday - private sector 1 day

11 March Saudi Flag Day National Holiday

Sep 22-25 National Day Holiday Government Holiday

It's worth also considering school holidays – almost 3 months – June - August

Mid-Year Holidays: two weeks during late December to mid-January.

Year-End Holidays: Around 12 weeks from early June until late August

Students also have the standard national holidays.

Islamic religious holidays start based on the actual sighting of a new moon's crescent. The Hijri calendar, as it is based on a lunar progression, is 10 or 11 days less than a Gregorian Christian calendar. These dates when dated in a Gregorian calendar are approximate.

Ramadhan 2024 11 March 30 days

Ramadhan 2025 1 March 30 days

Eid Al Fitr Holiday 2024 10 April about 7 days Government Holiday

Eid Al Fitr Holiday 2025 31 March about 7 days Government Holiday

Eid Al Adha Holiday 2024 17 June about 7 days Government Holiday

Eid Al Adha Holiday 2025 7 June about 7 days Government Holiday

Private sector businesses, especially service and retail, will often have a much shorter holiday period during these longer Islamic holidays.

Weather Saudi Arabia, in general, has sweltering summers, up to 50c+ and warm winters (November to February). In areas towards the coast, summer humidity is very high, especially directly on the coast, 85% is not exceptional. As perspiration will then evaporate more slowly - the body cannot cool itself quickly which can lead to Heat Exhaustion or even Heat Stroke. Also, on the coast, especially in The Gulf, fogs may form due to sharp nighttime air temperature drops in autumn. In the heights of the western mountains, temperatures are considerably lower by 10+c. In the far northwest in late winter (Jan-Feb), winter storms can spread from Jordan and beyond, bringing snow. Rain is rare throughout the country - though in the southwest, rain fronts spread from Africa from February - May. Note that all 'average' monthly temperatures given in media are what they say - the average of day and night, spread over a month - the daytime peak will be higher. For example - the average temperature in Jeddah in June may be shown on websites as 37c - however, the hottest temperature in Jeddah, so far, has been 52c - also in June, 15 degrees higher. In The Gulf summer, sea-water temperatures will top 30c - often 35c for weeks on end. The Red Sea will be several degrees cooler - rarely topping 30c in summer. In winter, The Gulf waters will range from 16-23c, and the Red Sea will drop to 20-25c. The temperature differences are mainly because of The Gulf being a shallow sea.

Saudi Flag - and Vision 2030

Flag: The flag has a green background – with white Arabic script – "There is no god but God; Muhammad is the Messenger of God.". This is the 'shahada' one of the 5

'Pillars of Islam' Page293. The flag, therefore, has special meaning and is absolutely not to be used on items that may be worn or damaged or used in a manner inappropriate for the word of God.

Media Within Saudi Arabia the media may be government owned, or self-censored to reflect the governments perspective. The internet is monitored and censored for what is considered offensive or subversive in any respect. Pornography or criticism of the government is included in this general area. As WhatsApp and similar phone apps operate in Saudi, it is reasonable to assume the government does have access to information transmitted, irrespective of any assurances to the contrary.

If you are arrested, prosecuted, or jailed for an offence against the law in Saudi Arabia, your own government is unlikely to be able to offer more than basic advice about lawyers who can act for you.

Government The Government of Saudi Arabia is a monarchy based on Islamic laws and culture. The King of Saudi Arabia, Salman bin Abdulaziz Al Saud, is the country's head of state. His son, Prince Mohammed bin Salman Al Saud, the Crown Prince, often referred to as MBS, was appointed Prime Minister in September 2022. This is the first time the Saudi King has not also been the prime minister.

The country is an absolute monarchy, and political power is concentrated within the Saudi royal family, especially the King and Crown Prince. There have been moves to reduce siloization of Government Ministries in favour of a centralised government. The government places restrictions on political expression, associations, and public assembly. Lese-majeste is covered under the country's royal decree on counterterrorism of 2 February 2014 and is robustly dealt with. The decree includes anything which "threaten Saudi Arabia's unity, disturb public order, or defame the reputation of the state or the king". Its scope extends to defamation etc of relatives of the monarch, dead or alive, and state apparatus.

The Council of Ministers, the Saudi Cabinet, is composed of around 30 members, including the King himself and the Crown Prince. Members of the Royal Family, have prominent and influential roles in all areas of Saudi Arabia, including politics and commerce.

Saudi Arabia does not have a formal written constitution – indeed regulations are more opaque than in Western democracies. The Quran and the Sunna (the traditions of the Prophet Muhammad) serve as the country's constitution. The legal system is also based on Sharia (Islamic law), with a system of courts that interpret the law in matters ranging from criminal offences to family disputes. There are no laws similar to the First Amendment or Habeas Corpus.

In 1992, Saudi Arabia established two advisory bodies, the Consultative Council (Majlis al-Shura) and the Provincial Council system. The Majlis al-Shura, composed of 150 members appointed by the King, selected "from amongst scholars, those of knowledge, expertise and specialists". There is a minimum 20% of the members who are female. The chairman is a member of the Al Sheikh family - descendants of Sheikh Mohammad bin Abdul Wahhab Page391 – the Al Sheikh family area also influential in many aspects of Saudi Arabia. The Shura Council provides the government with advice on public policy but does not have legislative powers.

The country is divided into 13 regions, each headed by a governor, who currently is a member of the Al Saud family, appointed by the King. These regions are further divided into governorates, sub-governorates, and municipalities.

Saudi Arabia has an increasing International influence. This is enabled as Islam was established within its borders; the substantial economic clout provided by oil; and the more recent very active use of both soft and hard power by the government.

A symbol of the government is present in many private homes and public places. The photo of King Salman, usually with a separate frame for Prince Mohammed, is on display. A third photograph of King AbdulAziz is frequently set in the middle of the King & Crown Prince. In some larger companies – each previous king of Saudi Arabia may have their own photograph of an equal size. Exceptionally, a photograph montage may have been used.

A focus of the government is **Vision 2030** www.vision2030.gov.sa. This is an ambitious plan for economic diversification, global engagement, and enhanced quality of life in Saudi Arabia. The plan was launched in 2016 by Prince Mohammed bin Salman. It will try and leverage the country's resources, strategic location, investment power, and centrality in the Arab and Islamic worlds. The vision has a number of pillars: including creating a thriving economy where everyone has the opportunity to succeed and a vibrant society in which all citizens can thrive and pursue their passions,. and an ambitious nation committed to efficiency and accountability at all levels, including building a government that is effective, transparent, accountable, empowering, and high-performing. Since the launch of Vision 2030, Saudi Arabia has implemented reforms in the public sector, the economy, and society as a whole. These efforts have led to improved government efficiency – through areas like web-based services, new growth and investment opportunities, greater global engagement, and enhanced quality of life for its citizens.

The government expects its authority to be unchallenged – by residents and visitors – and takes action to ensure compliance.

Economy: The national GDP in 2023 is estimated to reach US$1.061 Trillion (USA US$26.85 Trillion UK US$3.158Trillion all IMF figures). This makes it by far the largest Arab economy, its economy is greater than the other 5 Gulf Arab states combined. Oil and Natural Gas are the basis of this wealth; this is predicted to continue for the next century. Saudi Arabia is a moderately wealthy country in GDP per capita with around US$29,922 in 2023 (USA 80,034 & UK US$ 46,371, all IMF figures) – however, the wealth and income is concentrated towards the Saudi nationals, rather than the immigrant manual labourers. This means that the wealth of Saudi nationals will be greater than the raw figures suggest. Currently there is no direct income tax on personal income. However, there is Social Insurance (on non-Saudis 2% as the employer is directly liable for any health care costs and Saudis 22%, which is split between employee and employer), and Zakat (a religious tax @ 2.5% paid by Muslims). There are indirect taxes, such as VAT, and excise taxes on products such as tobacco. There are municipal taxes, customs duty, and hotel room tax (5%). Broadly, income from Oil, Gas and other government-owned industries is received by the government. This is then distributed through contracts and employment into the economy.

Education Saudi Arabia dedicates around 8.8% of its Gross Domestic Product (GDP) to education, nearly double the global average of 4.6%. The country, as a result, has a literacy rate of 98%.

The Saudi education model, free at all levels to nationals in state institutions, is overseen by the Ministry of Education and the Technical and Vocational Training Corporation (TVTC). The government supports the establishment of private kindergartens with technical and financial aid. School attendance is compulsory between 5-15. There are over 60 universities/colleges in Saudi Arabia; the oldest is the King Saud University, founded in 1957; the Princess Nora bint Abdul Rahman University was founded in 1970 and is the oldest female university. - providing education to over 1.4 million students in single-sex institutions. Overall most graduates, nationally, are female.

The King Abdullah government scholarship program, established in the mid-2000s, sponsors thousands of students each year to study at top educational institutions worldwide. As well as funding foreign university fees - a cost of living allowance is made of at least US$2,000. The use of this foreign education program is indicative of the government's focus on education and the perceived benefits of an education outside the Saudi system.

Population Capital: Riyadh, in the central plateau, is the capital, economic and population centre of Saudi. The Saudi Government assessed the mid-year population in May 2023 at 32,175,224. Saudi nationals 18.8 million – non-national 13.4 million. Males 19.7 million and females 12.5million – this imbalance is due to the substantial numbers of male immigrant workers in the country. Riyadh 6,924,566.00, Jeddah 3,712,917, Makkah 2,385,509, Madinah 1,411,599 and the Dammam conurbation at 1,386,166 are the largest cities. Except for Madinah - the majority of the population in each of these million+ cities are non-Saudi. 53% of the Saudi National population is under 25 years old. Of the non-Saudi population, 68% is aged between 25 and 49 - these are typically single males whose families remain in their home country. The government publishes a breakdown of non-Saudi nationals in the country - Bangladesh 2,116,192, India 1,884,476, Pakistani 1,814,678, Yemeni 1,803,469, Egyptian 1,471,382.USA 20,485 (females are by far the majority of American nationals), British 17,865 (with males the majority - Britain is the only Western European country detailed) and Chinese 14,619.

Uniformed Services The Saudi Arabian Armed Forces consists of the Royal Saudi Army, the Royal Saudi Navy, the Royal Saudi Air Force, the Royal Saudi Air Defense, the Royal Saudi Strategic Missile Force, the Royal Saudi National Guard, the Royal Saudi Guard Regiment and the Royal Saudi Border Guards. Military spending in 2021 was US$55.56 billion, broadly the same as Britain's military spending. In addition, there are the various Public Security forces, Special Tasks And Duties, Traffic department, Police department, Department of research and investigation, Criminal evidence department, Special Forces, Roads Security special forces, Diplomatic security special forces, Emergency special forces and Hajj and Umrah special forces.

MONEY, CARD USE, BANKS & MONEY EXCHANGE

The Saudi Riyal (SAR – sometimes within the country SR) has denominations of coins 1 riyal, 2 riyals - notes 5 riyals, 10 riyals, 50 riyals, 100 riyals and 500 riyals. Each riyal is subdivided into 100 halala. With coins 1 halala, 5 halala, 10 halala, 25 halala, 50 halala -

occasionally older people may call halala 'qirsh', the previous name of the coinage. The low-value coins are almost valueless; for example, 5 halala are less than 2cents.

SAR3.75 is the official fixed rate to one US$ - this means that the currency changes in value against the GBP, CAD, and AUD as they alter against the US$. Of course, buying & selling have a slightly different rate.

Saudi Cash

In the country, VAT levied at 15%, as well as other taxes that visitors rarely need to be concerned about - customs, social insurance, Zakat, etc. VAT is usually included in the price shown, as in Britain and Europe rather than an add—on as with sales tax in the USA - however, it's prudent to pay attention to it - especially on more significant expenditures such as hotel rooms and meals.

The government license and regulates all banks and money exchange companies in Saudi Arabia. Saudi Arabia has a large, visible banking sector. Most banks operate as Islamic Banks. All offer regular banking services. Staff will speak English - at least appropriate to their work. Major banks include The Saudi Awwal Bank (SAB, the local HSBC); Al Rajhi Bank, Riyadh Bank, and Saudi National Bank (the last three are the largest in the country). Working hours for all banks are 09:30-16:30.

ATMs are available throughout the country – with Arabic & English interfaces.. Irrespective of how you intend to pay for goods and services it will be prudent to make an early withdrawal from an ATM to verify that your card is compatible with the Saudi system – and so know that cash is available if required. It's doubtful there will be any issues in use. However, caution suggests that using ones attached to a bank property means the staff can help if needed. The service charge made against cash withdrawal depends on the bank that you use - and any specific agreement it has with the ATM provider. Typically you will be issued with larger denomination notes. If needed, change them within the bank or buy products in a large supermarket – many small shops do not carry sufficient change.

Money exchange companies are also regulated by the government. Exchange and transfer rates are incredibly competitive as their key customers are low-paid workers who transfer money home. This usually makes exchanging your own currency in Saudi Arabia more competitive – so no need to do this in your home country if it is a major economy with convertible currency. There are no worthwhile 'black market' exchange services. There is an informal, illegal transfer service, 'Hawala'. This originated centuries ago as a support to international merchants, but now also is used by the man on the street. The savings are minimal, the risk for a visitor is substantial, and the service should be avoided. Reputed companies include Al Amoudi Exchange, www.alamoudiexchange.com; Bin Yaala, www.byc.sa. As well as money exchange, most will provide transfer services like Western Union. Typical hours 08:30-22:00 (Friday 16:00-22:00).

Increasingly, even for small purchases in the very smallest shops, payment is by bank card, tap-and-go. You will have a small % service change through your bank. The internal system, Mada, is government-run. Domestically, it is compatible with Mastercard and Visa. However, maybe the card reader, on some occasions, will not accept a foreign card. This type of circumstance means that some cash should be held for payment. Google Pay & Apple Pay work in many locations.

Many large retail shops especially in Dammam, Jeddah and Riyadh will often accept the US$ & possibly Euro and other Arabian Gulf Currencies at good exchange rates. In smaller retail outlets that frequently deal with tourists, major currencies may be taken - with a slight premium against the exchange rates. Traveller cheques are only possible to use at the head office of a bank.

CULTURE

Language: Arabic is the official language; however, English is widely spoken and there are substantial numbers of Hindi/Urdu, Bengali and Tagalog speakers. Since 2021, English is taught from the 1st year at primary schools and in all other years. In general, there is a reasonable understanding of English, with many Saudis fluent to a well-educated native standard.

Family The Saudi nuclear family, Grandparents, Parents and Children form the key social unit in Saudi Arabia. The extended family, which includes first cousins and other cousins, creates additional units. Finally, the larger social unit, a Tribe, offers a social framework for its members and an identity familiar to other Saudis. The tribe's name is often the final part of a person's name 'Al xyz' (Al Balawi) – so an immediate association can be made.

A significant source of an individual's identity in Saudi Arabia is their Tribe. A Tribe is a group of people who share a common identity based, most times, in the belief they are descended from a single man and, by implication, his wives. However, maybe a Tribe is a historical accretion of smaller units that today share a collective identity.

Marriages are generally made with the parents' agreement, or the family has arranged or organised them. Marriages are often regarded as a legal agreement between the bride's and groom's families. A contract, Melcha (Milka), is drawn up and witnessed by suitable people, ideally including the Imam (religious leader) of the major local mosque. Typically, a dowry (mahr) is paid by the male's family to the female's, after agreement on what it should be. A theoretical upper limit is set by the government of SAR 50,000. This is different from, say, a marriage in a Hindu culture where a woman's family gives a dowery to the man.

Marriages from within the extended family account for a substantial proportion of marriages – approaching 40%. Within all marriages, first cousin marriages are common. Polygynous marriage is permitted in Saudi Arabia. Fertility rates (the number of children a woman has during her life) has declined rapidly to around 2.5% especially in major cities, so that now it is comparable to many western cultures.

The Shabka, a celebratory event, might be held by the families to present gifts. This celebration is followed by agreeing on the date for the marriage, which might be weeks or months away. Before the actual night of the wedding, a 'henna party' may be held for the females of the families, often nowadays in a hall specially built for weddings or hotel's ballroom. An event on the night of the marriage is held; the bride and females will have a separate venue from the groom and men. Only female guests usually attend the bride's party, perhaps with a strict no camera rule; however, the memory will be enhanced as guests receive a gift. At all celebratory events, the chief participants are at one end of the room and guests always formally greet them.

The men's event is complete with traditional dancing and music until, perhaps in a chain of hooting cars, the men's party leads the groom to his new bride. After marriage, typically at least one of the male children with his wife and children will remain living with his parents.

Within a family there is a male 'guardian', normally the father, whose permission is required by the family's females for many actions, including applying a marriage contract.

Traditionally, socialising occurs from within the extended nuclear family, with male members and female members forming separate groups during the week. Social activity, during the week, centres on coffee shops and modern malls, along with informal groups in parks and beachside locations.

At weekends, relaxing with the nuclear family is the focus, though as can be imagined, first cousins of both a husband and wife may be included as they are also the brother or sister of a spouse.

Town and Country Saudi Arabia has two non-religious intermingling cultures a Bedouin & Hadhr. Bedouin's were a nomadic population whose tribe may have had a territory enabling a form of a hunter/gather society to grow. The territory was acknowledged as their collective land that other people could enter with permission. Traits such as bravery alongside generosity, epitomised through hospitality, are core to Bedouins' culture. Alongside this culture is the 'Hadhr', a culture of settled people. The fixed location, based on agriculture & trade, for these Hadhr families allowed educational establishments to develop, commercial enterprise to develop fixed and social structures to grow. Honour of themselves as an individual and of their larger community is a key aspect of both these cultures.

Social Greetings

Greetings between members of the same sex is a matter of tradition, perhaps a 'cheek kiss', once on each cheek if you know of each other, maybe twice on the same cheek if you are more than acquaintances, a multiplicity if you are friends and haven't seen each other for a long time. A nose kiss may be given if they are perhaps from the same family. Occasionally, a person may kiss the forehead of another person; this is a sign of deference to that other person. Usually, during these greetings, the right hand is held, or the right hand is placed on the left shoulder of the other person.

Verbal greetings in Saudi Arabia are often formulaic and lengthy. Saudis enquire about the other person's health and family, and the other person reciprocates these. If between men, these enquiries are never about a man's wife, as traditionally this is considered disrespectful.

Between a Saudi and non-Saudi, a normal handshake will be used. Often the hand is held for a long time by people who are friends, it means just that – a friendship, nothing more. A male should wait for a female to offer her hand to shake.

Even if you have invited a Saudi person or group of Saudi people for coffee or a meal in a restaurant, there might be a good-natured disagreement after the meal amongst everyone who will have the 'honour' of paying for the meal. Each person will happily pay, especially if you are the only foreigner. However, if you have invited people insist; and accept the reciprocal invitation.

If invited into the 'Majlis' (sitting room) of a home, and you accept, remove footwear. Its possible that the house may practice gender segregation – if the house's females are present; however western males and females can expect to be hosted together. Often the host will not drink or eat with his guests, instead ensuring they are looked after, even if he has domestic servants. The hospitality may be through fruit (oranges etc and Dates) and Coffee. When the Coffee is finished, its time to express thanks and say goodbye. Do review the Dos and Don't's below.

Although achieving consensus is preferred, within Saudi Arabia decisions are top down and, except towards the very top, without having received any real delegation of responsibility or authority. This is the form of decision making in many businesses, where the culture is Arab and, to an extent, other Asian cultures. Even in the choice of restaurant, the senior person is deferred to. In businesses and areas such as meetings for work, a person is addressed using the type of their university degree or job title, followed by first name (not family name), Engineer Ahmed, Dr Fatima, His Excellency Khalid. To some extent, this explains some of the importance of achieving certification. Maybe a man is called Abu Mohammed or Abu Miriam; and here he is being acknowledged as a father (Abu). It is also a sign that he well known by the person who greets him, as they also know his child's name. A similar range of address terms are used for women though the term Umm, which means mother, is used.

Saudi clothing Clothing for both sexes is expected to be modest. Saudi men wear the white Thobe (it may be a dark colour in winter), either with a small stand-up collar (Mandarin style or western formal shirt collar). Both styles may have cuffed sleeves often worn with cufflinks. As well as the cufflinks, a stylish watch may be chosen, and frequently a pen in the Thobe's chest pocket. The Thobe is usually tailor made for the wearer, incorporating a choice of material quality, shade of material, overall design and fit. Under the Thobe, lightweight long sirwal pants are worn, and also a vest (undershirt). The Ghutra headdress is usually a heavily starched white cloth (the cloth may be red & white check or other design - especially in winter), formed from a square of material and folded once across two corners to form a triangle, the longest edge forms the front with the apex of the two shorter edges down the back. The headdress is worn in various styles according to the wearer's preference. Under the Ghutra is a small Ghafiya cap that provides some grip for the ghutra and stops the hair from touching the Ghutra. The black circle of rope, Agil, placed on Ghutra represents a previous use – a rope to hobble the front legs of a Camel; some religious men do not wear this on the Ghutra. In parts of the country a Turban may be preferred - though not on official formal or government work occasions. The men wear formal shoes, sandals or trainers/sneakers. Worn for prestige on special occasions such as weddings is a Bisht - a traditional long, white, brown or black lightweight Arabic cloak trimmed in gold thread.

The man's ensemble explicitly states the wearer's identity; he is a Saudi.

Saudi women typically wear a black (or another colour) cloak Abaya worn over the shoulders and reaches just above the ground. Over her head and covering the hair and neck is a scarf, Shayla, also known as a Hijab. Under this Abaya and Shayla may well be the latest fashion from New York, London, Paris or Milan, elaborate Lebanese style fashion or only jeans and T-shirt, along with western style underwear.

Society away from Jeddah, Riyadh, Dammam. Though women are an increasing part of the visible workforce (a stated 35%) and general public society, in areas away from the three major cities, Dammam, Jeddah, and Riyadh, women are less apparent in public. This means that female tourists are immediately more noticeable, more so if dressed in a style that is unusual in the region. Of course, there will be circumstances where women are very much present. Tuesday Market in Abha, which in any case is a larger town, is one example - as are events and leisure facilities targeted at families. Of course, times are changing, and every town and region will have its own social norms. Wealth is also noticeably different away from Dammam, Jeddah and Riyadh, especially in the northwest and southwest. NEOM, the massive development in the northwest, will eventually change income this area, the more successful it becomes. AlUla is already changing its region.

In general, though the younger population living in smaller towns may be well travelled, they will behave conservatively in their own district. Wherever you go a more positive response will be given to visitors who respect local traditions.

TOURISM OVERVIEW

The government is focused on diversifying the economy - part of this will encourage inward investment - much as Dubai did from the late 1970s; tourism is a crucial area. Currently the former CEO of the World Travel and Tourism Council is the 'Chief Special Advisor' regarding Saudi Arabia's tourism push. Locations such as AlUla illustrate this approach. Many of the operations there are government-operated entities, however the Royal Commission for AlUla actively supports small companies which provide suitable products & services. The stated aims include increased employment and diversification of the economy. The employment aspect will be obvious to visitors at AlUla. Tourism is also a part of the general re-branding of Saudi Arabia. Minor re-brands are illustrative, the previous cycle tour the 'Saudi Tour' has been renamed 'AlUla Tour'. The re-brand is targeting both the Saudi national and foreign audience. Its moving away from a pan-Arab & pan-Islamic identity to a more national identity; one with a more nuanced appeal. Though tourism visas have only been available since 2019, planning for permitting tourists into Saudi Arabia has grown since the Supreme Commission for Tourism was established in April 2000. World events, starting with the 11th of September attacks, put these plans on hold. In 2014, religious pilgrims were offered a 30-day extension to their stay to visit other areas of Saudi.

In this new, post 2019, tourism impetus, Saudi Arabia's pre-eminent place in Islam is emphasised along with associated historical structures, such as the mosques at Madinah. Non-religious historical sites, including AlUla and Diriyah, are being intensely developed, emphasising the ancient roots of the country and the lineage of the Al Saud family. In these sites, naturally, a curated viewpoint is provided. The country, however, offers a broad range of experiences for modern visitors – as it has done for people from Victorian period travellers though to foreign employees of ARAMCO oil company, and their families, since the 1930s. Alongside all this is an apparent focus to appeal to a Generation Z demographic (born from mid 1990s).

Purely leisure is being developed at vast NEOM and at The Red Sea resorts regions and at Qiddiya near Riyadh. Large scale pop concerts are held, featuring major stars of differing nationalities. Sport is a key element of this new tourism & branding Page18.

Despite the focus on leisure & tourism, what is missing (at the moment) is alcohol, which is an important part of a restaurant or hotel's income. The colossal spending in the northwest at NEOM & the Red Sea Resorts, and push into sports such as Formula 1 & the World Cup. might lead to change - perhaps local sensibilities/reactions may be found by allowing Diplomats to buy it. For example Heineken is a major sponsor/advertiser at Formula 1 & in Soccer.

Not all of this tourism development is simply for foreign visitors. Indeed, the introduction of inbound tourism has proceeded at the same time that many social changes in Saudi Arabia have also been made. These changes include the April 2018 permission for cinemas, music events and other popular entertainment generally, and the June 2018 permission for women to drive. Currently, internal tourism by residents is certainly being boosted & with the young national population in Saudi, events are targeting them in AlUla, Jeddah and Riyadh. These may dampen the regional appeal of Bahrain & Dubai in the mind & pocket of Saudi citizens (Dubai-Riyadh is a busier flight route than London-New York). At any event, expect some censorship to be imposed, for example a film shown in Saudi may have some editing to cut out a scene considered sexual. Cinemas are typically within major Shopping Malls, if you want to see a film.

A few service providers are noted – to allow you to at least have a start for needed research. Specialised activated such as Scuba have limited breadth & depth at the moment –**Game Fishing & Scuba** research through - https://swsdf.sa/ the National Accreditation Body.

Shopping In Saudi Arabia, the modern shopping experience is typically in a large modern shopping mall/complex. Here, depending on the individual mall, can be found major well-known franchised chains, including British stores, - Harvey Nichols, Marks and Spencer, Next and stores from the USA - Disney, River Island, Pottery Barn and so on. Local stores include eXtra, Home Centre, and Lulu they variously sell white goods, clothing and food (Lulu sell all). In these stores, bargaining is not usual, though seasonal sales are held. Staff will have a work-appropriate understanding of English. Especially in Dammam, Jeddah and Riyadh, there are several streets in each city that have a broad range of shops as a 'high street' type experience - though typically, these are driven along rather than walked. These usually have mid-priced businesses, often with branded goods, and some bargaining is not unusual - seasonal sales are held. In most population centres, there will be an area of low-cost retail stores, typically near the town centre. This is what to many visitors is a souq, such as Al Balad's Souq Al Alawi or the Tuesday Market in Abha. These will have un-branded or occasionally fake brands - negotiation is normal, and this acts instead of a sale - English will, mostly, be minimal. In these street-type settings - shops that sell a particular product type tend to cluster together, much like flocks of birds. So you will find many mobile phone shops close to each other, many footwear shops within a few steps of each other and so on.

For purchases of snacks and drinks, look for small supermarkets (grocery shops). In the main, these can be identified by a yellow graphic representing a shopping trolly (a government logo initiative) – negotiation/discount is not done here.

Small Supermarket & Shopping Trolley Logo (left)

Products like dates can be found in large supermarkets and specialised street shops. Larger supermarkets can be very good – with a wide selection of food, both locally sourced and imported. Familiar brands should be available, local versions are often on the shelves. When in larger supermarkets there may an assistant to help pack your purchases – for large loads tipping is appropriate as per petrol stations. In these and in small supermarkets plastic bags are used unnecessarily (in many shops they are free) – be clear if you do not wish one. Card payments are possible, and in larger supermarkets in major towns they may accept foreign currency at a reasonable exchange rate.

Previously, all businesses were required to close during prayer time - now they are no longer required to do so, but, especially in rural areas, many still do.

Sport Saudi Arabia is rapidly becoming a key player in many sports. There are an increasing number of major sports events held in the country. The Dakar Rally, held in Saudi Arabia since 2020. This motor rally is held from AlUla Page88 in late December to early January. In Diriyah Page143, the Diriyah ePrix, an electric motor race, is held in late January. In late January/early February, the AlUla Tour www.thealulatour.com cycle race takes place at AlUla. This is under the Tour de France umbrella. The LIV Golf tour is a Saudi-owned golf tour. It plays at Royal Greens Golf & Country Club north of Jeddah at King Abdullah Economic City Page54 during October. In December, Jeddah Page42 hosts Formula1 in the Kurnaysh; in December - it's a floodlit night-time event. A Formula 2 race can be seen on the same circuit in March. The Formula 1 race may be transferred to Qiddiya (Page134) southwest of Riyadh. or Saudi Arabia might host the event at each circuit. Numerous one-off events are held, including basketball, boxing, camel races, equestrian and tennis. Saudi has also made a move into yachting – with an America's Cup event, supported by NEOM, being held off Jeddah. In 2029, the Asian Winter Games will be held within the area developed by NEOM Page70 at Trojena. In 2034, Riyadh will host the 22nd Asian Games in Riyadh.

Football (Soccer) is rapidly becoming a focus for the government. International stars of the game have been recruited to play for local clubs, including some of the 18 First Division teams - Al Ahli (Jeddah), Al Ettifaq (Dammam), Al Hilal (Riyadh), Al Ittihad (Jeddah), and Al Nassr (Riyadh) - and more. Football's 2034 World Cup is also to be held in the country as there are no other bidders. These major events will require massive infrastructure upgrades – and may impact some areas covered here.

This focus on sports is not new, though it has accelerated recently. In the mid-1970s, Saudia (airline) became a major sponsor in Formula 1 of the Williams team - it was renamed Saudia-Williams and became champions. A member of the Royal family started the move into the English football league with a purchase of 50% (increased later to 100%) of current Premier League team Sheffield United in 2013.

SAFETY AND FITTING IN WITH THE CULTURE

Saudi Arabia is a conservative country, by natural inclination and requirement by the government. Within local society people behave in a way that fits in with the expectations of that society, whether it's the clothing worn, general behaviour or response to how they themselves are treated. Stand-outs may receive a 'cold shoulder' and more. As a visitor you will be given some elasticity depending on the specifics of the situation and if you are in the centre of Jeddah, or a small village near Buraidah. You are also treated, when you are a tourist, with extra grace as the government is making it clear that foreign tourists are in the country through the government's authority. Using your left hand will receive minimal attention, kissing in public will get more, and playing loud music outside a mosque at prayer times will get a quick, negative response. In general you will get a more positive reception if you adhere to the values of the society you are in. This covers the clothes you wear, the courtesy you show to others, your general behaviour and your obvious attempt to fit in with their culture.

The government wants you to have a positive experience, they also do not want local society to be disrupted by tourists.

Language Use Language that might be considered abusive or gestures that can be construed as offensive can attract police action. This might be even if they are made within the 'privacy' of your car, towards another road user. Penalties might include prison and fines. In all situations, remain calm and respond politely. If matters escalate - call the police Page22.

Social Intimacy Living together whilst unmarried is officially prohibited. Any intimacy (kissing, holding hands, etc) in public between men and women (this might include between parent & older child) can lead to arrest. Penalties might include arrest and a potential court case where the judgment can consist of a fine, a custodial sentence and deportation once the sentence is complete. This is especially so where the behaviour has caused offence. Do not assume that a foreign worker in a hotel will be more 'liberal' than the Saudi government. They may well come from a culture that is equally or more conservative.

LGBTQ+ Overall, the approach by the Saudi authorities towards LGBTQ+ people is similar to towards behaviour by heterosexual people, as above. Homosexual sexual activity will carry additional penalties. It's also illegal to be transgender. Transgender people travelling to Saudi Arabia are likely to face significant difficulties and risks if the authorities discover this. Review your own government travel advice Page22.

Safety Do's & Don'ts
Dos:
•Do review your own government's travel advice to Saudi Arabia Page22
•Do dress conservatively - cover shoulders and knees, avoiding tight/revealing clothing. Women should consider wearing an abaya in public – certainly wear clothing that is loose fitting and covers the body and limbs. Be respectful of the local dress code.
•Do use only your right hand for eating or accepting gifts. The left is considered unclean.
•Do ask before taking photos of people, especially women.
•Do stand when a senior person, particularly a Saudi, enters a room on a social or business occasion, - this is part of the social norm, handshakes are usually made along with polite comments.
•Do accept offers of Arabic coffee, 'Qahwa' Page276, and dates when visiting a Saudi home.
•Do respond with a positive viewpoint on Saudi Arabia in conversation.
•Do respect customs, and cultural and Islamic traditions when visiting Saudi Arabia.
•Do use formal titles or qualifications Page14 - these may include Royal Highness, Highness, Sheikh, Doctor, Engineer - followed by the persons first name - for example, Engineer Ahmed - when addressing Saudis until invited to use first names.
Don'ts:

Regarding any activity, entertainment or political commentary, the government makes a clear distinction between, for example, state-approved activity, such as comedy shows on TV, or dance routines at major pop concerts which are held at the approval of the government, and a similar activity created by an individual or group and uploaded on TikTok/YouTube. So despite, for example, Nicki Minaj, The Black Eyed Peas, Sean Paul, and DJs David Guetta and Tiesto playing concerts - individuals dancing to or performing their music on the street may well face prosecution under public decency laws. Despite the apparent sea-change and relaxed atmosphere, the country is extremely protective of external perceptions.

•Don't discuss politics or even obliquely suggest criticism of the royal family or country. Check - lese majesty Page8 to understand more.

•Don't publicly compare Saudi Arabia & its organisations unfavourably with other countries - or organisations.

•Don't criticise an individual, especially to their face. This is avoided even between Saudi nationals, and should 100% be avoided by a non-Saudi.

•Don't publicly carry or wear religious symbols - or products from other countries that may be opponents Saudi Arabia.

•Don't assume that it is only the government with conservative values - much of the local population (of both genders) is also very conservative - especially away from urban areas (as in your own country).

•Don't engage in 'pranks', especially publicising them on social media. The government writes "posting pranks on social media is a crime in Saudi Arabia, and it is classified as a violation of the country's Anti-Cyber Crime Law. The punishment for such crime ranges from SR500,000 to SR5 million (and) or imprisonment from six months to three years."

•Don't play loud music; this applies to car entertainment systems and within a building. Always turn music off at prayer times.

•Don't be close to an unrelated member of the opposite sex - especially a Saudi - for example, when using an escalator leave more space than you might in your own country - avoid absolutely being alone in an enclosed space - such as an elevator - with them. If needed, exit the space - it helps avoid potential problems for both people.

•Don't display public affection between opposite genders - who may appear to be adult.

•Don't engage in LGBTQ+ oriented issues - these may include same-sex affection, cross-dressing, discussing these issues and wearing clothing or symbols associated with LGBTQ+ issues. In June 2022 authorities seized products with rainbow colours or in rainbow packaging from shops in the country as they "violate the rules of Islam and public morals like promoting homosexuality colors" a Ministry of Commerce official stated.

•Don't use your left hand to shake hands, touch food, or gesture at someone.

•Don't accept food or gifts with your left hand.

•Don't display the soles of your feet - where possible. In many instances, this is not possible - an example connected with everyday life for Saudis is at prayers - when the row behind each row does have feet exposed to them_.

•Don't drink alcohol or eat pork products. They are forbidden and should not be available.

•Don't gamble - or bet on anything. This is proscribed in Islam.

•Don't photograph government buildings, palaces of members of the royal family, military sites or uniformed personnel.

•Don't photograph accidents - ask permission (if appropriate) regarding ones involving you.

•Don't bring into the country or use prohibited drugs. Saudi Arabia has the death penalty, and if convicted of drug crimes - your own government is unlikely to be of any help.

Note - that although alcohol and prohibited drugs are banned - they are illegally available. Do not show any interest at all in any offer to sell them to you - there is a death penalty for a wide range of crimes - including ones connected with banned substances. Alcohol was banned absolutely in 1952 by King AbdulAziz. It might be that Saudis engage in one or more of the don'ts. They understand the consequences and have their own support network if they need to deal with those consequences within Saudi Arabia.

Minding the do's and don'ts will help make any visit more positive.

A brief overview of an applicable law is available in Arabic https://laws.boe.gov-.sa/BoeLaws/Laws/LawDetails/3b96a591-47c8-4469-9abb-aa4700f1aa52/1

Ministerial Resolution No. 444 9 April, 2019. Though vague, key sections include Article 3 - "A person who visits a public place must respect the culture, traditions, customs, and values prevalent in the Kingdom. Article 4 No person shall appear in a public place wearing indecent clothing or clothing which bear images, shapes, signs, or phrases that violate public decency".

Safety Travel Advice Refer to your own government's safety advice for Saudi Arabia. Travel warnings of various types are placed within Saudi Arabia. The British government specifically "advise against all travel to within 10km of the border with Yemen". Yemen is a focus due to an ongoing internal & at times, external conflict - news-media will provide regular updates. Both Fayfa and Najran are within 10kms of the border. Advisories include a warning by the US government against travel within at least 50 miles (81 km) of the convoluted Yemen border. Areas within this zone include Farasan, Jizan, Dhahran Al Janoub, Abha, Fayfa and Najran. Most government's issues similar travel advice for Abha & areas south of its latitude. To the east, travel to Qatif, Tarout and Al Awamiyah, and centrally Al Qassim region are also sometimes advised against by various governments. The Iraq border is also an area where travel is advised against. This is noted by the British government as being a Saudi government requirement with "up to 30 months' imprisonment and a SAR25,000 fine". These restrictions may impact your travel insurance validity in any place under these exclusions.

Note that many of the areas covered by these travel advisories are where Embassy staff of many countries are prohibited from travelling to. This means that no face-to-face assistance is possible, and any person with any difficulty will have no direct support.

As a British citizen, for example, the British Government warns against 'all travel' or 'all but essential travel' to any destination before you get there, you may not be covered at all by your travel insurance – review your policy for specific details and its policy regarding your own government's travel advice.

The advice by your own government can be searched for within their foreign

ministry   websites.   Examples   include   www.travel.state.gov/destination;
www.gov.uk/foreign-travel-advice/saudi-arabia.   The   French   government
www.diplomatie.gouv.fr additionally notes specific security concerns in Jeddah.

General Safety For most visitors and residents, Saudi Arabia, is a safe country, with
few physical assaults or robberies. Although crime rates are low, crimes of all sorts do
happen in Saudi Arabia, though they are rarely reported. Use the same care about your
safety, credit card, passport and personal possessions as you would at home. Driving
may be the most worrying safety issue in Saudi Arabia.

Passive health and safety features in public places are often missing; these can be as
basic as not having handrails on steep stairs. It therefore pays to give more attention to
your immediate environment and the impact it may have on your safety.

Compared to many Western countries, the provision of support for people with any
sort of special needs may not be as developed everywhere. Contact any service provider
well in advance regarding particular requirements.

Driving standards will be different from those in your own country. Always drive
cautiously, Page35 and use the defensive driving technique - anticipating how situations
around you might evolve.

For most visitors the areas above are unlikely to impact their stay – for example if on
a group tour the service provider should deal with all these aspects in terms of where a
tour visits, and the capability of their staff. The information is given here for awareness
so that comprehensive, research can be made by each individual for their specific
circumstance.

Safety Emergencies
•**Ambulance: 997**
•**Coastguard: 994**
•**Fire etc: 998**
•**Highway Patrol: 996**
•**Road accidents: 993**
•**Tourism call centre: 930**
•**Police: 999**

The police have several divisions. For most visitors, the Traffic department, Road
security special forces, and general Police department will be the only ones they are
likely to be in contact with. Throughout the country, especially outside towns, there are
fixed and temporary road checkpoints. Here, identification and driving documents may
be requested. The checkpoints are typically police-operated, though the army may also
operate some. Slow down, stop if required or continue if waved through. Major
checkpoints will have high-tech security equipment, including overhead cameras with
the most up-to-date recognition systems.

Towns of, say, 6,000 people+ will have a police station. Unfortunately, the building
design varies, rather than a standard style, and may appear as a house or apartment
block - signage is usually only in Arabic; however, some have English. The signage style
also varies in design. The stations in larger urban areas have an air of security about
them; again, there is no common design.

CLOTHING TO WEAR

Both men and women are expected and required, by the government, to dress modestly. This applies to citizens, residents, and visitors. Also conceal Tattoos, though the HipHop stars performing in Saudi and Footballers playing might be covered, local culture may be offended by them.

When visiting, loose-fitting, non-opaque clothing is suggested. Men could choose long trousers and a comfortable shirt. Long sleeves protect against sunburn if you are sensitive to the sun. For women, again, loose-fitting trousers - or long dress/skirts. A blouse with a high neck and long sleeves is ideal. Wearing a head scarf is essential if visiting a mosque and is suggested when walking in remote villages. Wearing an Abaya (the black cloak) is no longer required for females - however, it helps merge into the crowd, if you wish. They are relatively inexpensive and available throughout the country - shades other than black are available in many shops. To protect against the strong sun, you are along the Tropic of Cancer, consider a hat with a brim & using sunscreen.

If visiting a mosque – footwear must be removed. Men should wear long trousers and conservative long sleeved shirt. Women should wear loose fitting opaque clothing, so that only the face, hand and feet are visible. Use a large scarf – and for an easy coverall do buy the black cloak (Abaya).

If visiting Saudi Arabia during Ramadhan be especially respectful of the dress suggestions when in public.

Beaches Wearing Speedo style trunks or Bikinis should be avoided, unless within a 5* hotel, & even then the hotel might have a policy requiring loose short style trunks just below the knee for men and a more modest one-piece costume for women. In public beaches women bathing will fall under the public modesty regulations, a Burkini might be acceptable - be cautious regarding this and observant regarding the local norms. Its far better to use hotel beaches. Pure Beach in King Abdullah Economic City (Page54) offers a private beach https://visit.kaec.net/ with general activities having a less restrictive dress code, +966558211919 from SAR200 pp on weekdays. In the east Dana Beach Resort south of Al Khobar Page257 www.dbr.sa has similar policies & services priced from SAR99

You, doubtless, will see residents of Saudi wearing clothing, or behaving, at odds with the government's expectations. They are aware of local requirements and, if making any infringement of local regulations, have a support network to deal with resulting issues. Minor consequences, such as short-term jail, are less likely to be totally disruptive to them than a visitor.

HEALTH

Ensure you have insurance to cover you for medical treatment, making sure you are covered for existing conditions, as you will have to pay for medical treatment in Saudi Arabia - see the entry visa insurance Page1. Emergency evacuation in case of serious accidents needs to be considered. Review your own government's health advice Page22. At least 8 weeks before your trip, check the latest country-specific health advice from your own government so you can have any vaccinations, if needed. Your own vaccine requirements and places you intend to travel to (or have travelled from) will cause considerable difference, even to a person you travel with. General information on travel vaccinations and a travel health checklist is available on the British NHS website www.fitfortravel.nhs.uk/home also https://travelhealthpro.org.uk. In the USA, review wwwnc.cdc.gov/travel. You may then wish to contact your health adviser or pharmacy for advice on other preventive measures and managing any pre-existing medical conditions while you're abroad.

Pay attention to medical advice regarding Hepatitis vaccine suggestions. Malaria and other mosquito-borne diseases incl Dengue. Respiratory infections of course include COVID-19 – in Saudi they also include MERS-Cov (a Camel born infection related to COVID-19 – but with greater mortality). Your health adviser may review outbreaks of other infectious diseases include Meningitis. During the Hajj period, the influx and concentration of people does increase transmission of air-born infections. Rabies is also a transmittable disease that they might review with you, as it is present in Saudi Arabia and any animal is a potential host and, if unvaccinated, an infection is commonly regarded by medical experts as fatal. Your health provider may offer advice about diseases carried by sandflies, ticks and water snails as these snails may carry Schistosomiasis (bilharzia), as any fresh water is a potential host to the snail. Other animals that can cause illness include snakes & and scorpions.

Consider the weather. In Saudi, winter temperatures of 30c in the southwest coast are not unusual - and summer temperatures throughout the country may approach 50c. These high temperatures can be fatal, especially with high humidity - even with non-strenuous activities - more energetic ones may be inadvisable. Ensure you drink water before becoming dehydrated.

In Saudi Arabia, most water for human use is desalinated. Transmission through pipes & storage in water tanks in the heat impact safety therefore ask your health provider for information regarding drinking water safety. Bottled, safe to drink water, is cheap and widely available. If needed to help with rehydration - isotonic drinks are available. The Japanese brand Poker Sweat is the most commonly available. It would be prudent to carry your up-to-date vaccination details, including COVID-19.

Health Care Health care in Saudi Arabia is a national system providing free universal health coverage through government agencies for Saudi citizens. The system is ranked among the top 26 in the world for high-quality health care. As the critical government body, the Ministry of Health is responsible for preventive, curative, and rehabilitative care. Health care in Saudi Arabia is provided without direct charge to all nationals at the point of use. There are over 2,500 health centres of various sizes throughout the country. Most small towns/large villages will have a health centre. Major cities will have hospitals comparable to those in the USA/UK and so on. All are under the supervisory umbrella of the Ministry of Health, although there is a separate system within the armed forces. There is a licensed private sector. This has every size of facility, from major hospitals, down to individual specialists. Major private hospitals include Dr. Soliman Fakeeh Hospital www.fakeeh.care/, International Medical Center Hospital www.imc.med.sa/ in Jeddah; Dr. Sulaiman Al-Habib Hospital Arrayan Hospital https://hmg.com/ in Riyadh, Saudi German Hospital in Dammam https://saudigermanhealth.com/en. Expect to find the doctors in larger hospitals speak excellent English and in others have a reasonable understanding. The visa into Saudi currently has mandatory health insurance - the insurance issuer will direct you to their partner hospital if a claim is made.

The Ministry of Health is not the only entity involved in health care provision. Several other government agencies, including the Ministry of Defense and Aviation, the Ministry of Interior, and the Saudi Arabian National Guard, offer primary, secondary, and tertiary care to specific enrolled security and armed forces populations. Additionally, the Ministry of Education provides immediate primary health care to students. The Ministry of Labor and Social Affairs operates institutions for the mentally ill and custodial homes for orphans.

In terms of budget allocation, the health sector has seen a significant increase over the years. From a budget of 39million SAR in 1956, the allocation rose to 68.7 billion SAR in 2011.

There are pharmacies in cities, towns and many large villages. You should have little difficulty in locating one. Private 24-hour pharmacies are found in cities - and chains that offer them include Nahdi www.nahdionline.com and Al Dawaa www.al-dawaa.com. A franchised Boots Chemist (UK brand) is available in shopping malls in Dammam, Jeddah, and Riyadh. Medicine is well-regulated by the government, and many products are price-controlled. Brands you are used to will be available or an equivalent. Staff will have reasonable to excellent spoken English.

Water Desalination In Saudi Arabia, most water for human use is desalinated; other sources are fossil underground water and a limited amount from water dams. Desalination is made by various means. Flash desalination mainly relies on the heat generated by power stations to evaporate water, which is then condensed. Reverse osmosis desalination is, in effect, a filtration system. A move into using solar-powered desalination has been made. All these desalination processes produce safe-to-drink water out of the plant. However - passage through pipes, which may be old, and storage in old tanks may result in some contamination. This means it is prudent to use bottled drinking water, which is inexpensively available nationwide. Grey water is often recycled into irrigation systems - for example, the landscaped areas in major cities.

Altitude in Southwest. Between Taif and Abha - the escarpment rises well above 2,000m, giving a much fresher climate. It also means that altitude sickness is a possibility - most especially in the higher areas, towards Abha, when taking exercise. Symptoms of altitude sickness include headaches, exhaustion, tiredness etc. Your health provider may suggest a rest period of several days and that paracetamol may relieve symptoms. Consult your own healthcare provider for individual advice.

RESTAURANTS AND HOTELS OVERVIEW

RESTAURANTS Lower-cost restaurants have been focused on in this book as they offer a different experience to most restaurants in Western cities. Many local restaurants away from major towns only have the sit-on-the-floor option, perhaps in a separate partitioned area for each group. In these, food is served on a tray – typically with dishes of rice, meat and usually a curry sauce. Eating with the washed right hand is the custom. Either bring cutlery with you or ask for some if you prefer. The food can be delicious in these lower-cost restaurants – though hygiene & service may fall short of, say, McDonalds or 5* restaurants. However, in most cases, food is freshly cooked. As a suggestion - in all except the best restaurants / McDonalds type- avoid salads/uncooked vegetables.

Throughout the country, there are small cafe-style options. These offer a variety of inexpensive snacks - often only as a 'takeaway'. The offering includes Shawarma bread (Pitta bread/ Malawach/Paratha) filled with meat, and Shakshouka (egg omelette with tomato, onion and spices) offered with bread, Naan etc. The cost - less than SAR10 - add in bottled water at about SAR2+. Self-catering accommodation (apartment style) means you can buy food from a supermarket and cook it at home, so you are certain what has gone into the meal.

As in most countries, there is a wealth of eating options in Saudi Arabia. Dammam, Jeddah, and Riyadh offer world-class restaurants to dine in, often within major hotels. In AlUla and Diriyah, there are a few reasonable options. So far, there are no Michelin-starred or 'destination' restaurants - doubtless, this is a government target. Major supermarkets like Lulu, Carrefour and Panda not only have a remarkable range of non-cooked food – but also many have a cooked food and ready-to-eat meal section. Usually, cutlery is available in their homeware section.

In many of these local restaurants - there are sections marked 'Families/Family Section' - where women & their family normally eat. If there is no family section, ask where to eat if a woman is in your group. Do not override local norms with your own preference regarding the location in a restaurant you wish to eat in. fitting in with local customs is the polite norm, especially in remote areas.

Most larger towns will have restaurants that specialise in the cuisine of the key non-Saudi workforce. Therefore, authentic Filipino, North Indian, South Indian, Turkish, etc., are often in the town centre. They will be inexpensive and of quality and price to attract back the resident population.

Throughout Saudi – most local restaurants work in Arabic or other Asian languages. The outside signboards are often only in Arabic, which means most English speakers (readers) will not be able to read a sign at a glance. The names given here are transliterations – so you could use them to ask for the place.

Do consider that in Saudi Arabia specific dietary needs may not be understood and that *catering for allergies may be impossible* because of the cooking methods used. Lower-cost restaurants and their small kitchens will certainly mix their cooking utensils - as well as add all sorts of ingredients to food. Unlike in many places in the UK you will not be asked about allergies – it is down to you to research. Staff may not really understand what an allergy – even with the best Google translation. If you are allergic to any food - it's best to avoid many of the restaurants listed here. Opt instead for upmarket hotel restaurants and specifically make your dietary needs clear to a supervisor in the restaurant you choose. Ensure they fully understand your meaning and are not simply agreeing, without comprehension.

Al Baik

AS WELL AS CHAINS OF FAST-FOOD RESTAURANTS YOU ARE FAMILIAR WITH, the country has local country-wide chains of fast-food-type restaurants – some may have a drive-through section – all may do a takeaway. These chains are not listed in this book for most individual towns. You will become familiar with them when travelling. They offer consistent standards and are well worth looking into - the non-McDonalds/KFC style outlets offer popular local-style food. You may find a calorie count on their menu items – but not ingredients or allergies; again, avoid these if you have any food allergies. These restaurant chains include **Al Tazaj** (www.taza.com.sa) – with a range including chicken & rice; **AlBaik** (www.AlBaik.com) – comparable to KFC & this is probably the most well-known chain; **Herby** (www.herfy.com - part of the same group as Panda supermarkets) similar to McDonald's; **Kudu** (www.kudu.com.sa) offering an extensive range of a mix between Arabic & western fast food. **Shawarma King** (https://shawarmakingsa.com/) is a shawarma-style fast food; **Zaatar w Zeit** is a complete meal selection of mainly Levantine-style food. **Al Romansh** (http://www.alromansiah.com/) – with its distinctive mauve-colour signboard, this country-wide chain offers traditional food, rice & meat-based menu – in a fast-food environment. **Raydan** (www.raydan.com.sa) is traditional rice and meat with side dishes, Saudi style). This is in the west in Jeddah and Abha – the restaurants are modern and clean – with a distinctive silver front – and red & blue details. Also in the west is **Khayal** - Jeddah, Taif, Yanbu, and Khamis Mushait, the food is well above average offerings. There is **Hashi Basha** (www.hashibasha.com) – a chain also specialising in traditional Saudi food - Hashi is a camel, and Basha is the Turkish Pasha. Camel meat has a premium price - Hashi Basha does offer chicken etc. **Hungry Bunny** www.hungrybunny.com.sa with burgers & fried chicken. Away from fast food is the small chain **Cafe Bateel** *** https://bateel.com/en/cafe/. These are bright, airy choices - well above the typical non-5* hotel restaurant food. The fast-food-style restaurant chains offer predictable food in a reasonably clean, well-run environment. Open for long hours, they are good to use when travelling. Finally - the Saudi coffee brand **Barns** https://barns.com.sa/en - has 400+ units nationwide - notably in petrol station forecourts.

Many restaurants use App based delivery services – https://www.tala-bat.com/ar/ksa/ and https://hungerstation.com/ alternatively www.careem.com. Even if you wish to dine in, use the app to check out the food & reviews.

Coffee shops, in addition to Barns, are found all over the country. Some are small takeaway kiosks in places like petrol stations. Others are remarkable and locally designed, with superb ambience, service and coffee. Even small towns may have a nice coffee shop/cafe for a break. Many of these offer not only Starbucks-type coffees - but also the local Qahwa - the Saudi coffee that differs from Western & Turkish brews.

There are a few specialised Tea shops, Tea Time is a Qatari franchise. However in many small restaurants tea if available -. Karak tea is a tea flavoured with spices that may include ginger, saffron, cinnamon etc, usually served sweet with milk. Bubble Tea, that is popular as it also can be flavoured to taste, will doubtless arrive as the local population does readily take up fashionable products.

Shisha restaurants serve food - but the chief attraction is smoking a Shisha (Water pipe, Hookah, Hubbly Bubbly). Smoking indoors is prohibited everywhere – surprisingly there may be some cases when Shisha pipes are smoked. Shisha, incidentally, has a 100% tax introduced in 2019.

Tipping is unexpected in the lowest-cost restaurants – however, staff wages, especially for non-Saudis, are very low, so rounding up - or a specific tip of some SAR would be good. Give direct to the service provider.

No offence is intended when any restaurant asks for payment against an order – perhaps they have been regular victims of dine and dash – it is not unusual in Saudi for staff to bear such a loss.

Prices are a broad stared grouping.

SAR 0-40 = *
SAR 40-80 = **
SAR 80-140 = ***
SAR 140-200= ****
SAR 200+ = *****

Remember that 15% VAT (dharebu) is charged in Saudi Arabia – check whether the quoted price includes VAT – typically it is included in a price, as in the UK and Europe, but especially on higher cost services its best to be certain.

HOTELS In this book, hotels listed are generally lower-priced options close to attractions in the town - for example, in Jeddah, the focus is on Al Balad and the Kurnaysh. You will be familiar with major international chains and what they offer. In each town, at most, a handful of properties have been included - rather than any attempt to be comprehensive - the book would be vast otherwise. Those noted are worth looking at, when compared to others at a similar price. There is no extensive review - as an online booking site will give the latest opinions and you can also readily compare them. In smaller towns or remote places like the Farasan Islands - a much larger percentage of all hotels are listed here - so that immediately, you can see if a town does have any hotels. For example, at Khaybar, there is a dearth of properties - their standard may not be right for you. A quick check of those listed here against the latest review on a booking service may quickly make a decision on visiting a town. Dammam, Jeddah and Riyadh offer hotels from the Ritz Carlton down in standard & fame.

Hotels in Saudi are far from cheap compared to North African Arab destinations; they are somewhat lower in price than Western cities. The Accor brands Ibis & Novotel may well offer the lowest-priced international branded properties in Dammam, Jeddah & Riyadh; look also for Golden Tulip. With a branded property, you will expect to have the service and quality the brand offers worldwide. The lowest-priced properties will be local operations. With these lower-cost local options, the accommodation is likely in good condition only in a new property. Lack of maintenance and poor housekeeping impact those hotels more than a few years old. Of course, there are many exceptions.

In AlUla, there has been tremendous promotion of the destination - and there are premium brands - such as the Banyan Tree. However, in AlUla, the greatest number of the limited number of accommodation options are in locally run properties, often converted houses. These have a premium price relative to the actual room offered because of the shortage of rooms at peak periods and the price uplift caused by the premium brands. Advance booking at AlUla is ideal - and often essential.

Many choices of accommodation in Saudi are called 'Furnished Apartments' - these are rented daily (or longer term - monthly rates will be available) and usually will have a small kitchen - possibly a separate sitting area and a bedroom, perhaps a couple - sometimes each bedroom will have its own bathroom. These properties may be competitively priced - and in Saudi are, of course, aimed at Saudis.

airbnb operates in Saudi Arabia. The local version **Gathern**, that is licensed and promoted by the Saudi government, is an alternative to consider. Choose carefully based on your individual situation, and gender compared to your host.

Camping is possible, with equipment from specialised stores including AlRimaya, and cheap tents available in stores such as Lulu. Avoid camping within proximity of settlements and take precautions for potentially problematic wildlife (see Health coverage) and issues with human residents.

There are many hotels in Saudi under local brands. **Ewaa Hotels** www.ewaahotels.com is a chain offering over 40 contemporary hotels - often with breakfast; **Narcissus** https://narcissushotels.com/ are a small boutique option; **Boudle** www.boudl.com is a low to medium-price brand - with reasonable hotels. **OYO** www.oyorooms.com is an Indian hotel brand that appears simply to provide marketing/software rather than property management in Saudi - all properties are in the lowest price brackets. **Al Eairy** hotels https://aleairybooking.com/ are owned by the Al Eairy family and managed from Qassim – using, in places, a strange impersonal kiosk system to book-in, not dissimilar to eGates at an airport. A Saudi-only Airbnb type offering is **Gathern** https://gathern.co/. Its properties cover the complete country.

In Al Balad Jeddah **Al Balad Hospitality** www.albaladhospitality.com will be opening in 2024 a number of Boutique style hotels (eventually well into the teens) .

These will be in original mansions, restored in keeping with their original style & decorated in a supporting manner.

There are some men only '**Youth Hostels**' – not usually offering a dorm type accommodation. They are attached to sports stadiums or other youth service. www.sayha.org.sa https://hihostels.com Individual ones are not included in this book.

Saudi Arabia hopes to have 320,000 new hotel rooms by 2030 - so there will be a flow of new properties to look for. The World Expo https://riyadhexpo2030.sa/ in Riyadh between October 2030 and March 2031 will be constructed just south of the airport and World Cup 2034 (Saudi Arabia was the only bidder) - will doubtless increase hotel construction in Riyadh.

Many lower-priced hotels use online booking sites to manage all bookings and payments and have no other online presence. In general, the on-site hotel reception staff cannot reduce the price compared to an online booking site - though an ask may pay off. Room prices will range from around SAR150 per night upwards. The lower price often does mean lower standards, perhaps unacceptably so. Some lower-cost rooms may have squat-type toilets, the vast majority will have a 'Shattaf' flexible hose for cleansing oneself after using the toilet. If using the lowest price hotels, it would be prudent to have in your bags shower gel & towel etc. These are easily & cheaply available in larger supermarkets etc. All rooms will have private bathroom and air-conditioning - free Wi-Fi is the norm; consider a VPN for security. If you have booked through an online booking service - follow up the booking confirmation with a WhatsApp message (or email) - to ensure they acknowledge the booking (rather rely on the automated response). This will also ensure you have their functioning mobile phone number. A text message is best rather than speaking to the staff - so that, if needed, a translation of your message can be made, and an appropriate response made.

In better hotel chains - tipping is normal, as in most Western countries. In lower cost hotels - as with restaurants - staff are poorly paid - so while tipping will be unexpected - a specific tip for help & good service is worthwhile. Many lower-priced hotels do not offer a restaurant service - other than a delivery from an outside operator.

Prices are a broad stared grouping.
SAR 0-200 = *
SAR 200-500 = **
SAR 500-800 = ***
SAR 800-1100= ****
SAR 1100+ = *****

TIPPING / BARGAINING

In Saudi Arabia amongst Saudi nationals, accepting tips may well be a new experience. However they are a key group the government wishes to benefit from tourism. Low paid, non-Saudi nations working in service industries may also be deserving of appreciation for good service.

It's preferable to tip in SAR - or, if not, US$. SAR is better as it is immediately usable without using a money exchange. Never give foreign coins - they are useless as they cannot be exchanged – drop them in charity boxes in the airports etc.

In 5* hotels, tip as usual in Western capitals, perhaps slightly less generously. Better restaurants may add a service charge. A tip (around 10%) for good service is appropriate. In small, lower-cost hotels and restaurants, tipping is unusual. However - the staff.especially the non-Saudi nationals in these are poorly paid, earning perhaps US$250-400 a month - so why not leave a tip for good service as you would to their better-paid equivalents elsewhere? Give direct to the service provider to ensure they receive it.

At petrol stations, which are attendant service, round up the bill if paying cash or hand over a few SAR if using a card - again, the wages are low.

If on a private guided tour, consider SAR300+ per day to the guide - if there is a separate driver - consider SAR150+ a day. If on a group tour - with, say 10 clients - a guide tip of SAR30 per person per day - and for 4x4 drivers, SAR20 per person per day. If on a bus tour (perhaps off a cruise ship) with, say 30-50 people in the bus - SAR15-20 per person per day with instructions to the guide to split it with the driver. on the organised tours attached to experiencealula.com tip if you have had a truly exceptional experience.

There is not a 'Baksheesh' culture in Saudi Arabia, begging is prohibited, though it does happen discreetly.

Bargaining If shopping in a street-type souq like Al Balad or the Tuesday Market in Abha, negotiation is the norm. If you are buying a T-shirt with "I love Saudi" on it - the discount is likely to be far more - who knows, it might be 50%. If you are buying gold, 5% may be all that's possible. This bargaining differs from the intense encounter you may have experienced in Egypt or Morocco. It's more of a social interaction, don't get into a heated argument over any negotiation- walk away if you don't like the 'offer'. If you are uncomfortable negotiating and know what you want to buy - pop into several shops to find which offers the lowest price and then return to that one.

TRAVELLING AROUND

Tour Operators There are an increasing number of local tour operators. More established ones include www.husaak.com; www.palmsland.sa; https://hayatour.com; https://saudiarabiatours.net;   http://alboraq.com.sa;   https://alulaguide.sa; https://amazingtours.com.sa.   https://saudiarabiatravelandtours.com/   For **Scuba Diving** – research through https://swsdf.sa/ the Saudi national body. There are other local service providers - such as short sightseeing boat trips, 4x4 trips, hiking. In all cases - check your own insurance conditions & enquire about theirs. Caveat emptor in all cases.

There are non-Saudi tour operators providing tours - both private tours and group tours. Many will offer a land-only service - where you fly into the country independently, and the program starts on your arrival in Saudi Arabia. A bonded company from your own country will provide peace of mind. These foreign operators will certainly use a Saudi company to handle much of your experience in the country.

Tourist Sports Activities From Hot-Air Balloons, Zip-wires, through mountain trekking to Scuba Diving, Saudi Arabia has a wide range of potential activities outdoors. Stable weather and generally low levels of inbound leisure tourism - add to their attractiveness. Many companies will be new in the field, though well-established ones have catered to the resident population for years. All companies in Saudi have to be registered specifically for the activity they undertake (such as tour provider) with the government.

Though Saudi Arabia has vast sandy beaches, few are used for sunbathing – see Page23 for clothing – if you need to sunbath a 5* hotel is perhaps a good choice.

INTERNAL TRANSPORT

Uber & Other Taxi Services. App-based taxis are available in major towns. Look for Uber, Bolt, Careem (Dubai-based Uber-owned), Jeeny. Smaller towns often, unfortunately, do not have Uber-type services. Jeddah, Madinah, Riyadh, Hofuf and the Dammam area do have services. Expect to be picked up within 10 minutes of ride confirmation. The driver (expect a Saudi, often doing a second job) might work under multiple services - it may be worth your while to have a couple of apps on your phone in case one service doesn't have availability.

If you hire an App Based Taxi – your fare is, roughly, known based on planned kilometres & time. As usual unexpected diversions, or traffic delays may cause an increase in the cost, calculated by Uber etc. The driver of course will have your pick-up location and destination on his own Uber app. It will also show the suggested route. However drivers may have a second phone, and use Google Maps for the route, in the belief it is up to date regarding diversions and traffic conditions.

However if for any, unlikely, reason you use a non-App based taxi, fix the price firmly before getting in & do not accept a suggestion from the driver "You Decide", there will be quite a good chance that on arrival the taxi driver will actually decide.

International Coach Services - SAPTCO https://saptco.com.sa coaches run between Saudi Arabia & Abu Dhabi, Ajman, Bahrain, Dubai & Sharjah. Dammam & Bahrain and Dammam & Abu Dhabi. Obtaining a Visa in advance is suggested, and may be required by the SAPTCO management, irrespective of any web-site claims. Services were previously offered to Jordan, Kuwait and Qatar – if useful, check the website to see if there have been re-introduced.

Long Distance National Coach - SATRANS (used on maps here) also called SAT https://satrans.com.sa/ has long-distance coach services between larger towns.SATRANSis a joint venture by SAPTCO & Spanish transportation company ALSA. This is a new venture replacing the previous SAPTCO Intercity operation. – so there have been changes in routes, bus terminal stations and so on – there will be more changes. Wherever SAPTCO is mentioned for an Intercity route – check SAT. Local services and International routes are still provided by SAPTCO.

The SATRANS coaches are air-conditioned and should have a functioning toilet. Longer distance journeys will have a stop for refreshments from a roadside restaurant. It's advisable to book the seat in advance – a couple of days or so is usually ok except on holidays, when longer will be needed. Online booking is ideal – as the in-person counters are often busy. Dammam's station is south of the

SATRANS - SAT coach

Kurnaysh on 11th St - south of the local bus hub. In Jeddah, it's within the car park area of Al Sulimaniyah Train Station (local bus 14 goes to Al Balad) – previously it was just west of Al Balad. The bus station in Riyadh, is in the southern Azizia district off Route 500 (local bus services 7, 9, 660, 680). Major routes have several departures daily.

Local Bus Services - There are local bus services in Dammam, Riyadh, Jeddah as well as Madinah & Taif - provided by SAPTCO. A change to electric buses is moving forward. These local buses operate on fixed routes with specified stops, whose signs may be difficult to see. A bus might stop on demand if requested by passengers within the bus - see if other passengers do this. Payment is through a plastic tap-and-go type card. This card is purchased for SAR10 on the bus or at a hub - and is then topped up on the bus for the fare. Fares are SAR3.45 per ride. Unfortunately, although the company, SAPTCO, operates in other towns and uses the same system in each, the cards are currently not interchangeable. Buses typically operate 07:15-midnight.

Metro Saudi Arabia will shortly have three Metro systems.

Riyadh may open its 6-line network in 2024. The Yellow line will service the airport. It will have a link to the Princess Nourah Bint Abdul Rahman University Metro circuit, which is a separate private system for the university. The Yellow line then links with the Blue Line. The Blue Line is the key line in Riyadh. It runs north-south, broadly along the arterial King Fahd Rd and is linked with all the other lines. It serves many of Riyadh's key tourist sites. The Orange Line Metro will service the Riyadh-Dammam station. A bus service may be initiated to offer a service from the local area to each metro.

There is a third Metro system in Makkah (the city is not covered in this guide). This will expand from the current single line to five – construction on these additional four lines has not started.

Train Saudi Arabia has 3 modern passenger Train services.

Between **Riyadh, AlAhsa and Dammam**, www.sar.com.sa - operates several times daily. Between **Riyadh and Qurayyat**, in the north of Saudi Arabia, a sleeper service operates once a week. Services between **Riyadh and Hail** operates a couple of times a day - and there is 4 times a day service between **Riyadh and Qassim** - these to the north are all on the same line. The newest service is the Haramain Rail Service www.hhr.sa (the website might transfer to www.sar.com.sa) – this connects **Jeddah & Madinah**. Stations on this line are- Madinah Station, King Abdullah Economic City Station in Rabigh, **King AbdulAziz International Airport**, Jeddah's **Al Sulimaniyah Train Station** and Makkah Station (only used by Muslims). There are a dozen services daily between Jeddah Sulimaniyah and Madinah. All use excellent carriages and engines, providing a smooth ride.

The trains on all three lines are typically punctual. Two classes should be available, and there are some luggage restrictions. Travel in all Saudi trains is by assigned ticketed seating (or bed) only, with no subsequent self-selection of seat.

The staff may reallocate seating if needed, perhaps for social reasons. Most impressive is the Haramain Rail Service, where the trains reach 300kmph between Jeddah and Madinah. Online booking is suggested for all services - if there are issues with doing that, in-person counters are available at each station. Unfortunately, there is no connectivity between the mainline Train Stations in Riyadh until the Metro opens.

Airport & Airlines Saudi Arabia has numerous airports. There are three major international ones - **Jeddah** - King AbdulAziz International Airport; and **Riyadh** -

King Khalid International Airport; **Dammam** - King Fahd International Airport. These are served by many airlines - including low-cost cost such as Wizz Air. Jeddah does have a train connection - though the town's station in Jeddah is also far from the centre. Secondary international airports include Abha International Airport, AlUla Prince Abdul Majeed bin Abdulaziz International Airport and Madinah Prince Mohammad bin Abdulaziz International Airport. Domestic airports serve most major cities.

Local airlines include Saudia www.saudia.com which is the original flag carrier for Saudi Arabia. A new airline founded in 2023 (probably launching flights late 2025) is Riyadh Air www.riyadhair.com - a second flag carrier. As Saudia relocates operations to the west coast it is likely that Riyadh Air's hub focus will be Riyadh.

Interior Saudi train

There are three other locally owned airlines; flyadeal www.flyadeal.com; Flynas www.flynas.com; Nesma www.nesmaairlines.com Saudi owned – managed from Egypt. Many other airlines fly into Saudi Arabia, including Air Arabia, British Airways, Emirates, KLM, Lufthansa, Qatar Airways, Turkish Airlines & Wizz Air.

Ferries International Ferry services operate out of Duba Port Page69 to Safaga, Egypt and Jeddah Page42 to Sawakin in Sudan (subject to the security situation). Namma Shipping Lines www.nammamarinesservices.com handles these. Their offices in Jeddah - Baishin St, Al Hindawiyah. +966126487203 Ext. 170, +966509090570 Email amajid@nesma.com

Domestic Ferry services run between Jizan Page234 and the Farasan Islands Page239. Operated by MACNA https://macna.com.sa King Fahd Rd (opposite port) +966173340227

Seaports on the West Coast, **Duba Port** commercial & passenger, **Jeddah Islamic Port** - commercial & cruise, **Jizan Port** - commercial & passenger , **Jizan** - commercial & leisure east coast

and on the east coast, **Jubail King Fahd Industrial Port** Commercial (Oil) , **Dammam King AbdulAziz Port** - commercial & the old town for cruise. On all ferry services – specifically ask the company regarding Visa requirement. If possible, get this as an Email / WhatsApp message and anticipate that a Visa in advance of arrival will be required.

Car

Car hire companies are available at major airports and within towns. There are international brands such as Avis, Budget, and Hertz that will have websites in your country. Local brands include Abu Diyab https://rent.abudiyab.com.sa, Yelo www.iyelo.com. To rent a car in Saudi - a driver must be 25+ and have held a full licence for 12+ months. An international Driving Permit is good to have - only the 1968 (Vienna) version is recognised. Full insurance - CDW - should cover for accidents, less a deductible. A credit card is also needed - to pay, and they hold a deposit against traffic fines and accidents. Typically, cars are automatic – however manual gears are ideal in off-road situations, especially sandy ones. You will have up to 250km daily allowance (unless you take a longer-term hire) - this will almost certainly result in an excess mileage (kilometrage) when hired on a daily rate, as distances in Saudi are long. Look at the kilometre charge - from around SAR0.40 per kilometre (4x4 has a much higher kilometre charge). When renting a car - check carefully for damage, inside and out. Ensure there is a spare tyre and jack, etc. Make certain that the power supply - for phones, etc does work. Ensure that documentation of ownership – (called a mulkiya) is given to you - it is normally as a photocopy and that the rental agreement is kept by you. This should have the phone number of the company and take the mobile number of the official in the office who dealt with you – phone them to ensure it functions – and ask for a WhatsApp contact. Finally - make certain no fines are outstanding against the car from previous renters - if there are any, refuse the car. If the authorities notice the hire car has outstanding fines - you, the current renter, will be expected to pay on the spot – the vehicle might be wheel clamped.

On the car's return, check about any damage and traffic fines. The traffic fines are important as, in theory, they are digitally attached to your passport record in the central government system and payable before leaving the country to the car hire company, which removes them from the record. During normal government hours, Page5. fines might be payable by you at the three major airports (if offices are open) - but it's best not to count on this in case it impacts your departure.

Small-engine cars are, of course, more economical, but given the vast distances involved in driving through Saudi, and mountain heights, they may lack pulling power, especially on mountain ascents (see Page38 for driving tips). All cars will have air-conditioning.

DRIVING

in Saudi Arabia can be a pleasure - out of major towns, the traffic on roads is often sparse. Driving habits are not as bad as might be reported - but nonetheless, with a young population and powerful cars, driving habits can be shocking & dangerous at times. However - stay alert and always anticipate any oncoming issues. Saudi Arabia drives on the right-hand side of the road (the driver sits on the left of the vehicle, as in Europe and much of the world). There is a mix of traffic light-controlled road junctions, flyovers (overpass) and underpasses and a few roundabouts (rotary). Signage's text is in Arabic and often English, with speed and distance signs in kilometres. However, the numerals in remote areas may only be in Arabic numerals – rather than the Western Arabic numerals (as used in Europe & North America, etc).

Driving regulations are comparable to most Western countries. These include not leaving the scene of an accident, fines for illegal parking, penalties for not wearing seat belts, using phones, etc. Naturally, alcohol and drug use are absolutely prohibited. The maximum speed is mostly up to 120kmph, with lower speeds down to 45kmph.

There are usually numerous petrol stations in Saudi Arabia's towns. They often are locally owned rather than a nationwide chain. A station might have recently closed permanently; therefore, don't absolutely rely on getting to any very remote stations with a near-empty tank. On intercity highways, petrol stations are less frequent, at an extreme with several hundred kilometres between - this is most especially the case in less populated areas in the northwest. It's prudent to fill up if a tank falls to around half-full. The stations are attendant service, as the staff are low paid, they will appreciate a small tip (a riyal or two) – of course to be given if they wash a screen. Simply say 'full' 'mumtaz' for premium or 'aadi' for regular. Petrol (called locally Benzine) cost octane-95 SAR2.33 (less than US$0.63) in late 2023 - the price is set by the government.- payment can usually be made by card as well as cash. Many stations have additional businesses around – such as small shops, cheap restaurants, ATMs and so on.

Open road - and livestock on it

If there are no toilets in the petrol station itself, ask to use the toilets in a restaurant or mosque, usually to one side of the main mosque building. Cleanliness may not be ideal - & toilet paper is not used – rather the Asian style of washing is always practised – usually a flexible hose is next to the toilet.

A road network of four and three-lane motorways crisscross the country - even in cities, the lanes may be exceptionally wide by European standards. Despite the 140kmph speed limit on a few major highways - it's best to assume a maximum of 120kmph on any major highway. Over speeding is, unfortunately, almost encouraged by roads being broad and relatively traffic-free out of town. Most cars will have cruise control to help avoid breaking the speed limit. Other speed limits drop to 45kmph in town. Often, major out-of-town roads are fenced to restrict livestock entering the road. However. always be alert regarding camels, goats, sheep and donkeys on the roadside. Baboons are also a potential road hazard in the mountain areas south of Madinah. Major highways typically will have two numbers – the Saudi national network – for example Highway 5 (with a green background) & a pan-Arab network – the equivalent for this Highway 5 – it's the pan-Arab highway number M55 with a blue background.

Fixed location and mobile speed radar with still and video cameras include sophisticated recognition systems including the number plate & face; allow the imposition of fines including for phone use. The equipment includes overhead gantries.

Hands-free phone holders are available in most shops selling mobile phones, so digital maps can easily be used without holding a phone and subsequently being fined.

Roads might be poorly signed, whether regarding restrictions such as speed limits or directional signs. This means that digital mapping is often essential for travel by car and navigation.

Road up towards Abha

Though overall, roads provide a good driving experience, in some areas, road design and maintenance are not ideal. This includes speed humps (speed breakers or sleeping policemen) that are not marked and if hit at 120kmph may cause damage to the vehicle. Roads may occasionally expand from single lane to dual carriageway - with a sharp right onto the extra two lanes for your roadside - you might continue straight - driving onto the oncoming dual-carriageway traffic. Road surfaces may be heavily cracked on minor cross-country roads - therefore having the potential to damage tyres as well as being a distraction when driving. The surface of some major roads might be broken up, even on routes between important towns – this might extend to potholes. These poor design and maintenance issues are reasons why driving after sunset should be avoided.

If you have an accident – photo the scene if you can do so safely. Contact the car-hire company and ask for their advice. At some stage, the police, - perhaps the fire or ambulance service may need to be called Page22. Do not leave the scene unless advised to do so by an official – however, do keep all people in a safe location and place hazard warning signs and the vehicle hazard warning lights.

There are frequent official checkpoints. An army checkpoint might be within a few kilometres of a police checkpoint – both have authority. Slow down and be able to stop if required; frequently, you will be waved on. The checkpoint might be looking for people in the country illegally or with illegal substances. Always have all official documentation to hand. On minor roads, for example, in mountainous areas in the south near the Yemen border, they may turn you back.

Driving Hints. Out of town, It's best not to drive from sunset-sunrise as roads are poorly lit – if at all. Plan your day - and distances to avoid nighttime driving. Defensive driving techniques should be practised – planning ahead and trying to anticipate what other drivers may do. In the southwest high mountains, cloud cover may reach ground level, all be it that the ground is at 2,000m. This requires driving as you would do in your own country during fog.

When driving a vehicle down a steep mountain road – use the gears to slow the vehicle. The equivalent of gear 2 may be right. Constant use of brakes when going down a hill, may cause brakes to overheat and fail – possibly resulting in a crash. The sharp hairpin bends encourage drives to cut corners, especially on the way down – so its best to be very alert for this.

It's best not to drive 2WD cars off-road – this will automatically invalidate your insurance and, potentially cause damage to the vehicle, and perhaps put your life in peril if it cannot cope with the rough road conditions.

In the rain, leave wadis quickly to avoid flash floods. The water is surprisingly fast – and carries debris with it – adding to its force. If a road is flooded above axle height & you can't see the bottom of a water-filled area be cautious. A wait for the water to subside is better than getting stuck. Flowing water may have rocks or debris below the water. If you can't walk through it to test (because of the water height) – your vehicle is unlikely to pass through – indeed if the passenger section is well sealed the vehicle might float along with the water flow. Alternatively, watch others cross first. Do not tailgate them through - if they stop, you will be forced to do so as well. Where the water is widest, its often shallowest and slowest.

It pays to know where the engine's air intake is and how low it is. If water is drawn into the engine through the air intake, the engine may stop working. It might have flooded because of a hydrolock – petrol and especially diesel engines can get this. If the engine has flooded and stalls in water, tow it out. The engine will need to be dried out. If you are lucky, it will start – if unlucky, engine may have been destroyed and general electronics need replacing. As an additional incentive to avoid crossing flooding roads, the government says, "Crossing valleys and canyons while they are flowing puts your life in danger and is a violation punishable by a fine of up to SR10,000 ($2,700)". This is issued as a shocking number of vehicles are carried away by flooding wadis. Be cautious on mountain roads as rocks and stones may fall, or have fallen, onto the road.

If driving in remote areas – advise people where you are going and when you will return. Bring lots of drinking water. All occupants should always wear seat belts – especially when off-road as bumpy roads do cause lots of jumping around which may cause heads to hit the roof.

The major advantage of a 4x4, for some drivers, on rough tracks, is the greater ground clearance it gives rather than simply having a 4x4 traction. This will be clear if using a 2WD – and the vehicle grounds its chassis over even a slight hump in the rough road. In sand light 4x4 will help ensure the vehicle doesn't get bogged down.

As off-road driving does require concentration and, at times, strength, it's best avoided when tired. Usually, staying on a track will give compact surfaces - and at least keep the vehicle on a route between places other people have been.

On gravel roads, brake and turn progressively – gravel gives little grip to tyres, and sharp wheel movements may cause lack of traction and the vehicle might slide off the road. Dust clouds behind vehicles can block

typical road sign, southwest Saudi

the forward view of vehicles behind. Stay back from other vehicles to avoid their dust.

Travelling even with suitable vehicles in a Sand Desert without considerable experience and at least 1 additional vehicle is unwise.

It's common practice for driving in sand, to let air out of tyres using the recommended reduced pressure for your vehicle; the pressure will depend on the vehicle and tyre. This spreads the vehicle's weight over a greater surface – this means the vehicle is less likely to sink into the sand. Engaging light 4x4 before entering the sand will power all wheels, giving extra traction. Tyres need to be reflated when driving on tarmac roads.

If using a 4x4 in desert conditions – ensure safety equipment is available – including traction boards, very heavy-duty tow ropes (10tons + to allow for inertia) and long so that the rescue vehicle can stay clear of the area that has trapped the car.

Using 4x4 consumes larger quantities of petrol, and having drinking water for all passengers before desert trips is ideal.

If stuck in sand, spinning the wheels may sink the vehicle down to the axle or even worse to the chassis – in which case another vehicle is needed to tow it out. Digging around the wheels and creating a clear a drive route out – may help especially if using sand-boards or suitable track material for the wheels to run on. In a rescue situation, even the strongest tow rope can snap under sudden strain – and the whiplash can be fatal – its ideal if people stand clear. After clearing a route - & placing sand boards, secure the tow rope to the correct tow point in both vehicles – a plastic bumper/fender cannot hold a 2-ton vehicle being pulled out of deep sand.

When pulling – a gradual increase on the ropes tension will help avoid the vehicles and rope being put under an impossible sudden strain. It goes without saying that having two vehicles stuck will dramatically increase problems.

If extraction is impossible, unless there is a clear, short walk to a place of safety it may be safer staying with the vehicle - as a vehicle is more easily seen by rescuers and provides shade. Walking a long distance in high temperatures without water can lead to disaster. Call for expert help via the car-hire company if needed.

There are no toll roads, at the moment, in Saudi Arabia.

CHAPTER 3
LOCATION GUIDE

Saudi Arabia is vast - around 2,215,000 sq km - at almost ten times the size of Great Britain at 228,919 sq km and about 25% of the 9,629,091 sq kms USA. Driving distances are significant - and with stops on the way, the time taken from place to place can be surprising to a European driver. There are limited areas where a 4x4 vehicle is needed - so a saloon car is often all that's required. Always remember that on a rough/sand road - the insurance of a saloon car will not cover any damage see (Page35)

The area from **AlUla** Page88 south through **Jeddah** Page42, **Abha** Page196 to **Najran** Page181, is rewarding to visit. Read your country's travel advisories Page22 for all areas. If you decide on travelling through the southwest, a tight seven days - or much more comfortable 10 days will work here - a round journey taking the coastal route from Jeddah to **Jizan** Page234 - then either **Najran** and up to **Abha** or go to Abha directly. From there, travel along the mountain plateaux, with fantastic views west over the wooded escarpment and villages below and continue to **Taif** Page224 & back to Jeddah. Alternatively, from Jeddah - drive north to **Yanbu** Page65 - then visit **Madinah** Page75- **AlUla** - page88 **Khaybar** Page107 and up to **Dumat Al Jandal** Page166. Drive south to **Jubbah** Page162, **Hail** Page157 and back through Madinah to Jeddah - this is through arid country. For a short turnaround, consider Jeddah with Al Balad Page44, the Kurnaysh & Abdul Raouf Khalil Museum Page50- then travel (flights available) to AlUla. If you have more time, add Madinah - by **SATRANS** (fully Saptco Alsa Transportation) coach https://satrans.com.sa/ or Haramain Rail Service www.hhr.sa – possibly drive the entire round trip. **Riyadh** Page124 is also good for a long weekend. Visit the National Museum Page127, Masmak Palace Page129 and **Diriyah** Page143. If you have more time, take the train to **AlAhsa** Page262 from Riyadh.

Away from Jeddah and Riyadh, you may find that when you visit a historical tourist attraction, it is practically deserted, for some visitors this may be a pleasure. The downside to many places away from these cities is that so many historical places are closed and cordoned off by fencing with no officials to help visitors, making them impossible to get close to. Also, scheduled openings could be regarded as target timings - so relax and go with the flow. Private Museum costs, where charged, are generally below SAR30. They are more of a personal collection with the quantity of items, rather than quality and curated, the apparent preference. While perhaps understandable to a modern Saudi national, many exhibits need information cards. Without these, they may lose their importance to a visitor.

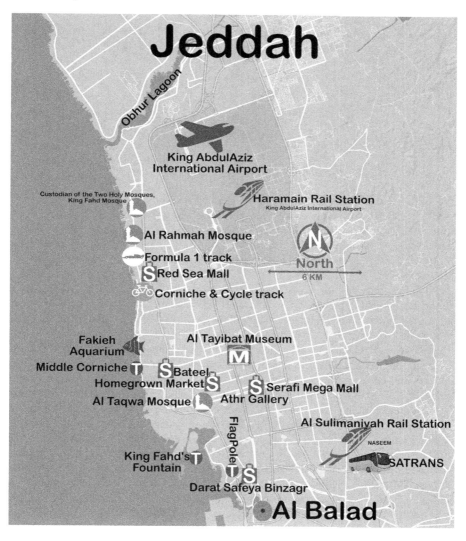

CHAPTER 4
JEDDAH

Jeddah / جدة GPS - 21.484226, 39.187584 Population (appx) 3,712,917

A quick overview of the Geography - The topography around Jeddah and much of Saudi Arabia's Red Sea coastal areas is varied, with a coastal plain of alluvial sand, salt flats (sabkha soil), and fossilised coral reefs. Further inland, the hills and mountains comprise metamorphosed sedimentary and igneous rocks, including granitic batholiths.

A brief history - Jeddah has been settled for over 2500 years. Legendarily, it was founded as a fishing hamlet by the Qudaa tribe, who migrated from Marib in Yemen after the historic dam gradually failed - between 145BC-557AD despite attempts to increase its capacity.

However, Jeddah was officially established as a city in AD647 by the Caliph, Uthman bin Affan. The site is in what is now Al Balad, and this remained the entirety of Jeddah until the early 20th century. The reason for its foundation was strategic - Jeddah's location on the shores of the Red Sea made it an ideal transhipment port for trade, as it's at a convergence zone of winds - coming from the south & north. A different type of ship would be used for an onward journey, needing a transfer of goods. It was also the nearest coast to Makkah. As time passed and the Islamic Empire spread, pilgrims travelling to the holy city of Makkah increased in numbers. Jeddah's accessibility by sea provided a crucial link for traders and pilgrims alike, leading to its rapid growth as a prosperous trading hub. The Tulunid dynasty, of Egypt, acquired rule over the Hijaz from the Abbasid Caliph Al Mutazz in 868. The Hijaz was then under Egypt's authority until Egypt's conquest by the Ottomans in 1517.

In the 10th century, Jeddah witnessed the rule of the Fatimids in Egypt, from AD969 for over 200 years. They had originated in northwest Africa and then conquered Egypt and with it ruled over the Hijaz. This brought a period of cultural and economic growth, further enhancing Jeddah's significance as a trade centre in the region. It's from the Fatimid period that the Sharifs of Makkah rose to rule much of the Hijaz.

Jeddah came under threat from the Portuguese fleet based in India in the early 16th century. To defend against the Portuguese attack, a wall was constructed around Jeddah in 1509 by Amir Husain Al Kurdi. Restored gates from the wall still stand today in Jeddah's historic Al Balad district. The Portuguese attacked Arab vessels in the Red Sea and attempted an unsuccessful siege of Jeddah in 1517.

Portugal's Arabian Sea fleet - 1507

The co-Sharif of Makkah, Abu Numayy II bin Barakat II bin Muhammed, who ruled with his father, Barakat II bin Muhammed Sultan, went to Cairo aged 11, in 1517. The purpose - to acknowledge the suzerainty of the Ottomans, the new rulers of Egypt & the Hijaz. In exchange for that loyalty to Sultan Selim I, the Sharifs were confirmed as rulers of Makkah etc. The Ottoman Sultan assumed the title of Servant of The Two Holy Mosques, the Al Saud kings use it, (or depending on the translation from Ottoman) as 'Custodian of the Two Holy Mosques'. By 1525, under Sultan Suleiman the Magnificent, Jeddah was re- fortified and a naval fleet of 18 ships was based at Jeddah. The Portuguese were considered a potent threat.

Under Ottoman rule, Jeddah continued to prosper as a commercial hub, facilitating the annual influx of Hajj pilgrims. Goods from Asia, Africa and Europe were imported, repackaged in Jeddah, and sold to pilgrims heading for Makkah and Madinah as well generally through Hijaz.

Trade in Jeddah was adversely impacted by Napoleon's invasion of Egypt in 1798 & the Levent. The British blockade against his forces increased the slump. Disruption was intensified when the expansionist Abdulaziz bin Muhammad Al Saud conquered Taif in 1802, Makkah in 1803 and Madinah in 1804. Sharif Ghalib bin Musaid, who fled to Jeddah, had an opponent looking down at him from the mountains. Though Ottoman forces initially held Jeddah for the Sharif - by 1806 the Al Saud forces had occupied the town. Regulations were put in place, conforming with the views of the Al Saud.

The withdrawal of the French from Egypt in 1802 and the consolidation of power in Egypt by Mohammed Ali Pasha in 1805 resulted in the Ottoman's new ruler, Sultan Mahmud II, requiring Mohammed Ali Pasha to reoccupy the Hijaz. After a patchy start by his commanders, Mustafa Bey occupied Jeddah in January 1813 - with Mohammed Ali Pasha arriving in October 1813. By 1818, Mohammed Ali Pasha's son Ibrahim had captured the Al Saud capital, Turaif, at Diriyah.

The rest of the 1800s to the 1st World War saw Jeddah under the control of Egypt, Britain and the Ottomans at different times. But in 1916, Ottoman power finally ended with the Arab Revolt against their rule. The Revolt was led by Hussein bin Ali, the

Sharif and Amir of Makkah, who declared himself King of the Hijaz & of Arab Lands and later, Caliph of the Muslims in 1924. It was a short-lived rule. Amir Abdulaziz bin Abdulrahman Al Saud conquered the Hijaz, including Jeddah, by 16 December 1925 – he assumed the title, King. He was on various dates Sheikh, Amir or Sultan & final King – depending on the date as he rapidly grew his territory, for simplicity of reading, Amir or King are used in this book.

With Saudi control, King AbdulAziz started developing Jeddah into a modern hub. It became Saudi Arabia's main port as the economy shifted from agriculture to an oil financed economy. Pilgrimage traffic boomed, and Jeddah Islamic Port was established in 1976.

Today, Jeddah has exploded into Saudi's second-largest city, with almost 4 million people. It focuses on commerce, industry and tourism. Millions of Hajj pilgrims pass through each year en route to Makkah and Madinah. The gleaming new King AbdulAziz International Airport opened in 2019 to handle all the travel. Now over 1,300 years old, Jeddah remains a thriving, bustling city straddling tradition and modernity. The engaging Al-Balad district recalls Jeddah's legacy as the historic gateway to Islam's holiest site.

What to see in Jeddah

AL BALAD

This old core is, for many visitors, the principal tourist area, though Scuba diving might run it a good second or first for a few. Previously, Al Balad was a walled town; now, only isolated heavily renovated, fortified gateways remain. Part of it is a registered UNESCO World Heritage Site (outlined in its map), nominated in 2014. The nominating document states, "The historic centre of Jeddah, within which is located the nominated property, constitutes the most outstanding traditional urban centre in Saudi Arabia and on the Red Sea. Its surviving houses underline the impressions conveyed by earlier visitors; with its fine coral houses, ribats (a sort of caravanserai) and mosques, Jeddah was a major Tihamah town whose international character long predates the modern period". The area of the UNESCO site is not large, at 17.92 hectares. From north to south, it's a kilometre and from Al Dhab St (this road is also written as Al Dhahab or Al Zahab – using a non-Gulf interpretation of the Arabic first letter as Z) to the east 500m. Al Dhab Street marks the general western side of the UNESCO site. A non-UNESCO area to the west of Al Dhab St is also interesting - this area is, at most, 500m west-east. Though less old, it has a similar atmosphere and is also an area to walk in.

Redevelopments around Al Balad are taking place immediately north, east & south of Al Balad. Since October 2021 many sq km of previous lower-cost housing & business have been demolished. Emaar Square (Jeddah Gate) by Emaar the UAE property developer, a small pocket 3km northeast of Al Balad, is nearing completion - which may give an idea of the rest. This redevelopment means that, as historically, Al Balad is defined by the four gates – Bab Jadid (Madinah) in the north, Bab Makkah to the east, Bab Sharif in the south and Bab Al Fardah to the west. Another area around the southern Kurnaysh (previously called Al Andalus) is being redeveloped and falls within the Jeddah Central Project www.jeddahcentral.com (chaired by Prince Mohammed bin

Salman). This will be redeveloped as a major leisure & tourism project with a harbour for cruise ships. It may have some areas open from 2027.

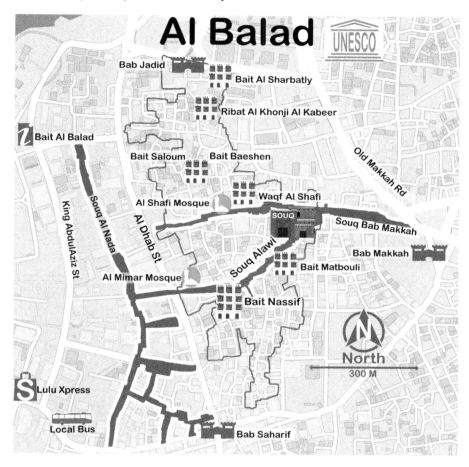

Motor vehicle access into Al Balad is restricted, with street barriers manned by uniformed officials – access to hotels is possible on request. Paid parking (SAR3 per hour +VAT– free from 23:00-08:00 and all-day Friday) is available in the central Al Balad area. Car parks are available on the western side of Al Balad. Given the short walking distance from the roads that ring Al Balad – consider getting a taxi to drop you off – its easiest around Bab Jadid, and walk in. Electric scooters are available for hire (from SAR35)– and golf-style chauffeured buggies (from SAR50) offer a 'tour' option.

Al Balad is undergoing a major makeover – with old buildings being renovated and repurposed. This means some side streets may have access restrictions – and some old houses may be closed while restorations are done. Irrespective – the whole area is enjoyable to walk around. Give yourself half a day – or more if you like people-watching, enjoying older housing or simply window shopping.

There are an increasing number of small cafes here – and there are small groceries to buy water. West of the UNESCO part of Al Balad the more modern area is still largely pedestrianised, with modern shops, including gold shops, Rolex watches official outlet, electronics, and a nearby local bus service hub.

Alley Al Balad

To the northwest is **Bait Al Balad** - an information centre & more; unfortunately, it's away from the UNESCO area.

With the warren of streets and random closures, Al Balad is best enjoyed by simply wandering through and enjoying the sights. **Al Dhab St** is a street that runs through the entire north/south central length of Al Balad from **Bab Jadid** (Bab Madinah) in the north to **Bab Sharif** in the south. In the middle of Al Dhab St is **Souq Alawi's** junction that leads through the UNESCO site for less than a kilometre from Al Dhab St in the west – to **Bab Makkah** in the east.

A Souq is simply an area to shop, rather than only an Aladdin-style covered market - though there are cities in the Middle East where Aladdin might feel at home. Running off Souq Alawi are numerous other streets that make this a fascinating area to wander around – it's largely car-free - with shops open to the street. The shops sell men's headscarves, perfumes, sports gear, food and much more.

Al Mimar Mosque (not open to non-Muslims) is at the junction of Al Dhab St with Souq Al-Alawi. This was recently reopened after renovations. A date in the mihrab of 1093Hijra (AD1682) suggests this as its foundation. However, it has been ascribed to 1263Hijra (1847) and built, it is said, by an Ottoman governor Mustafa Mimar Pasha. The raised elevation suggests that flooding may have been an issue when it was built.

Another historic mosque is **Al Shafi Mosque**, which has signed directions, north of Souq Alawi. The mosque is named after Abu Abdullah Muhammad bin Idris Al Shafi (767-820AD) - a Bani Hashim theologian and governor of Najran. This mosque is locally said to have been founded earlier during the Caliphate of Omar bin Al Khattab (died AD644). The minaret probably dates from the mid-13th century. The courtyard in the centre allows light to enter, air to circulate, and people to flow through. This mosque was restored from 2011 and is currently open to non-Muslims. Out of courtesy, request permission to enter (this also ensures that the permission to enter has not been withdrawn) - wear clothing as on Page23 and try and visit away from prayer times - so ideally, visit from 08:00-11:00 Sunday-Thurs. Just east of Al Shafi Mosque is a building 'Waqf Al Shafi' whose rental provided financial support to the mosque.

The key locational building in Al Balad, and the most attractive old house, is **Bait Nassif Museum** (bait means house), open daily from 08:00-23:00 – currently free to enter. The building's direction is well-signed in Al Balad. This was built by Omar Nassif in 1881. It is a 5 or 6-story building (depending on how you count floors) with the principal entrance facing north onto Souq Alawi - and a secondary entrance on a side street to the west. The white plastered facade includes typical Rowshan/Mashrabiya - the wooden projecting windows characteristic of the wider Arab world. In origin, Bait Nassif was a merchant's style of house with broad, shallow stairs for possible pack animals to use, accommodations for visiting merchants and finally, the upper floors for family members. The house is now laid out to reflect its importance after King AbdulAziz used it. Later, King Faisal purchased the house from the grandchildren of Omar Nassif.

The houses of Al Balad were typically built from blocks of fossil coral (locally called Al Mangabi) stones. Look for new Al Mangabi blocks where a house is being renovated. Wood beams (locally named Takaleel) spread the weight over a row of stone blocks. The stones are covered with plaster (often lime, locally called Nourah) for insulation and aesthetic purposes. About 150m east along Souq Alawi from Bait Nassif is **Bait Matbouli**.

Shop selling Sandals in Al Balad

This is still a private house on three floors with furniture and artefacts hours 17:00-22:00 entry cost cash SAR30. **Bait Baeshen**, about 350m north of Bait Nasif, built around 1856, has a similar layout to Bait Nassif and is open 18:00-22:00 free at the moment. **Bait Saloum** opposite Bait Baeshen, has intermittent openings. Not currently open, but these may open soon - **Bait Noor Wali** the house with the green Rosan on Souq Alawi between Al Mimar Mosque and Bait Nassif and a collection of several houses near **Ribat Al Khonji Al Kabeer**. To the north, east of Bab Jadid, is **Bait Al Sharbatly** 10:00-17 Sun-Thurs. This four-floor house was constructed in 1917 for Sharif Abdullah Al Abdali. He was a merchant, trading through the Red Sea and occasionally into India. Ownership was then purchased by Sheikh Abdullah Abbas Sharbatly, who was also a Red Sea merchant. It has recently been sympathetically restored after being largely abandoned, though without furnishings which are contemporary to its age. Nowadays it often holds arts and cultural events.

Al Shafi Mosque - Al Balad

MODERN JEDDAH

Since an announcement in 2016, there have been some Mosques that non-Muslims can visit in Jeddah outside prayer times. All are best visited – Sunday-Thursday – in the morning before 11:00 to avoid prayer times. "Non-Muslim visitors must respect the sanctity of the mosques and not to desecrate the holiness of the houses of Allah", according to officials. Conservative clothing is expected. Males should wear long, loose-fitting trousers – and a traditional long-sleeved shirt. Women, to be clothed so that only feet, hands and face are exposed –a headscarf and loose-fitting garments - are ideal – and a black Abaya (cloak) is even better. Though the ability to visit is a government permit – worshippers in these mosques may be unaware of this - so always ask permission to enter 'mumkin?' and avoid interfering with the prayer of any worshiper. Of course – just as this permission was granted – it might also be withdrawn.. Specifically mentioned in the announcement were - **Al Rahma Mosque** (previously the Fatimah Mosque) on the Kurnaysh, which is often called 'The Floating Mosque' as it has been built over the sea on pillars. Inside the prayer room is a discrete mezzanine floor or balcony with mashrabiya, where women may pray. **King Saud Mosque** on the corner of Route 271 and Habib Bin Amru Street (about 4.5km drive north of Bait Nassif). This is one of Jeddah's largest mosques, and its plain multi-domed exterior is matched by its simple interior – though the newly gilded mihrab does draw attention. Off the northern end of the Kurnaysh is the **Custodian of the Two Holy Mosques, King Fahd Mosque**. This looks like it had just been transported from Morocco & is in an area of royal palaces near Roshan Mall on the Globe Roundabout.

Bait Nassif - Al Balad

Al Taqwa Mosque is just south of Al Nahda Road on Abdullah Al Matri Street (8km north of Al Balad). This small mosque is a local congregational mosque built in 1987. The young Imam - Nabil bin Abdulrahim bin Yahya Al-Rifai (www.nabeelalrefaei.com) – is an acclaimed reciter.

Al Tayibat Museum (Abdul Raouf Khalil Museum) 21.580446, 39.176661 www.musaksa.com 9:00-12:00/17:00:21:00 Sat-Thurs Closed Friday. SAR80. Its roughly a 13 km drive north of Al Balad on King Fahd Rd opposite the part of Jeddah University. This is a private museum that opened in 1996, founded by the late Sheikh Abdul Raouf Khalil. The exterior is in the style of a 19thc home and Mosque in Jeddah. Inside are exhibits over three floors – offering an overview of Saudi Arabia. The ambience is an old-fashioned museum. If you are touring Saudi Arabia, this is worth visiting to get a taste of what's to come.

King Fahd's Fountain Kurnaysh Rd. This sea fountain (north of the port off Al

Salam Palace) has been a landmark in Jeddah since 1985. It has the world's tallest water jet of, over 260m – as with the entire seafront of Jeddah this is good in the late afternoon as the sun-sets. 200m southeast if this is a massive **Saudi Arabian Flag** - once the world's tallest flagpole. **Middle Kurnaysh Sculpture Park** on Al Andalus and Kurnaysh (also called Al Corniche Rd or Al Hamra Kurnaysh). Open-air sculptures on the edge of a lagoon. They include pieces from the British sculptor Henry Moore.

Al Tayibat Museum

Serafi Mega Mall access from Al Sayyida Khadija St (off Setten Rd 10km drive from Al Balad) 21.561452, 39.186694 (8km north of Al Balad). A large four-floor – mid-price range shopping mall, though it is losing stores and 'footfall' to newer malls. It has an advantage of good parking. Leisure facilities including bowling & ice skating. A major supermarket has an excellent choice and a range of dining options, including the popular Al Baik.

Athr Gallery 10:00-14:00 / 17:00-21:00 Sun-Thurs 15:00-21:00 Sat www.athrart.com. Located upstairs in the Serafi Mall office building - Prince Mohammed bin Abdulaziz Street (just west of the junction with King Fahd Road) opposite IKEA. This contemporary multi-discipline art gallery is a hub for Saudi and Arab artists, with occasional exhibitions. If you are interested in the art scene in Jeddah, this is the place to visit. They also operate in AlUla.

Scooter rental

Darat Safeya Binzagr https://daratsb.com/ 10:30 - 14:00 Sat - Thu, King Abdullah Rd, about 6km north of Al Balad, is the base of the contemporary Saudi artist Safeya Binzagr.

Homegrown Market www.homegrownmkt.com On Saud Al Faisal Street in Ar Rawdah district. This is a retail outlet for local Saudi designers of fashion and clothing.

Fakieh Aquarium hours 10:00-23:00 (Fri midday-23:00) adults from SAR65 www.fakiehaquarium.com Al Kurnaysh Road This is a relatively small aquarium – with a claimed 200 species on show incl Dolphin & Seal. Watching captive sea life, especially Dolphins (SAR80), is not for everyone – however this is very popular. Check the website entry policies.

Red Sea Mall Sat-Thurs/10:00-01:00 Fri: after midday prayers - 01:00 Fri www.redseamall.com King AbdulAziz Road (about 25km drive north of Al Balad) Shopping is a key leisure activity in Saudi Arabia. Its major shopping malls frankly have

little to choose between them. The Red Sea Mall on the north part of King AbdulAziz
Rd is a mid to upper-price mall that is well-established in a location with other leisure
options close to it. There are numerous eating options in most shopping malls.
However, most are Western franchises and retail outlets that are a mix of Western and
local brands.

Cycle Hire - Kurnaysh

North of the Red Sea Mall is the 'City Walk' an amusement area. The **Formula 1
Racetrack** is 500m west of Red Sea Mall. It's set in the landscaped and popular seafront
of the **Kurnaysh** that extends for many kilometres. As it's west-facing – this is a great
place to be at sunset and is very popular with the locals in the evening - who picnic here
and fish. **Cycle Hire** (from SAR30) - & a car-free riding route (enquire at the hire shop
exactly where you may cycle) is south of the Formula 1 track. There are plenty of places
to have snacks (McDonalds, Tim Hortons and many local brands). The **Al Rahma
Mosque** (Page49) is in the northern section of the Formula 1 track. A bit further north,
past the Formula 1 track along the Kurnaysh, is the **Jeddah Yacht Club & Marina**
www.jeddahyachtclubandmarina.com. This is a possible visa entry point for private
yachts into Saudi Arabia, if it is pre-organised - check with the Marina regarding this.
There are several restaurants here.

Some 2km east of the Red Sea Mall is **Art Jameel** Sun-Thurs 10:00-20:00 Fri
14:00-22:00 Tues closed www.hayyjameel.org on Arwa bint Abdulmutalib Street. This
is a purpose built complex in Jeddah's spreading northern frontier. The focus is on art
and culture – with resident artists, workshops, temporary exhibition, cinema, shop and
so on. It has been in partnership with the UKs Prince's Foundation – now the focus has
shifted to a more Arab-centric and modern one.

Obhur Lagoon area (around 50km drive north of Al Balad) has private beaches as
part of hotel and chalet complexes on a creek area northwest of King AbdulAziz

International Airport. Contact several to find rates which fluctuate depending on local demand. King AbdulAziz Road is on one side, and Prince Abdullah Al Faisal Street on the other. The hotel beaches are small and at weekends become crowded. Coral Beach** +966126560702, Mangrove Beach Resort ** www.mangrovebeach.com Prince Abdullah Al Faisal Rd beach front & pools. Boat trips depart from a small marina Samaco Marina +9668002440366. The area is popular with younger people and families for the activities available in a calm lagoon setting – search out sea-trips, Jet-Skis and so on.

Obhur Lagoon from flynas

North Obhur is another area with sea-based activities - focused on a lagoon. Based around the Sheraton Marina +966122341871 – about 60km drive north of Al Balad. These activities include Jet Ski, Schiller Bikes and Scuba Diving http://Hadda-jscuba.com/. Most of these are busy at the weekend as their target clients are residents of Jeddah.

Jeddah Tower, in Jeddah Economic City – just adjacent to Obhur, is planned to be the world's tallest building. However, construction was halted for some years; it resumed in late 2023.

King Abdullah Economic City (KAEC) www.kaec.net is north of Jeddah; about 110km drive from Al Balad. Based in KAEC are major companies, Mars, Total Oil, Pfizer and Lucid cars. At **Royal Greens Golf & Country Club** https://royalgreens.net/ north of Jeddah at King Abdullah Economic City is the annual LIV Tour in Saudi during mid-October. There are hotels. private beaches Page23 and housing, though at the moment, the area is underdeveloped. KAEC is served by Al-Haramain Rail and Highway 5 (M55).

In the south of Jeddah - is **Al Saif Beach** South of Jeddah 21.168305, 39.171811 its a 50km drive. This public, free-to-use beach area has some facilities on a natural shallow lagoon. Public parking and landscaped areas add to the facilities. It is overlooked by a power plant with a water outlet a couple of kilometres offshore.

Festivals The Jeddah Summer Festival is a month-long festival from late June to late July. Spread in various locations, it is a family-oriented event. Check local papers or the Arabic www.jeddah.gov.sa.

For **Game Fishing & Scuba** research through - https://swsdf.sa/ the National Accreditation Body. In Jeddah **Coast Anglers** can be found through https://www.in-stagram.com/coast_anglers/ and **Haddad Scuba** https://haddadscuba.com/. Certificates for Scuba will be needed – PADI / BSAC.

~

RESTAURANTS & HOTELS IN JEDDAH

The stared* price is for a low-cost option within the restaurant or hotel – not the most expensive choice.

Where to eat in Al Balad.

Adventures & Hobbies Restaurant** (13:00-midnight) www.adventures-hobbies.com 100m southwest of Bab Jadid. A quirky, small, casual restaurant – serving local cuisine. **Al Bukhari Restaurant** * (11:00-23:00) on Al Dhab St. A low-cost Saudi-style food (meat & rice-based). **Baeshan Seafood** **(13:00-23:00) just off Souq Al Nada St., One of several fish restaurants here. Most are sitting on the floor style. The cooking style in all these is local – with fish & rice. **Baissa Mandi**** midday-02:00 rice and meat in a Saudi/Yemeni style on Al Dhab St northern end. Just on the corner of Al Dhab St (near Baissa Mandi) is a small local bakery - **Forn Al Sheikh***, - selling traditional local bread and pastries; it's a takeaway.

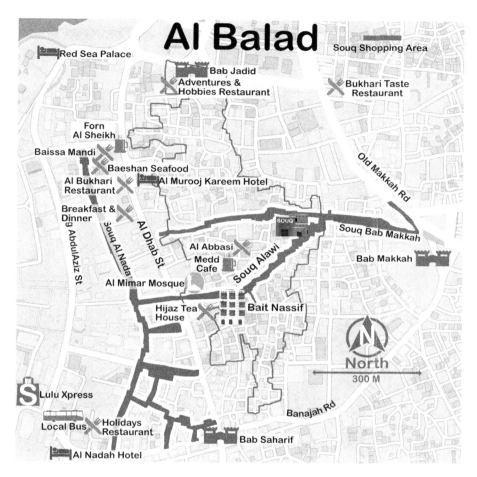

Some places to consider eating in

Breakfast & Dinner * (06:00-11:00/15:00-23:00) on a side street west of Al Dhab St (opposite Broast Hanoo) – cheap & quick street food & drink - here you could choose 'Shakshouka' and egg omelette with tomato etc. with Lebanese (pitta) or other flat bread – Shakshouka is ubiquitous in Saudi as a cheap, quick snack. **Diyab Coffee** * (09:00-23:00) and **Medd Cafe** * (08:00-23:00) are a couple of coffee shops less than 70m north of Bait Nassif.

To their northwest -is **Al Abbasi Restaurant*** (07:00-midday/07:00-23:00), a small operation offering light local Arabic-style meals. **Hijaz Tea House*** (09:00-23:00) on Souq Alawi opposite Al-Mimar Mosque. A small coffee shop-style option also with light meals – focusing on tourists. It could do with an upgrade - they are overwhelmed at times, and service suffers.

Medd Cafe

   Holidays Restaurant * 10:00-Midnight Fri 13:30-midnight * 012 649 4947 Al Bahr Street – southwest of Al Balad by a street market, just off the western end of Salah Al Din St Indian food with rice and meat-based food. In the northeast is the popular, well-priced **Bukhari Taste Restaurant**** (one of a chain) +966543660849 11:30-midnight on Old Makkah Rd - this is a central Asian style option with simple decor and authentic, low-priced rice and meat food.
   Where to eat away from Al Balad in Jeddah. Many visitors almost inevitably eat at night, in or near their hotel and during the day where convenient. However, Jeddah has an excellent range of restaurants in a mid-price bracket. In Jeddah, the better restaurants are in the 5-star hotels and the more modern city area towards the airport. Our stared price is for a low-cost option within the restaurant or hotel – not the most expensive. With few tourists away from Al Balad – they are catering solely to a very demanding local clientele and need that repeat business. In general, the food will be freshly cooked for you. The service may not be as good as you would hope for, but typically, the cost

will be less than in a European or North American equivalent. To give you an idea of options to eat in, a few are below – of course, there are also the western franchises such as McDonalds, Starbucks and so on. **Al Sadda Restaurant**** www.alsaddahrest.com/ +966126673545 11:00-01:00 Palestine St (and Hira St & Tahlia St branches in Riyadh) A southwest Saudi/Yemeni style restaurant, meat and rice-based, with cubicles to sit on the floor, with cushions. **Ash Café*** 07:00-midnight 054 104 5110 - just west of the junction of Al Madinah Al Munawarah Road & Quraysh Street in As Salamah – this is a small local start-up with excellent coffee and a limited selection of cakes. **Cup & Couch Cafe** ** 06:30-23:30 Al Yamamah St (just south of Mohammed Ibrahim Masoud Rd) Beautifully laid out, with a variety of seating options - a local, trendy coffee shop that does expect 'smart casual' and at times may be overwhelmed by the number of customers – but these go toward making a more interesting experience. **BACO**** 13:00-01:00 +966500034378 Boulevard Mall, Ali Abou AlUla St - Asian Latin fusion in a casual, stylish atmosphere. **Belajio Resort****** 09:00-02:00 +966920003409 Kurnaysh Rd (surrounded by the Formula 1 track) west of the Red Sea Mall are several seafront leisure facilities that run from the Planetarium in the south to Belajio Resort adjacent to the Red Sea Mall. Bellagio Resort is a couple of artificial islands (400m west of the Red Sea Mall) with several restaurants, both indoor and outdoor seating. The Red Sea Mall has a good choice in its popular food-court.

The Hilton near the Kurnaysh offers alternative restaurants like the **Ginger Leaf** **** (19:00-midnight) **Brew92 Café**** (one of a chain in northern Jeddah - all are good) 07:00-midnight +966540576421 Sari Rd Coffee and light meals - a good option for quick meals if you are in a rush. **Falafel Al Sham Restaurant*** is a local chain serving – falafel, mainly as a takeaway. **Khayal Restaurant**** www.khayalrest.com The hours are practically 24 – with a break at dawn and midday prayers. Prince Sultan Rd off Hira St. This is a very popular Levant-style restaurant – often bustling. They offer a wide range from Shawarma-style sandwiches – though to overwhelming mains. They have branches in Taif & Yanbu. **Le Traiteur****** www.letraiteur.com.sa/ 13:00-midnight Abu Al Abbas Bin Abdulmutalib. From the name – it's training you to enjoy modern French cuisine. **Makan** **** 13:00-01:00 +966530814100 Mohammed Al Tayb Al Tunisi (off Prince Mohammed bin Abdulaziz St) Indian fusion style. A delightful setting, Mainly north Indian style food. **Naranj Restaurant***** 15:00-midnight www.naranjsa.com On Abdul Maqsus Khojah Street A Syrian restaurant (about 14km drive from Bait Nassif) elegantly decorated appropriately. Both indoor and courtyard dining. Service can be patchy in courtesy, but overall, it is a pleasant experience – always check the cost with VAT before ordering. **Nino***** - http://nino-me.com/ Palestine St junction with Al Andalous. Simple in appearance, it's an Italian restaurant.

Shakshouka egg dish - with Naan style bread

Pink Camel** 08:00-23:0+553206187 Ibrahim Al Jafali Street west of Median Road, Al Hamra A small restaurant with coffee and light food. Outdoor seating. **Qaymariyya*** – Hamid Al Jaser +966126622221 Modern, bright Levant style Sheesha Cafe. Stop by one of the small outdoor sheesha places, or if smoking is not your cup of tea, try some Arabic coffee instead. **Street Fifty Six**** 15:00-23:00 +00542077601

Ahmed Al Attas Street in Al Zahara east of the Kurnaysh Attractive and authentic Asian style' street food' along with a United Nations of other influences, served with universal French fries. **Sura****** - +966568767234 Prince Saud Al Faisal St 12:30-23:00 Korean dining by style and cuisine.**Accommodation**

Hotels in Jeddah are far from cheap compared to North African Arab destinations; they are some what lower in price than Western cities. Lower cost options suffer from lower standards in housekeeping & maintenance, due to poor or no management. As the city has spread north towards & beyond the airport, the choice of hotels has also grown in those areas. There is a good range of 5* hotels, including the **Ritz Carlton******* www.ritzcarlton.com - between Al Balad & the Kurnaysh, **Waldorf Astoria******* www.hilton.com both overlook (but are not next to) the sea. For value for money, consider the **Hilton** **** www.hilton.com, which also has a choice of good restaurants and overlooks the open ocean on the northern part of the Kurnaysh near the Waldorf. Farther down the price scale is the city hotel **Movenpick Hotel City Star** *** www.movenpick.com on Al Madinah Al Munawarah Road with 228 rooms in what could be called a Louis Farouq style, and with three dining options.

Alternatives include the **Radisson Blu** (a couple of locations) ** www.radissonhotels.com in a less ornate style. **Red Sea Palace Hotel** ** +96626428555 King AbdulAziz Rd – an older hotel well located for Al Balad. There are numerous budget hotels – **Renz Hotel** * +966126725111 on Palestine Rd is near several other reasonable low-cost options. The **Ibis Jeddah** Malik Road** www.accor.com, northeast of Al Balad, offers a pool and a couple of dining options (they have exceptionally dynamic pricing – aimed at maximising occupancy).

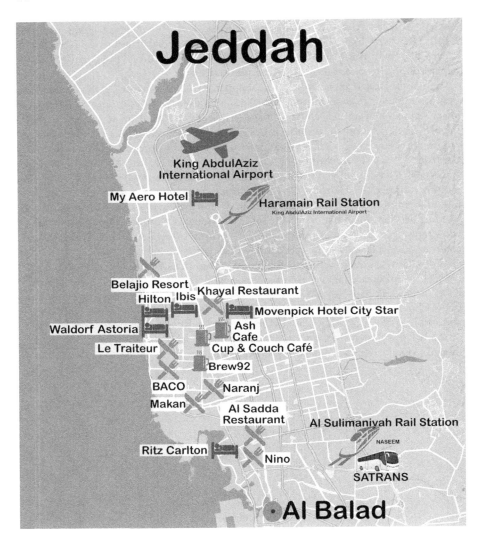

INSIDE AL BALAD, THE HOTELS CERTAINLY NEED UPGRADING - THE **AL Murooj Kareem** Hotel* +966126445052 is convenient, and on Al Dhahab St. Less central, but within walking distance of Souq Al Alawi, are the basic **Al Nadah Hotel** *+966126471158, two other hotels are outside the main Al Balad area, just southwest of Al Nadah Hotel - **Prime Almina** Hotel** +966552151020, **Touq Balad** Hotel** +966126490756. There were more hotels in Al Balad's area – the redevelopment of old properties by **Al Balad Hospitality**, www.albaladhospitality.com, will mean boutique style options open, as in Souq Waqif in Doha. These will open from early 2024.

If needed, an airport hotel is at King AbdulAziz International Airport (www.myaerotel.com).

GETTING AROUND JEDDAH

Jeddah is a rectangular city, around 1,000sqkm, with the administrative area around 1,600 sq km. Urban development sprawls to the north and south where the coastal plain allows for extensive spread. To the east, the mountains act as a barrier and to the west is the Red Sea. In the north of the city, the arterial roads out of Jeddah run north-south. They feed into Al Nouzhah St/Route 217 – which links up to Highway 5/M55 that leads north to Haql & the Jordan border. In the east, use Setten Rd, also called King Fahd Rd, to link up with Highway 80 (M50) and onto Highway 15 (M45), which goes north to Madinah or up into the mountains at Taif. To the south, Al Andalus & Al Falah roads feed traffic onto Highway 5 (M55), which leads south to Jizan.

Key modern shopping areas are Prince Mohammed bin Abdulaziz Street, Madinah Al Munawara Road and Prince Sultan Street with their malls. As with all Saudi towns, the car rules - with minimal public transport and multi-lane highways which ease traffic flow and impede pedestrian progress. However - Al Balad is quite easy, indeed a pleasure, to explore on foot - and the Kurnaysh (seafront street also Corniche) is also walking-friendly.

Jeddah's local public transport is largely provided by **SAPTCO Bus**. They operate between 05:30-22:30 with frequency at least every 20 mins during the week and as often as every 35 mins on a Friday. Payment is through a plastic tap-and-go type card. This card is purchased for SAR10 on the bus or at a hub - and is then topped up on the bus for the fare. Fares are SAR3.45 per ride. Unfortunately, although the company, SAPTCO, operates in other towns and uses the same system in each, the cards are currently not interchangeable.

The local buses are typically used by non-Saudi workers. Men sit in the larger rear section, women in the front.

The southwest area of Al Balad – east of Lulu Xpress, is the hub for various routes – including bus 13 to the Airport and bus 14 to the Al Sulimaniyah Train Station (every 50mins). There is a supervisor at this Al Balid bus hub who can help with questions - this is a 'temporary' location moved from near Bab Makkah due to the redevelopment there. With all the redevelopment it may move again.

The main SATRANS **coach** https://satrans.com.sa/ long-distance coach station was also relocated from near Lulu Xpress, to the Al Sulimaniyah Train Station. An alternative transport is the Careem green and white minibus. These run west-east along Prince Mohammed bin Abdulaziz Street (Tahlia Street – named after Tahlia Mall), north-south on Prince Sultan Road, and Hira Street west to east. These buses are hailed by the Careem app and boarded from fixed points along the route, with a cash payment to the driver (SAR3/SAR5).

Bus Al Sulimaniyah Train Station.

Taxi services include Uber with a minimum of SAR12 for 12 minutes and SAR0.50 per minute afterwards. Careem taxi is a good alternative - they currently accept cash and credit card payments; other options include Bolt. There is a wide range of car rental options in Jeddah, both from the airport and the city. Avis.com, Hertz.ae, and Budget.com are available with compact Japanese and cheaper Chinese automatic options provided.

Unless you especially enjoy driving yourself in a congested city, use either a taxi or bus. Using a taxi for the last kilometre will help when using a bus, if on a budget. This also means that parking will not be an issue.

≈

GETTING TO JEDDAH

Flying into Jeddah is through King AbdulAziz International Airport www.kaia.sa, whose new terminal opened in 2018. Initially, it was only used by Saudia, with other national carriers relocating starting with Etihad at the end of 2019. There are separate entrances depending on the class of your ticket. The terminal serves international and domestic flights and is about 25km from the Madinah Gate in Al Balad. The new terminal is substantial, perhaps a kilometre long- with 2 wings at each end serving more than 40 gates. Use the terminal trains (APM) and travelators. At the arrivals entrance, it has that essential for a modern airport- a vast aquarium. There is an entirely separate terminal for Hajj pilgrims.

At the airport, parking for 21,000 vehicles is immediately outside the terminal, with a pick-up and drop-off directly at the terminal entrance.

Airlines using the airport include Air Arabia (low cost), British Airways, Emirates, Etihad, flyadeal (low cost) domestically, flydubai (low cost), Gulf Air, Kuwait Airways, and Oman Air. Riyadh Air, the new airline, will be added to the choice – finally Wizz Air, also low cost.

Road connections to the airport are good, principally the Prince Majid Road.

A train https://sar.hhr.sa/ operates south from the airport terminal to Jeddah Al Sulimaniyah Station (reopened after a fire caused its closure in 2019) and onto Makkah (this section to Makkah is, of course, for Muslims only). The same line goes to the north via King Abdullah Economic City (Rabigh Station) to Madinah. The Haramain rail into Jeddah Al Sulimaniyah Train Station is hardly worthwhile as that station is farther away from the Kurnaysh than the airport, and almost as far to Al Balad. However, a public bus, 14, runs between the Al Sulimaniyah train station (from the furthest area of the road drop off/pick up) and Al Balad. The bus operates from 07:15 to midnight every 50mins appx. Direct from the airport into Al Balad is Bus 13.

Al Sulimaniyah Train Station

SATRANS coach https://satrans.com.sa/ (previously SAPTCO buses www.saptco.com.sa) offer excellent connections to Jeddah from numerous cities and towns, including Riyadh, Abha, Tabuk and many more. The Jeddah – Riyadh service runs several times daily and costs from SAR190 single for the 12-hour trip. The SAPTCO service was also several times a day between Jeddah and Abha, the new SATRANS website does not list it as of compilation of this book. The Jeddah SATRANS coach station has moved to the train station at Al Sulimaniyah. It previously was just west of Al Balad, on Baishin Road, about 1.5km walk southwest of Bait Nasib in Al Balad. Use bus number 14 for travel into Al Balad.

Ferry services operate between Jeddah to Othman Digna Port at Suakin/Sawakin Sudan (the historical port now leased by Turkey), 50 kilometres south of Port Sudan. Tickets from Namma International Marine Services Co.(www.nammamari-nesservices.com) on King Khalid Rd – outside the port about 2km to the east. Review their carriage terms carefully and ensure any payment receipt is for the total charge. Vehicles (from SAR2000) & passengers (from SAR900) are charged separately. The ferry takes 12-14 hours. The time to organise your car may take a full day – ensure you plan this several days in advance with the office & review your foreign ministry's travel advice into Sudan. Remember that 15% VAT (dharebu) is charged in Saudi Arabia – check whether the quoted price includes VAT.

CHAPTER 5
YANBU TO THE RED SEA RESORTS VIA RABIGH

Rabigh رابغ GPS 22.799916, 39.036668 - Travelling north from Jeddah to Yanbu is a tedious drive – on the broad express Highway 15 (M45). Rabigh is passed before arriving at Yanbu. Rabigh's area is home to King AbdulAziz University and has a Train Station of the Haramain service. The town was one of several attacked in December 1182 by the crusader Raynald of Chatillon during his conflict with Saladin.

Yanbu ينبع – GPS - 24.078670, 38.059037 **Population** (appx) 258,777. **A brief history** - Yanbu has been associated with several historic ports whose actual location is unknown. The most probable link is with Charmuthas, a port in the first centuryBC. Its location may have been the creek – 15 km northwest of Yanbu Al Baha. The Roman Prefect of Egypt, Aelius Gallus, may have used Yanbu as the disembarkation port for his failed invasion of Yemen – there are other candidates for this port. Yanbu grew substantially as the main port for Madinah after the Ayyubid dynasty developed it. The Caliph Ali bin Abi Talib had estates in the inland area of Yanbu Al Nakhl. Yanbu Al Nakhl was a key stopping place in the Egyptian Pilgrimage route due to its abundant water springs. The Sharif Qatada bin Idris (died AD1220) was born in Yanbu, and it is from him that the later Sharifs of Makkah descended. In October 1811, the army of Egypt landed in Yanbu under the command of Mohammed Ali Pasha's son Tusan – their intention to defeat the Al Saud forces in Diriyah.

More recently, Lawrence of Arabia arrived in Yanbu Al Bahr on 2 December 1916, moving on to Yanbu Al Nakhl (then called Nakhl Al Mubarak) – at the start of his involvement in the Arab Revolt. He stayed in the Yanbu area until 2 January. 1917. As with so many towns in Saudi Arabia, the town wall was demolished after the 2nd World War as the population increased, security improved and money from oil flowed around the kingdom. In Yanbu, its wall was torn down in 1948.

Lawrence of Arabia's house - Yanbu

Yanbu's southern coastal area of Al Sinaiya is a vital part of the industrialisation of Saudi Arabia. It was established in 1975, along with Jubail on the east coast.

Night Market - Yanbu

YANBU HAS A LIMITED NUMBER OF ATTRACTIONS. AN EXTENSIVE landscaped area runs along the beachfront for around 8 km along Kings Abdullah & Khalid roads in the residential area southeast of Yanbu Al Bahr and northwest of Yanbu Al-Sinaiya. In Yanbu Al Bahr – the critical area of interest is immediately west of the port. This includes an area of pop-up fast food stalls opposite the small area of older houses that have been or are being renovated. Several restaurants, mainly fish, are associated with a small souq area, the **Night Market**. A small Visitor Centre cum museum (10:00-21:00 – Fri 13:00-21:00) is west of the collection of old houses. This offers a quick, free, insight into the Yanbu area. To the east, a small art centre, **Al Saagh**, has occasional music events. To the rear of the old housing, opposite an area with trees, is the reputed **house of Lawrence of Arabia**. It's currently not open – and is heavily restored.

Northwest of Yanbu – is **Barracuda Beach**, the start of the excellent **Scuba/snorkelling** of Yanbu. Several Scuba diving operators in Yanbu offer diving the islands offshore - including the Iona wreck - 10 km to the west. Check out Yanbu Divers +966543166655 about 9km northwest of the port & Coral Reef Divers – on the main highway King AbdulAziz Rd +966563363606 near Taraf Yanbu Hotel.

A **Flower Festival** is held in February/March in Al Sinaiya's 'Celebration Park' south of Highway 5 (M55) 15kms eat of the port in Yanbu Al Bahr.

Driving east out of Yanbu Al Bahr on the road to Madinah, AlUla, and Khaybar is **Yanbu Al Nakhl** GPS 24.322712, 38.416404. Here about 47 km from the port area of Yanbu Al Bahr, to the west of Route 328, water springs irrigate areas of agriculture. The very scattered plots with agriculture are in sunken areas – perhaps the elevated land areas are 'tells' where centuries of mud-brick housing have collapsed into a mound, alternatively the gardens may have been dug down to give gravity-fed water flow from the spring.

≈

EATING OPTIONS THE TOWN HAS A GOOD SELECTION OF RESTAURANTS and is worth eating here even if driving elsewhere.

The most convenient restaurant options are around the Night Market, especially **Al Marsah Sea Food** ** 11:00-23:00 +966544291010 & **Ozone Seafood Restaurant** *** 13:00-01:00 +966143251738 with rooftop dining - on the main highway King AbdulAziz Rd - east of Yanbu Al Bahr. **Khayal Restaurant** **, 10:00-23:00 (Fri 16:00-23:00) at Yanbu Mall, Ali Bin Abi Talib St (Opposite Al Jarir Books) www.khayalrest.com Levantine food. This is one of a small chain – Jeddah, Taif, Khamis Mushait.

Accommodation Yanbu also has a reasonable selection of places to stay - at the lower cost end - **Al Dhakiya Apartments** * - +966554017617, a small block of apartments on King AbdulAziz Rd about 5km drive from the port. **Cities Inn Hotel Apartments** ** +966590001928 not far from the sea - near the **Radisson Blu** *** www.radissonhotels.com - both are southeast of the port.

Getting there

North of Jeddah, after 260kms, is **Al Rayes** town, west of Highway 5 (M55), with a lagoon, white sand beaches and turquoise sea. **Aljar Resort** ** +966554255600 overlooks the lagoon but, unfortunately, is separated by a road.

Yanbu is an easy but monotonous 350km drive north along Highway 5 (M55) from Jeddah. From Madinah in the mountains - Yanbu is a more interesting drive of around 230km using Routes 8028 & 328. SATRANS does have a small bus station northwest of the old town – off Khalid bin Al Walid. As with cities away from Dammam, Jeddah and Riyadh - there are no local bus services and poor taxi options. The Red Sea Resorts are also on Highway 5 (M55) – about 220km northwest of Yanbu. Expect some restrictions due to the construction work in this area.

Umluj 24.9609117,37.1230593 املج is a small settlement, 151km along Highway 5 (M55) from Yanbu. A restored Emirate Palace (FOC when open), in effect a fortified house, and small souq are adjacent to the local fishing harbour. Several small restaurants line Highway 5 (M55) and cluster around the Emirate Palace. Umluj makes a convenient stop on any drive north, towards Jordan.

The Red Sea Resorts / منتجع البحر الاحمر - الشورى - GPS - 25.505424, 37.000404 Just over 200km north along the coast from Yanbu & almost 600km north of Al Balad, is one of Saudi Arabia's new resort areas, 'The Red Sea' www.theredsea.sa. The Red Sea collection is focused on a series of offshore islands. The locations include Shura Island, Sheybarah Island & Ummahat Island (**Ritz Carlton** & **St Regis**). Here is an airport Red Sea International & Sea Plane options at Hanak. Amaala (also part of the Red Sea Resorts operation) is a less ambitious project just south of Duba.

CHAPTER 6

DUBA TOWN & DUBA PORT

Duba / ضبا - GPS - 27.348626, 35.695084 **Population** (appx) 39,543
Probably the only tourist attraction in Duba is King AbdulAziz Castle. 10:00-12:00 16:00-19:00 - Fri 16:00-19:00 (currently closed for renovation). It dates from 1933 and is set in the central area of the town - as an administrative and, in the early days, as a defence place. Inside is a small prayer room and rooms arranged around a courtyard.

Some places to consider Eating In. - There are a few restaurants in Duba. On the main highway, King Abdullah Rd Al Marajan Fish ** +966507406117 is easy to get to - it's next to Marsa Duba Hotel ** +966500087145 which is an option to overnight in.

Duba Port/Oxagon/NEOM Port / ميناء ضبا - GPS - 27.557048, 35.556664 Duba is the port will be used by NEOM for the core of its planned Oxagon floating industrial complex. From Duba Port - ferries currently sail to Safaga in Egypt. Namma International Marine Services Namma International Marine Services Co. Ltd., (Namma Shipping Lines) www.nammamarineservices.com 5th Floor, Hotel Jeddah Trident, Port Road, Al-Hindawiya +966-12-648 7203 Ext. 170. Closer to Duba Port Naama Marine www.nammamarineservices.com on King Abdullah Rd. Next to it is Al-

Bassam Foundation for Marine Works info@bassamdubagroup.com +966509176813. Alternatively, Mubashir Agency +966 56 277 9308 akhatab1987@yahoo.com just north of roundabout Duba town (opposite football ground) in Duba Town. Check the services - there may be a standard slow ferry (overnight service) or a new faster catamaran twice a week - 1200 passengers/ 110 cars. Passengers can book relatively easily (an Egyptian Visa is required before boarding) - cars need more organising & time.

GETTING THERE DRIVING NORTH ALONG THE COAST FROM YANBU - DUBA is a small town reached after a tedious 470km drive on Highway 5 (M55) from Yanbu. Thirty kilometres north of Duba town is Duba Port. SATRANS coach does offer a service here. Check carefully about this coach service - as the port and Duba town are a long way apart.

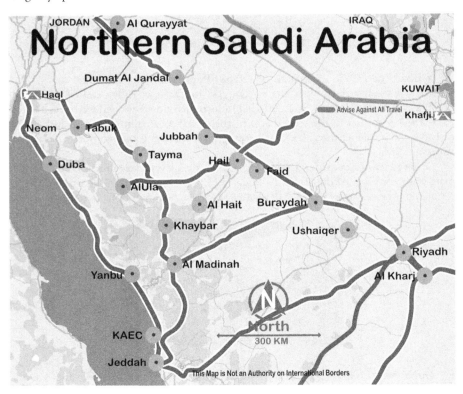

CHAPTER 7
NEOM, SHARMA, WADI AYNUNA

NEOM / نيوم - GPS - 28.067699, 35.238028 www.neom.com. This is the US$500 billion+ (yes, that billion with a B) poster child of Saudi Arabia's new focus on re-branding, diversification generally and leisure tourism. Many of the intended projects have an avant-garde design, familiar to architecture and sci-fi aficionados from the 1960s onwards. NEOM's projects (at the moment there are 10) include 'The Line,' a remarkably ambitious linear city enclosed within a mirrored shell. This is planned to stretch 170km east from Ras Al Sheikh Hameed (Ras Sheikh Humaid) on the Gulf of Aqaba. Within its 500m width its intended to have 'no roads, cars or emissions' with a high-speed rail system among the transport options. As this is a key project it is likely that major events will be associated with it, in much the same way as Trojena is planned to host the Asian Winter Games. Excavations to prepare the ground for around 50km are underway.

Just north on Gulf of Aqaba is the planned small collection of hotels called Leyja. Another remarkable project is **Trojena**, which is expected, to be a winter sports resort and host to the 2029 Asian Winter Games, amongst other things. It's 2,000+ meters above sea level, within an arid landscape around Jabal Lawz – from Highway 5 (M55) at Al Sharaf Route 394 leads east through this region's dramatic scenery towards Tabuk. Hotels brands, such as the Chedi, will be a feature. Currently, beach games are held on the coast near Sharma, & triathlons at **Ras Al Sheikh Hameed** see www.neom.com for dates etc for these events – a shuttle bus is also available from Tabuk for these sporting events. Much of the NEOM general area (including areas around Duba and Wadi Tayyib Al Ism) is currently a restricted zone for these massive planned building projects. Smaller projects within their 'sustainable regional development' umbrella include Epicon & Siranna.

What's there From **Sharma**, though to the Gulf of Aqaba is a series of islands and lagoons that are part of NEOM. These are served by the NEOM airport & much farther south Duba port. The islands of Tiran and Sanafir that straddle the Strait of

Tiran into the Gulf of Aqaba, were ceded by Egypt to Saudi Arabia in 2017. A key focus is **Sindalah Island**, opposite the Strait of Tiran at the mouth of the Gulf of Aqaba. Sindalah Island is a luxury accommodation complex with a marina and world-class yacht repair centre. The eastern region of NEOM includes several mountain peaks - including Jabal Lawz - the highest in the region and one with a good elevation above the immediate surroundings. The area was associated with the Biblical Mount Sinai since its linkage by Ron Wyatt in the mid-1980s.

NEOM

Wadi Aynuna / Leuke Kome / وادي عينونة / ليوك كومي / - GPS - 28.086408, 35.183745 **A brief History** - East of the coastal developments of Sindalah (NEOM) and Sharma is the historic archaeological area in Wadi Aynuna that possibly was the Nabataean trading town of Leuke Kome that functioned from 2nd centuryBC - 7th cAD. The visible remains are located on the northern bank of Wadi Aynuna. The remaining low walls suggest a fortified building, perhaps for warehousing and adjacent small settlement. The small fishing port of Al Khuraybah may have been the harbour's location.

   Getting There The coastal hub of NEOM is around 1,000 km from Jeddah - using Highway 5 (M55), passing Yanbu. There will be regular flights eventually.

CHAPTER 8
AIN MUSA, MAGHAYER SHOAIB, WADI TAYYIB AL ISM AND THE JORDAN BORDER

This general area has numerous small sites that have acquired a Biblical connection. Access while all the tourism works connected with NEOM will change. from Highway 5 (M55) at Al Sharaf Route 394 leads east through this region's dramatic scenery towards Tabuk.

Ain Musa / عين موسى - GPS - 28.396427, 34.751054

On the coastal road, towards the Jordanian border, at **Maqnah** is Ain Musa - a couple of perpetually flowing water springs (Ayn is the Gulf Arabic for water spring). The spring is a kilometre east of Maqna, just south of Route 8746, in an area of scattered Date Palms. The nomenclature doubtless adds momentum to Jabal Lawz's association with Mount Sinai.

- tombs Maghayer Shoaib

Maghayer Shoaib / مغاير شعيب - GPS - 28.488213, 34.999586 **Population** (appx) 16,583 **A Brief History** - The previous name of Maghayer Shoaib was Midian Shoaib which references the Biblical & Quranic Land of Midian which is generally accepted to be to the east of the Gulf of Aqaba, and Shoaib (Shuyab named Jethro / Reuel in the Bible's Exodus) the land's priest/king. After fleeing Egypt, Moses is said to have helped Shoaib's daughters and married one, Zipporah.

What's there - Near the town of **Al Bidea** - Maghayer Shoaib 10:00-18:00 Sun-Thurs 16:00-18:00 Fri-Sat FOC is a collection of tombs (overall about two dozen) cut into the rocks which are stylistically Nabataean. There is little information about them - however, the area must have had some wealth, from trade, for these tombs to be created.

Getting there Maghayer Shoaib at Al Bidea town is another location off the coastal drive, in western Saudi. On Highway 5 (M55), it's about 680 km from Yanbu - about 120km south of the Saudi/Jordan border.

Wadi Tayyib Al Ism / وادي طيب أسم - GPS - 28.559925, 34.801549 The impressive coastal road to the Jordan border is built against steep cliffs. Partway along is Wadi Tayyib Al Ism, a steep gorge cut into the mountains. This area is locally linked to Moses - especially Exodus 15-27 - Elim with its springs and palm trees. Wadi Tayyib Al Ism is temporally closed due to work connected with the Leyja 3 hotel resort under NEOM, which will be constructed inside the valley. The spring is about 7km (walk) inside the wadi from the coastal highway.

Wadi Tayyib Al Ism - with Sinai in the distance

Haql & the Jordan Border / حقل / الحدود - GPS - 29.299881, 34.951977 **Population** (appx) 25,652. Haql is the last settlement before the **Durra** / **Aqaba** border on Highway 5 (M55) into Jordan. It's some 1,100km between the border and Jeddah. The border crossing is quick both ways - except at weekends - and especially slow during Eid, the Hajj and Umrah. Though currently buses do not operate, they used to. If they do restart operations between Jordan into Saudi - obtain your Saudi visa online to save hassle at the immigration counters - and vice versa. In Haql, there are several petrol stations. Aqaba has a better range of hotels and restaurants.

CHAPTER 9
MADINAH

M adinah / المدينة المنورة - GPS - 24.465637, 39.610507 Population (appx) 1,411,599

A quick overview of the geography - Madinah is set with an arid landscape - of granites and basalt fields. To the south are the lava flows from numerous volcanos in Harrat Rahat stretching south towards Makkah. The volcanos have been active as recently as AD1,256. **A brief history** - The holy city of Madinah (officially Al Madinah Al Munawwarah), has a long and rich history dating back thousands of years. Located in the Hijaz region of present-day Saudi Arabia, it was originally called Yathrib and was inhabited by a mix of Jewish and polytheistic Arab tribes.

Around the 6th centuryBC, the city was dominated by three prominent Jewish tribes - the Banu Qaynuqa, the Banu Nadir and the Banu Qurayza. They lived peacefully alongside the pagan Arab tribes of Aws and Khazraj for several centuries. However, conflict arose in the early 7th centuryAD with the arrival of Islam.

Madinah is revered as the place where the first Islamic community was established and flourished under the leadership of the Prophet Muhammad. He relocated to Madinah from Makkah in AD622 after liaisons with the Aws and Khazraj. This journey of exodus (Hijrah) marks the beginning date of the Islamic era, Hijri. The Prophet unified the tribes under the banner of Islam and made treaties with the Jewish tribes, forming the Constitution of Madinah. After eight years in Madinah, Islam became firmly established as the dominant faith.

After Muhammad died in AD632, he was buried in the house of one of his wives, Aisha. The burial location is now immediately below the **Green Dome** of the Prophet's Mosque (Masjid al-Nabawi). This mosque became the second most sacred site in Islam after the Kaaba in Makkah.

Many companions of the Prophet lived and taught there, making it a crucial hub for preserving and developing Islamic knowledge. Over the following centuries, Madinah grew as a significant religious and scholarly centre in the Islamic world. Pilgrimage to the Prophet's Mosque and tomb became an increasingly important, non-obligatory, ritual for Muslims.

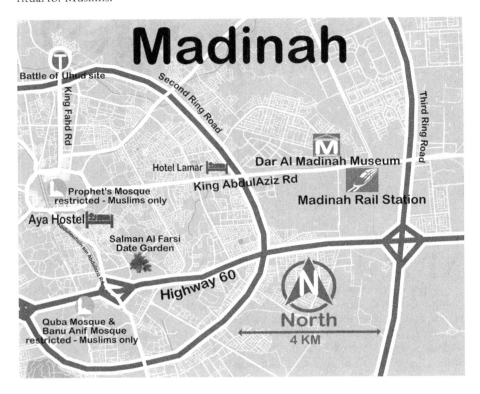

MADINAH'S SIGNIFICANCE AS A RELIGIOUS DESTINATION GREW UNDER THE Mamluks of Egypt, who controlled the Hijaz region from 1250-1517AD. They invested heavily in expanding and decorating the Prophet's Mosque and developing infrastructure for pilgrims. This helped cement Madinah 's place as the second holiest city after Makkah.

In 1517, the Hijaz came under the control of the Ottoman Empire, which continued to improve access and safety for pilgrims travelling to Makkah and Madinah. However, in 1805, the first Saudi State led by Abdulaziz bin Muhammad Al Saud briefly occupied Madinah before Ottoman rule was restored.

In 1925, Madinah was conquered by the Saudi ruler Amir AbdulAziz Al Saud without heavy fighting. He became King of the Hijaz in January 1926 - the title had been created by the previous ruler, Hussein bin Ali Al Hashimi - and King AbdulAziz Al Saud added Nejd to this title. He went on to establish the modern Kingdom of Saudi Arabia. This began significant renovations and expansions to the Prophet's Mosque under Saudi patronage.

Today, the Prophet's Mosque remains the enduring symbol of Madinah 's sacred status in Islam. Millions visit every year to pray at the site of Muhammad's tomb and walk in the city where he established the first Muslim community. While some pilgrimage sites have been lost to development and religious dogma, Madinah's place as the second holiest city for Muslims worldwide remains unchanged.

Prophet's Mosque - Madinah

Orientation

The Prophet's Mosque is in the centre of Madina – within ring-roads. From the Prophet's Mosque is The First Ring Rd (King Faisal) then Prince AbdulMajid bin Abdulaziz, and The Second Ring Road (King Abdullah). There is a potential Third Ring Road (King Khalid) that is not complete in the north. The First Ring Road encircles the Prophets Mosque and the hotel area and Al Baqi Cemetery. Within this area is a largely pedestrian street layout. A substantial vehicle underpass (Prince Abdul Mohsen bin Abdul Aziz Rd) is below the Prophets Mosque's area.

What to see - Madinah has only been officially accessible to non-Muslims for a few years. There will be many Muslims who are not aware that a non-Muslim is permitted to visit – many might be shocked that they can. If you are a non-Muslim, discretion is suggested, especially in your clothes. Ideally, dress as if visiting a mosque when you are visiting Madinah – this after all is the location of the second most revered site in Islam. Males should wear long, loose-fitting trousers – and a traditional long-sleeved shirt. Women should wear clothing so that only feet, hands and face are exposed –a headscarf and loose-fitting garments are ideal – and a black Abaya (cloak) is even better.

It's possible to approach the Prophet's Mosque to the Perimeter Wall & Railings. This permission can of course change without notice – and the security guards are empowered to take appropriate action.

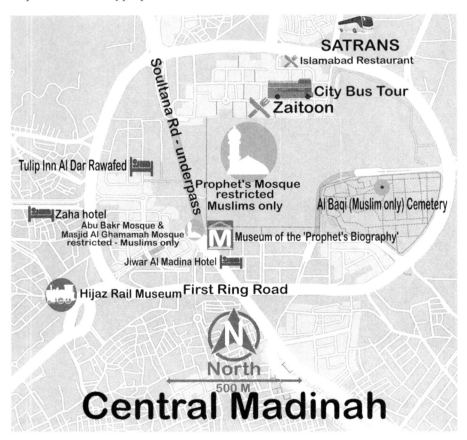

Today, the **Prophet's Mosque** encloses about 460,000 sqm, and the mosque itself is just under 100,000 sqm. Further expansion is currently being made in the northeast corner. Apart from the mosque especially the **Green Dome**, the courtyard's umbrellas are the most noticeable feature when viewed from outside. These can open and close automatically to create shade. The **Al Baqi Cemetery** (to the east), is where several members of the Prophet Mohammed's family are buried (near the mosque). Close associates are also buried here, as are some modern dignitaries. The graves are now simple, in the style preferred by the current authorities, with only head/foot stones and no inscriptions. Elaborate mausoleums were demolished over the last 200 years.

South of the mosque is a museum of the **Museum Of The Prophet's Biography** https://med.salamfairs.com.sa/ 05:30-22:00 SAR40. This modern exhibition gives an overview of the Prophet & Islam.

Immediately west of the mosque are two small mosques, **Abu Bakr Al-Siddiq Mosque** and **Al-Ghamama Mosque**. Both, in origin, date from the time of the Prophet Mohammed and were used by him.

To the southwest of the mosque (near the government offices) is the **Hijaz Train Station** daily 09:00-16:00/17:00-22:00 – Friday 17:00-21:00 SAR10. Also within the building is the **Madinah Museum**. The building is the original Ottoman construction and is almost a twin of the station in Damascus from where the trains originated (see Page84).

Hijaz Rail Station & Museum

Inside, the museum is well laid out, with a suggested flow to see the exhibits, and provides a good overview of Saudi Arabia and its history & culture. Organised in 14 sections, from the pre-Islamic culture and on through the time of the Prophet Mohammed into the 20th century. The artefacts are labelled and include clothing, household items, weapons, and ceremonial products – including incense burners and currency. The actual trains are currently not currently on display. Within the museum's grounds is a mosque, **Al-Saqiya Mosque**, dating from the time of the Prophet Mohammed and associated with his military action.

Check opening information about the Hijaz Train Station & Museum – it's in an area of redevelopment and access may be restricted. Hopefully pedestrian access from the Prophet's Mosque will be improved. The Hijaz Train Station is separated from the Prophet's Mosque by the First Ring Road. To walk to it from the mosque, about a kilometre east it's possible to walk, with care, under the First Ring Road; then turn west past the government offices. A similar option exists 400m to the north. Bus 403 stops south of the Hijaz Rail Museum, as does City Sightseeing **Hop-on-Hop-off bus** (enquire with staff regarding this stop).

About 4 km south of the Prophets Mosque are a couple of historic mosques. The **Quba Mosque** might be the earliest mosque ever built as a separate structure. The Prophet Mohammed reputedly started its initial construction immediately after his move from Makkah to Madinah to avoid conflict in Makkah. It has been completely rebuilt since that period. On the edge of a date plantation about 500m southeast of Quba Mosque are the remains of a smaller mosque, the **Bani Anif Mosque** (Masjid Musabbih), used by Mohammed. The Qibla wall of this mosque might be original to his time. East of these mosques is **Salman Al Farsi** date garden 07:00-23:00 with a shop selling dates. This is a historic location associated with buying the freedom of a Persian slave, Salman Al Farsi, facilitated by the Prophet Mohammed.

Dar Al Madinah Museum is 8km to the east of the mosque and a couple of kilometres northwest of the modern train station off King AbdulAziz Road and Prince Murquin bin Abdulaziz St. Sat-Thurs 11:00-19:00 Friday closed. SAR25. This is a modern museum, with most of the information in Arabic only. The museum duplicates, to a large extent, the Madinah Museum in the Hijaz Train Station. However, this has dioramas that illustrate the mosque's development in Madinah (information written in Arabic).

Southeast of Madinah are **lava fields** off the Madinah – Madh Adh Dhahab Rd (Route 8258). These include volcanos that erupted in 641 & 1256. Around Madinah are extensive Date Oasis - the dates are sought after due to their origin.

∼

DINING - THE AREA WITHIN THE FIRST RING ROAD, THAT SURROUNDS THE mosque, is almost completely devoted to hotels, restaurants, and retail businesses. Of course, the hotels have restaurants appropriate to their standard. For proximity to the mosque, these hotels are as convenient as anywhere for a meal - and suggested to use. Other than within hotels, immediately north of the mosque, look for **Zaitoon** ** (Levantine / International food) +966543163461 12:30-midnight - to the rear of the same building with McDonald's and KFC. There are numerous restaurants in this area, but not all are as good - and I noticed others also called Zaitoon! On the northern section of the First Ring Road is **Islamabad Restaurant** * 06:00-midnight with inexpensive Pakistani-style food.

∼

ACCOMMODATION - THERE ARE INNUMERABLE HOTELS IN MADINAH. IN general, the hotels here, understandably, carry a premium price adjusted for the season, so during the Hajj prices increase. Package tour groups of pilgrims are the key clients - if you intend to stay within the First Ring Road, early booking is suggested. For more distant hotels, the demand is not as intense. Consider **Tulip Inn Al Dar Rawafed** *** www.tulipinnaldar.com - choose a room facing east as they directly overlook the mosque. The area that this hotel is in has a good selection of similarly priced hotels. **Jiwar Al Madinah Hotel** *** http://jiwaralMadinah.com is to the mosque's south. Farther away - **Hotel Lamar** * +966148315828 to the east on the Second Ring Road (Route 333), **Aya Hostel** (this is a normal hotel) * +966555691373 east of Fatima bin Muslim St (southeast of the mosque). In the west - just outside the First Ring Road **Zaha Hotel** ** zahahotel.sa-Madinah.info and further out **Taiba Suites Hotel**** +966535169999 - to the west on the Second Ring Road (King Abdullah Rd).

Haramain Trains - Madinah

GETTING THERE THE **HARAMAIN TRAIN** IS A GREAT WAY TO TRAVEL TO Madinah from Jeddah or the Airport - it's just under 2 hours travel time - at up to 300kmph. Making the visit by the Haramain train could be a fantastic part of the overall experience. Many passengers will be undertaking Umrah – or the Hajj if you choose to visit during these overwhelmingly busy times of the year. Many may wear Ahram

(Ihram) clothing, white oblong cloths – worn by men and often by women. The purpose may be to show the equality of all Muslims.

There are luggage restrictions - & economy/business seating. Book online - https://sar.hhr.sa/ - though online payment may be glitchy. See if it works without going through a VPN – check that the site is HTTPS. The alternative is to book in person, though inexplicably that has been impossible except on the day of travel (this, of course, may be changed). The cost from SAR143.75 Jeddah-Madinah one-way (its seasonally adjusted). Travel in all Saudi trains is by assigned ticketed seating (or bed) only, with no subsequent self-selection of seat. The staff may reallocate seating if needed, perhaps for social reasons. Immediately in front of Madinah station are buses for the city centre. Look for bus route 300. Uber taxis can also be picked up in the same general area.

By road, it's some 450kms from Jeddah - mainly on Highway 15 (M45). Research SATRANS coaches from Jeddah – SAPTCO used to operate here and though Madinah is not currently on their route listing. North of the northern section of the First Ring Road is the previous SAPTCO coach station (possible SATRANS coach station). From Riyadh by road - it's around 900km. Check out Uber, Bolt & Careem app taxi services. and poor taxi options.

There is a comprehensive web of bus routes into Madinah.

A **LOCAL BUS SERVICE** WITH 6 LINES operates, up to 24 hours a day depending on the route. Bus route 300 links the train station with the city centre, about 500m north of the mosque (a hub for 3 other lines). Payment is through a plastic tap-and-go type card. This card is purchased for SAR10 on the bus or at a hub - and is then topped up on the bus for the fare. Fares are SAR3.45 per ride. Unfortunately, although the company, SAPTCO, operates in other towns and uses the same system in each, the cards are currently not interchangeable.

There is a **Hop-on-Hop-off bus** in Madinah https://city-sightseeing.com/ from SAR80. There are two routes - check the validity for use before booking. A principal stop is north of the Prophet's Mosque. The route extends to the far north of the city centre. It includes, on the edge of the Second Ring Road, the location of the Battle of Uhud, an early battle between the Prophet Mohammed & the Quraysh in Makkah.

CHAPTER 10
HIJAZ RAIL HIGHLIGHTS

Hijaz Rail highlights / سكة حديد الحجاز ة **A Brief History** - The idea for the Hijaz Railway was conceived from the 1870s by the Ottoman Empire, which sought to connect Damascus in modern-day Syria to the holy city of Makkah in present-day Saudi Arabia. The railway aimed to facilitate the movement of Muslim pilgrims travelling to Makkah for the annual Hajj pilgrimage, as well as to bolster Ottoman influence in the region. A line would connect Istanbul with Damascus.

Financial backing for this ambitious project came from various sources. The Ottoman government itself invested in the mammoth project and donations came from subscriptions by Muslims across the Ottoman Empire and especially Muslims in Egypt and British India. A tax was also levied on almost every person under Ottoman rule, in addition a tax was levied on Hajj pilgrims. With this finance model, construction of the 1,300 km line began in 1900. German engineers and companies played a crucial role in the construction of the railway, solidifying Germany's ties with the Ottoman Empire. A similar project was constructed through the Ottoman territory of Turkey and Iraq - in concept this started in 1871 & was intended to run from Berlin to Baghdad & ideally the ports of Hamburg - Basra.

The construction of the Hijaz Railway held several advantages for the Ottoman Turks. Economically, the railway provided a means to transport goods, people, and resources more efficiently across the vast desert terrain of the Arabian Peninsula. The Bedouin tribes however lost much of their business providing transport and pilgrimage services. Militarily, the railway provided tactical advantages by allowing the Ottomans to exert greater control over the region. With a faster means of troop deployment and supply transportation, the Ottoman Empire hoped to safeguard its interests and suppress any potential uprisings or rebellions in the Hijaz region more effectively. The Sharif of Makkah would have his independence eroded. Unfortunately many of these hoped for benefits to the Ottomans failed to materialise. Early on – the plan to build onto Makkah was abandoned – a financing issue.

The Hijaz Railway stretched from Damascus, through the Jordanian town of Ma'an into Saudi Arabia and to Madinah, covering around 1,300 kilometres.

The First Attack by Lawrence of Arabia. The Hijaz Railway faced resistance from various quarters, including from the Arab Revolt, which sought to overthrow Ottoman rule in the early 20th century, during World War One. One of the most iconic figures associated with this resistance was T.E. Lawrence, better known as Lawrence of Arabia. On 26 March 1917, Lawrence helped lead a daring attack on the Abu Al Naam (Aba Al Naam) Station 135km northwest of Madinah. This aimed to disrupt Ottoman supply lines and weaken their regional control. The Arab forces then conducted a series of attacks, destroying bridges, derailing trains, and disrupting operations along the railway.

Following the defeat of the Ottomans in World War One, the railway fell into disrepair and lost its significance as a major transportation route.

AlUla Hijaz Rail Station

What's there - Surprisingly, the Hijaz Railway stations, and Ottoman Forts protecting them are still mainly standing - their rails and trains, however, are a different story. Scrap metal is easy to transport & sell. A 4x4 is ideal to reach many - as they may be several kilometres off the tarmac road. Despite their remoteness - many (probably all) are enclosed by the wire fencing you will be familiar with at so many historical sites. Most of the buildings will however be clearly visible. The stations are around 25 km apart. Driving north from Madinah, Highway 15 (M45) passes three stations over about 44kms - all on the road's west. At **Al Hafeera**, about 35km northwest of Madinah 's centre, is a station & Syrian Hajj fort. Further north from Al Hafeera (about 7 km) to the west of Highway 15 (M45) are the remains of an **Umayyad period castle** - with Byzantine-type brickwork - crumbling away. Swing northwest off Highway 15 (M45) after about 50 km (at Al Mulaylih petrol station) onto a minor road leading northwest. **Al Buwayr** has a scattered group of station & train wrecks around 100km from Madinah.

Abu Al Naam Station is reached after another 35 km. Abu Al Naam, with the station buildings, is where Lawrence of Arabia first attacked the railway (Lawrence wrote Aba an Naam). It's about 5km off the tarmac along a rough track needing 4x4. After Abu Al Naam, along the same road, round 180km from Madinah is **Hadiyah** GPS 25.541248, 38.739951. This is under 10km drive east of the main road - a new junction & minor road leads east. Here is a collection of buildings and train wreckage, all enclosed by the mesh fencing and, a kilometre to the north, the partial remains of a bridge. Do look at the main site from the northern section of fencing – you may get a much better view.

In **AlUla**, the Hijaz Train Station and abandoned carriages are in the southern area of the town (Page89). At **Hegra** (Page94), the station, fort and sheds are in the north of the site, now part of the Chedi Hotel. North of Hegra, the railway broadly follows Route 375. The most interesting station is at **Al Muadhem** (Al Muaazam etc). Here is not only rail infrastructure - but under 500m away to the northwest - an Ottoman pilgrimage fort & water cistern, dating to AD1622, next to a small rocky hill. The Ottoman fort has collapsed inside, but the exterior walls and corner towers are in good condition. The inevitable fence here is a double structure. There appears to have been extensive digging of pits surrounding this fort. The station at **Tabuk** is within a small museum (Page102).

~

GETTING THERE. THE REMAINING HIJAZ TRAIN STATIONS AND FORTS ARE strung between Madinah, via AlUla to Tabuk - a few even a bit further north. It's about 700 km between Jeddah and Tabuk by road. Given that many of these buildings are fenced off (though visible), it's worth planning to see them as an add-on to a drive elsewhere rather than the purpose.

CHAPTER 11
ALULA, DEDAN, HEGRA

AlUla / العلا - GPS - 26.626065, 37.915508 **Population** (appx) 40,760 **A quick overview of the geography** - AlUla is in a sandy valley enclosed by ochre sandstone mountains that rise to just under 1,000meters above sea level & 300 or 400 meters above the valley floor. Farther west is Harrat Uwayrid, a basalt lava field - which is passed if driving to Tabuk.

A broad overview of AlUla. The area is one of the key focus places for Saudi Arabia's diversification. It's under the Royal Commission for AlUla www.rcu.gov.sa chaired by Prince Mohammed bin Salman. The plans for the area are substantial – both in terms of the infrastructure and general cultural focus. Supporting all this will be a planned hospitality training centre at AlUla.

The hub for most activities is the **'Winter Park'** visitor centre - access to the west of the flyover. An office there can handle bookings - alternatively, in advance, use **https://tickets.experiencealula.com**. General information can be provided, with staff speaking good English. Toilets are here - and bus departures to Dedan & Hegra - and if operating to distant Khaybar and Tayma.

The three heritage components at AlUla with adult entry cost (including transport as required) are Dedan SAR60, Hegra SAR95 and AlUla 'Old Town' SAR70. These can only be visited as part of an organised tour - booked through the Winter Park office or online at www.experiencealula.com. You must fit your schedule to their tour departures if you are a solo traveller. Arriving before the booked time-slot is suggested – 15+ minutes is worthwhile. The only way to make an actual visit into Dedan and Hegra is in their provided transport. As these are relatively new operations its possible changes will be made based on feedback.

The modern town of AlUla is spread along Route 375 (sections are also called King Fahd Rd & Bin Ziyad Rd) in a spectacular broad valley setting. While currently there is no public transport - a 50km tram system is planned. A flyover in the town's north leads west into the Winter Park and up to a plateau, with a small cafe & viewpoint overlooking the valley & the date oasis. If coming from AlUla town & the south a turn is needed on Route 375 to the north of the flyover. It's worth making this stop, on the plateau, towards the start of your visit - it will orient you. The views are stunning - and on a clear day, Hegra is just visible. At all times, the sandstone escarpments and date plantations look magical. It's best from late afternoon - as the sun drops and floods the valley with golden light. There is a cafe next to the car parking on this plateau.

AlUla towards Dedan and beyond Hegra

At the start of the ascent to the plateau is AlUla Adventure Hub. If your adrenaline needs increasing, there are activities such as rock climbing, a Zip-Line (SAR180) a kilometre length & around 200m drop from the plateau and a giant swing. There are trekking trails in the areas, including through the surrounding mountains. Look for **Oasis Heritage Trail**, near the Old Town – and **Mujdar Mountain Trail** in the mountains above. If you will visit the plateau - before making the ascent, book future excursions at the Winter Park - you can plan your time in AlUla when you know what schedule is available for you.

The AlUla website also gives details of other named areas of the AlUla region, **Wadi Al Fann**, (full opening in 2026) with its art installations in the open air. Immediately east of AlUla Old Town is **Daimumah**, with a western and eastern area. Here are dining options in the date palms, and activities to draw you in – including walks (the paths are currently open to non-escorted individuals) &

Cycling - AlUla

hands-on practical cultural activities through experiencealula.com run by https://nomuhub.com/. Many events & activities are seasonal and weather-dependent, such as **Hot-Air Balloon Flights** (SAR100) limited season - from north of Hegra. Annual events include - **Desert X AlUla** a contemporary art festival, mid Feb-mid March, The **AlUla Tour** cycle race www.thealulatour.com, **Dakar Rally** www.dakar.com, **AlUla Trail Race** (running) and other similar races, Polo, and **Custodian of the Two Holy Mosques Endurance Cup**, for long distance horse events, the focus location is on Highway 70, east of the Winter Park. Of course it's great to see an event not held in European & North American countries. Camel racing is held late February & March with prize funds in the millions of UD$ to attract the best participants – check experiencealula.com for dates. In addition, various music events are held during 'Winter at Tantora' late December through to late January, & 'Azimuth' in late September, and so on. Some are free to view - others may be pay-to-enter. These pay-to-enter include **Maraya** - a mirror-covered concert hall hidden in a valley north of the Winter Park. In short, some one-off activities may be held throughout the year - check www.experiencealula.com for dates.

Tours from AlUla have also been provided by coach to distant Tayma SAR295 and Khaybar SAR215 – it's a full day excursion. Check at the booking office regarding these as they are currently seasonal. Adventure tourism is supplied by the well-established **Husaak** www.husaak.com operating since 2014. Bike Hire is available from '**Wheels**' +966538707143 06:00-11:00-16:00-19:00 (Closed Monday). The shop is on a side road about 5 km northeast of the winter park. Next to the Bike Shop is a minor station on the Hijaz Rail, **Wadi Hashish**. Other activities – try Roller Skating – just north of the Old Town, Horse Riding at **AlZhra Stables**, www.instagram.com/alzhra_stable 200m north of entrance to Dedan. Minor natural attractions include **Elephant Rock** (frequently closed for events) off Highway 70, east of the Winter Park, and a seasonal **Dates Festival** (weekends September-October) in the same area off Highway 70. The only worthwhile museum in town is not currently open. It's in the central area on King Fahd Rd. AlUla is probably the only place in Saudi where advance accommodation booking is needed.

Somewhat off the current tourist's experiences, but within the AlUla umbrella, is the Arabian Leopard. AlUla is one of the focus sites for its future.

~

HOTELS AND ACCOMMODATION

Eating options - The considerable promotion of AlUla as a leisure destination has increased the choices of where to eat. Most are to the north of the modern town area. The hotels which are hidden in the mountain's canyons offer a choice in great surroundings. There are also ever increasing and constantly changing new options around AlUla Old Town. These are comparable to restaurants in your home country. They are very easy to find from within the Old Town and though very worthwhile are not mentioned here as some may be pop-ups, many may be seasonal, others may have closed, for a new flavour of the month to open. In the modern commercial areas south of the 'Old Town' a few to consider include - The '**Pakistani Restaurant**'* 07:00-13:00 on the junction of King Fahd and Makkah Al Mukarramah (just south of the

Museum) offers a good choice of Pakistani food (meat and rice-based) - with indoor & outdoor seating. **Dermas Corner Restaurant** ** just west of the souq in the new town has local Saudi-style meat and rice dishes - 11:00-midnight. **Yemeni Taste** ** 06:00-11:00/19:30-midnight just east of King Fahd St near the souq - does exactly what it says on the tin. **AlUla Palace** * midday-midnight - south of a government ministry west of King Fahd St. is far from a palace - but offers reasonable Saudi-style food. There are also pizza and fast-food restaurants. Worth a stop is **AlUla Farmers Market**, near the Hijaz Train Station. Here is a mix of market stalls and a couple of small places to eat in - most places here should be open midday-22:00.

    Places to sleep in - AlUla has fewer hotels than its marketing results demand. This is despite a slew of luxury properties in the canyons to the north of town. This means that hotels are priced higher than elsewhere in Saudi Arabia. This price point is reinforced as more luxury hotels open. Among these premium-priced options are **Banyan Tree, Chedi, Habitas**, and **Shadeen Resort** (base for the AlUla GCC Heads of State Meeting). Apart from these, consider the established **Al Harbi AlUla** ** +966148843100 in the main (northern area) of the new town - it's a bit north of the closed AlUla Museum. **Sweet Inn** ** +966551580531 in the southern region of AlUla and nearby **Abraj** *** +966550364596 also in the southern area of the new town. Farther south is Al **Wateen Hotel** **** +966568555214 and **Waad AlUla***** +966500662343, both in AlUla's south, on Route 375. They both take full advantage of hotel scarcity in their pricing. East of Route 375, look for **Queen Hotel**** +966506994887, which offers more competitive value. This southern area will probably be the focus for more hotels - it's around 10km south of AlUla Old Town. At the moment most available properties in AlUla are converted houses - privately owned and in the side streets in one of the areas of newer housing south of AlUla Old Town. Some owners of Date and other farms offer accommodation within these. These private houses & farms will have only a few rooms available – and may only operate in the winter months. Advance booking is more important in AlUla than elsewhere in Saudi Arabia - with a follow-up suggested to secure the reservation.

∿

GETTING TO ALULA

AlUla is best reached by road from Jeddah via - Highway 5 (M55) and Yanbu, then Route 328 - it is about 730kms. From Riyadh, it's almost 1200km via Highways 65 (M35) and 70. There are SATRANS coach services (from Jeddah via Madinah & Riyadh via Hail / Buraydah) - and flights into **Prince Abdul Majeed bin Abdulaziz International Airport**. The airport is under renewal, to increase capacity from 400,000 per year - to 6 million. There are several car-hire companies in town, including Alamo, Theeb, and Yelo. All transport is best booked well in advance. As many towns away from Dammam, Jeddah and Riyadh - there are no local bus services and poor taxi options –Uber does operate a small service.

∿

DEDAN

Dedan / ددان **A brief histor**y - The kingdom of Dedan (Dadan etc), emerged along the incense route in northwest Saudi Arabia sometime in the 7th centuryBC. It was also known during its later stage as Libyan, after its rulers. The capital, Dedan, was located at a large oasis, now called AlUla, which provided a vital stopover point for caravans travelling through the inhospitable desert landscape that surrounds it. The city's position on the incense route between the Arabian Peninsula, Egypt, and the Levant, a critical trade network for aromatic spices and perfumes, brought considerable wealth and influence to the region.

Archaeology indicates that Dedan had a complex society with skilled artisans and craftsmen. Intricate carvings, jewellery, and pottery have been unearthed at various sites across the kingdom. As a trading hub, Dedan also had contact with diverse cultures from across the ancient world. Cuneiform inscriptions reveal that they traded extensively with the Assyrians. There are also indications of cultural influences from ancient Egypt, Mesopotamia, and the Levant.

Politically, a monarch ruled Dedan. While the king held absolute power, the kingdom's administration was handled by local governors appointed to oversee large settlements. Taxes were collected from the lucrative caravan trade that traversed Dedan's territory. Relations with neighbouring kingdoms seem to have been peaceful, as maintaining regional stability was beneficial for commerce.

In the 6th and 5th centuriesBC, Dedan flourished, and grand temples, tombs, and other monuments were constructed across the kingdom. This was Dedan's golden age when arts, literature, and culture thrived. The Deadness developed a unique script and language which still can be seen in surviving inscriptions. Long-distance trade expanded significantly during this period, enriching the kingdom immensely. Luxury goods from across the then-known Middle East have been found at archaeological sites from this era.

However, Dedan's prosperity was disrupted in the 4th centuryBC by the growing ambition of the Nabataean Kingdom located to the north. Seeking control of the lucrative incense trade, the Nabataeans began encroaching on Dedanite territory. This marked the beginning of Dedan's demise as an independent kingdom. Over the next century, Dedan was gradually absorbed by the Nabataeans despite resistance. Their unique culture, script and language disappeared.

Book tickets online A bus will take you to Dedan after about a 15-minute drive from the assembly point in the Winter Park.

In **Dedan** - as in each other heritage location in AlUla - a 'Rawi' (storyteller) can give you some information about the site. Though Dedan has archaeological digs and cliffside tombs, these are currently not included in the tour. However, light refreshments are available, and a small information centre tells you what you are missing. From Dedan, another drive leads to **Jabal Ikmah**. Here, a plethora of Dedanitic and Lihyanite inscriptions and other rock art are inscribed on sandstone cliffs. In the reception area (this is in addition to the one at Dedan) - there is an opportunity to chisel your name in small pieces of rock - and have more small refreshments - coffee & candied fruit. These Dedan visits are unlikely to be the most memorable of your time in AlUla, unless the archaeology at Dedan is included for visitors.

Inscriptions Jabal Ikmah

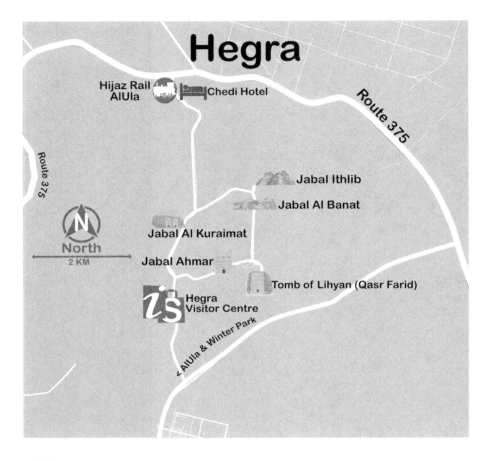

HEGRA

HEGRA / الحجر **A BRIEF HISTORY** - THE ANCIENT CITY OF HEGRA, KNOWN previously as Madain Saleh, has an intriguing history that spans thousands of years. Having water supplies in a remote desert area in northwest Saudi Arabia, it was a vital settlement along ancient trade routes.

According to Islamic tradition, the city was inhabited by the people of Thamud, known for rejecting the Prophet Saleh and, as a result, incurring divine wrath. The ancient Nabataean kingdom eventually took over the site under Aretas IV (around 9BC to AD40). As a hub for Nabataean trade, Hegra thrived. The Nabataeans were skilled engineers who constructed elaborate tombs cut into rock cliffs around Hegra – like Nabataean Petra. The oldest tomb dates from 1BC the last AD75. These served as burial sites for wealthy merchants and demonstrate an architectural fusion of Mesopotamian - with Assyrian 'crows steps' (corbie step), and Nabataean style.

Around AD106, the Roman Empire annexed the Nabataean Kingdom taking control of Hegra through the Legio III 'Cyrenaica'. The Roman fortifications and other buildings (not currently open) are on and around a hill 400m northwest of Jabal Al

Ahmar. Official inscriptions have been excavated. However, the quick shift to Sea Trade and the Emperor Theodosius prohibited making offerings including incense to pagan gods, after AD381 must have reduced trade through Hegra, which became a backwater.

For centuries, Hegra sat almost forgotten in the desert, only visited by the Hajj caravans. In October 1326, the traveller Ibn Battuta passed through on his way to Makkah - he wrote, "Here, in some hills of red rock, are the dwellings of Thamud. They are cut in the rock and have carved thresholds. Anyone seeing them would take them to be of recent construction. Their decayed bones are to be seen inside these houses". In the mid-18th century, the Ottoman governor of Damascus, Asad Pasha Al Azm, constructed a fort at Hegra to secure the surrounding region.

But by the 1870s, the crumbling ruins of Hegra were still largely unknown to the outside world. That changed with the arrival of the British explorer Charles Montagu Doughty in 1876 – who accompanied a Hajj caravan on part of its journey. He became the first European to thoroughly document the mysterious tombs and other ruins of the ancient city. Doughty's writings re-introduced Hegra to the Western world.

By 1908, the Hijaz Railway was working through Hegra, linking the settlement by rail to Damascus and Madinah. A small station was constructed, but the remote spot still remained off the beaten track. Bedouin tribes lived among the ruins into the 20th century.

The forgotten Nabataean tombs of Hegra were finally recognised as a world treasure in 2008, when UNESCO designated it as Saudi Arabia's first World Heritage Site. The site has had archaeological teams under the long-term direction of Dr Laïla Nehme, the Lebanese-French archaeologist.

Within the area encircled by the Hegra's internal road was the settlement (vestiges are covered by soil) of about fifty hectares, surrounded by a wall. Inside this wall, the housing was of mud brick - currently, it's fenced off. The central mesa here has a small temple complex on its summit, - the priests must have had mountaineering skills to reach it. To the west, north & south of the settlement was a large area of sub-surface water - the reason for its locational choice.

Whats at Hegra

From the assembly point in the Winter Park, a bus will take you to Hegra after about a 20-minute drive. Check experiencealula.com for full information. There are various versions of an experience at Hegra, from a non-guided bus transport to a private option with a 'Rawi'.

There are various styles of tomb, from simple tombs cut into the rock, having undecorated facads, tomb 92 at Jabal Al Kuraimat with the decorated arch over its entrance and most typical, the Hegra, (and later more elaborate Hegra Style) with its 'crows-steps' (also called stepped gable, or corbie step), architrave and Egyptian style cornice.

Stops may include Jabal Al Kuraimat, Jabal Ithlib with the triclinium – a 3-sided seating arrangement, Jabal Al Banat, Tomb of Lihyan

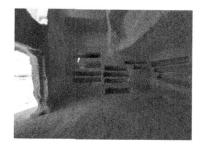

Interior Tomb 26 Jabal Al Banat

(Qasr Farid) and Jabal Al Ahmar. The Hegra tombs were created by cutting the rock from the top down, as can be seen from a few unfinished tombs tomb high in the rock faces - including at Jabal Al Banat. The crows-steps on these are the only part completed. **Jabal Kuraimat** has tomb 100 - with an Egyptian-style cornice and the typical crow steps. Created for Tarsu bin Taym & his family in the reign of the Nabataean King Malichus II (ruled 40-70AD). It's inscriptions, almost uniquely, mention the settlement's original name, 'Hijr'.

Jabal Al Banat has several grand tombs - tomb 22 is the joint oldest at Hegra - dated to 1BC. This tomb was placed under the protection of the gods Dushara - Hegra's patron god; Manat, an essential goddess at Makkah and in Arabia, she looked after destiny, fate, and the time/the future; and finally, a funerary Nabataean goddess, Qaysha. The tomb's owner, Aydu bin Kuhayl, had all possible afterlife problems covered. The tomb of **Lihyan bin Kuza** (Qasr Al Farid) is the most recognisable tomb, its isolation does make it stand out. The crow steps surmount an Egyptian-style cornice. Below are 4 Nabataean-style columns. The eagle above the entrance is a symbol of the goddess Dushara. **Jabal Ithlib** has the triclinium called locally the "Diwan". A triclinium was a dining area - possibly associated with the shrines in the short valley leading deeper into the rock. Here it is cut directly from the rock.

Jabal Al Banat - Hegra - UNESCO site

The drive covering the tour of Hegra is around 7 km. The bus will stop at various sites - check with the driver or officials if it's possible to extend your stay at a particular location (it should be) and catch the next bus; they do not allow people to explore on foot, and restrict entry to tombs. At each stop is an official - or several - to regulate visitors - and provide some information.

Despite its regimented organisation - a visit to Hegra is rewarding. Compared to

Petra - it is less impressive - almost domestic in comparison – it was not, after all, the capital of the kingdom. The openness of the site and far lower numbers of visitors, with its hassle-free nature, adds to the pleasure of a visit. The make this a very worthwhile visit. Seasonal events may be held, at Hegra - check the AlUla website in case there are any when you visit.

At the end of the tour - there is a **gift shop** with original products for sale - in a local character.

The former **Hijaz Rail complex** (station with fort, etc.) is being subsumed by the Chedi hotel, to its east.

~

ALULA OLD TOWN

AlUla Old Town / العلا القديمة A **brief history** - The old town of AlUla was built in the 13th century. This was one of a succession of settlements from Dedan, Hegra and the Umayyad settlement of Al Mubiyat (also called Qurh/Qarah etc) which is 20kms to the southeast. Though mainly mud-brick – unsurprisingly, AlUla also used the stones of the old Dedanite ruins nearby. It was built as a semi-fortified settlement - about 500 meters long whose house walls provided the outer town wall. The small Musa bin Nasir Fort, on a natural outcrop of rock, must have been both a lookout and final place of defence. AlUla became the primary settlement of the region until modern times. Between 1901 and 1908, the Ottomans built the Hijaz to Madinah rail through the area. The railway had three stations in the area - AlUla, Wadi Hashish and Hegra.

In the later 20th century, the new town centre was established south of the original town. The last family is said to moved from the older town by 1983, whilst the final service in the old mosque was held in 1985. Both the ruins of the medieval town and the site of Dedan now lie within the administration of the modern town.

The organised excursions in AlUla 'Old Town' leave from the information centre - behind the mud brick housing - near the base of the mountains west of the town. Follow the paved walkway/road to get there - it's a very obvious route. Along this route are shops and places to eat. Souvenir shops sell products made locally. If you wish to buy something, there are lots of choices that won't break the bank - and, importantly won't break on your flight back. The shops sit next to places like Dunkin Donuts - a great dichotomy about the country.

The AlUla 'Old Town' tour meanders through the narrow walkways of **AlUla' Old Town'**, escorted by a Rawi. The town itself is mud-brick housing, at most a couple of stories high. Restoration work is ongoing, so minimal areas are currently possible to see - and these are building shells rather than furnished. The end of the tour is an ascent up to the small **Musa bin Nusayr Castle** perched on a rock outcrop. This gives excellent views of the town and valley. Check the www.experiencealula.com site for other activities - including walks (**Oasis Heritage Trail**) through the date gardens. To visit AlUla Old Town, make your booking - and arrive independently - west of Route 375 / King Fahd Rd.

AlUla Old Town from Musa bin Nusayr Castle

CHAPTER 12

WADI AL DISAH

Wadi Al Disah / الديسة - GPS - 27.633915, 36.518995
A quick overview of the geography - towering ochre coloured Sandstone columns and mountains create the valley at Wadi Al Disah. These sandstone formations are also found through to Wadi Rum and into Petra. The green of the vegetation fed by a stream add to the striking scenery, that overshadows AlUla by some margin.

Wadi Al Disah with flowing spring water feeding date palms, rush and pink-flowered Oleander (a poisonous plant) is a superbly attractive - but out-of-the-way place. Wadi Al Disah has practically no services - a few overpriced farm stays for accommodation and no restaurant at the moment. Despite all this - the spectacular scenery is a magnet - and at weekends and holidays, the area is packed. At the entrance to the wadi where the tarmac runs out, you may find a few local people with 4x4 who can take you (SAR200+) on a trip deeper into the valley, which meanders for 10 km+ before opening into drier canyons. Indeed, a saloon car could not venture in. As with many tourist spots in Saudi Arabia, this is earmarked for development.

Getting there - Northwest of AlUla - a superb drive of almost 300km leads to Wadi Al Disah. A journey over the mountains from the north off Route 375 (junction left after 12km to the north of AlUla flyover) & an un-named road onto 8443, then 8790 & 8756. The drive is the epitome of driving pleasure in Saudi, with empty roads surrounded by rugged, superb scenery. From Tabuk Highway 80 (M50) and then 8756 are less interesting than Route 8900 and 8790 which are more attractive as a route from Tabuk, and not much slower - both are under 250km one way.

Wadi Al Disah

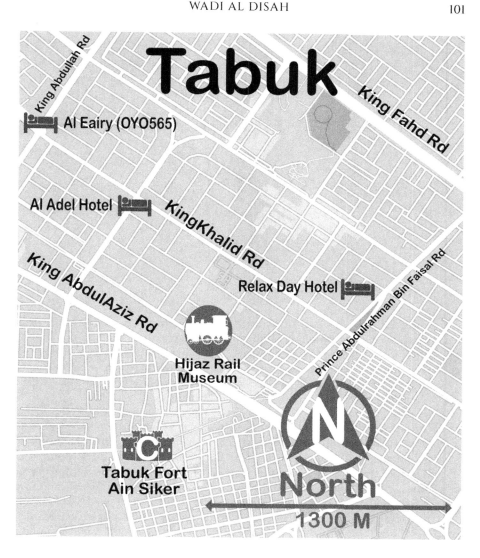

CHAPTER 13
TABUK

Tabuk / تبوك - GPS - 28.388040, 36.562555 **Population** (appx) 594,350 **A brief history** - The area around Tabuk has been inhabited since prehistoric times. In the 3rd millenniumBC, during the Bronze Age, it was an important stop on trade routes connecting Mesopotamia, Syria, Egypt and the Hijaz region of Saudi Arabia. Ancient inscriptions and other archaeological evidence indicate it was inhabited by various nomadic tribes.

In the 1st centuryAD, during the Roman era, Tabuk became a military outpost and trading town. The Romans used it to project power and control trade in the region. In AD631, a Muslim army led by Prophet Muhammad himself passed through Tabuk on its way to attack the Byzantines in Jordan. This event, known as the Expedition of Tabuk, marked the growing power and expansion of the new Islamic state – forcing the Byzantine army to withdraw before any battle. For several centuries, Tabuk continued to prosper as an important stop on Hajj pilgrimage routes between Syria and the holy sites of Makkah and Madinah. Its strategic location made it prized by various Muslim dynasties. Local Bedouin tribes, however, maintained autonomy in the surrounding areas.

In 1517, Tabuk was incorporated into the Ottoman Empire along with the rest of the Hijaz region. The Ottomans invested in Tabuk, seeing its potential as a commercial and military centre. They built Tabuk Castle in the city centre in 1559 with water cisterns (Ain Sikar – the Sweet Spring) for use on the pilgrimage route. The Ottoman grip on Tabuk ended in the early 20th century as their Empire collapsed. In 1916, during World War One, it was briefly occupied by the forces of the Arab Revolt led by Sharif Hussein of Makkah and the British officer T.E. Lawrence (Lawrence of Arabia). Finally King AbdulAziz Al Saud incorporated Tabuk into his kingdom in the mid-1920s.

In recent decades, Tabuk has grown rapidly as part of the modern Kingdom of Saudi Arabia. With investments in infrastructure, education, and healthcare, it has become an important regional centre. New hotels, resorts and archaeological sites in the region have also made it a minor tourist destination. Agriculture, military, and government services are the mainstay of the economy.

Hijaz Train Station Museum

Tabuk has a couple of places to consider visiting. The **Hijaz Train Station Museum** 08:00-15:00 - closed Friday & Saturday - FOC is on the main King AbdulAziz Rd. This has a modern building to house a carriage and Tubize 0-6-0T locomotive, built in 1893 for Ottoman railways. The building seems to have been built to have a larger museum collection so it will hopefully acquire more of interest. Less than a kilometre walk southwest is **Tabuk Fort** (Ain Sikar) FOC 08:00--20:00 Sun-Thurs (Fri & Sat 16:00-18:00). This is a small 2-floor Syrian Hajj fort - with an adjacent water cistern. It was built under the Ottoman Sultan Sulaiman the Magnificent after 1520 - and improved in 1652 under Sultan Muhammad IV. The information focuses on the region's association with the Prophet Mohammed in AD630. The fort and spring, though small, are impressively constructed. Tabuk however is a long drive for these two minor places of interest.

Northwest of Tabuk is **Jabal Lawz** 2500+m - the area around it, branded within NEOM as '**Trojena**', will, apparently, have one of the most environmentally sustainable ski slopes in the world for the Asian Winter Games 2028.

The area involved with work for NEOM & Trojena is currently off-limits. North of Tabuk are large areas of pivot fields - the large circular irrigated fields that grow grain and fodder. The irrigation attracts insects and rodents - and in winter migratory flocks of Black Kites. Elsewhere, vegetables and fruits are grown. Look for citrus, Fig, Grape, Peach, Olive, Potato and onion. There are no local bus services and poor taxi options. SATRANS coach does offer limited inter city connections.

Black Kites at Pivot irrigation

∾

DINING AND ACCOMMODATION OPTIONS. DISAPPOINTINGLY - IN TABUK, local cuisine restaurants are poor, and there is a dearth of reasonable options to eat in Tabuk – search out the country-wide chains like AlBaik. The chain options are included on Page27 - unfortunately, away from the town centre. **A selection of accommodation** - Better hotel options are away from the town centre,. However, in the town centre, consider the **Relax Day Hotel** ** +966144223735 Prince Abdulrahman Bin Faisal Rd, **Al Eairy (OYO565)** * www.oyorooms.com King Abdullah Rd, **Al Adel Hotel** * +966144221515 King Khalid Rd. The best option is right out of town - **Millenium Hotel** ****, www.millenniumhotels.com, slightly less good is the Hilton Garden *** www.hilton.com.

∾

GETTING THERE TO TABUK. FROM ALULA THERE ARE SEVERAL ROUTES. One cuts north off Route 375 (west of Hegra) and passing the turn to Wadi Al Disah and continuing to Highway 80 (M50) is around 400km - it's a scenic route almost all the way. Here, the villages are noticeably less prosperous - and again, the lack of services along the route is noticeable. An alternative is to take Route 375 north from AlUla. This follows the Hijaz Rail for much of the drive into Tabuk. Around 150 km from Tabuk is **Al Muadhem Station**, Page86. Continuing on Route 375 - and taking Highway 15 (M45) (with a detour towards the east and a double back towards Tabuk on Highway 15!). The drive is about 400km. Between Dumat Al Jandal & Tabuk - it's around 430kms - using Highways 80 (M50) & 15 (M45). Ensure you have a full petrol tank before starting on the road in this region - & fill up, if possible, when the tank reaches half-full. Tayma and Tabuk are about 270 km apart - all on Highway 15 (M45). Tabuk is in an isolated position in the far northwest of Saudi Arabia.

road between AlUla and Wadi Disah - off Route 375

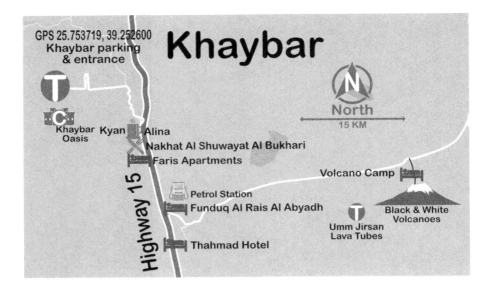

CHAPTER 14

KHAYBAR & BLACK AND WHITE VOLCANOS

Khaybar / خيبر - GPS - 25.753784, 39.252197 **Population** (appx) 15,888
A quick overview of the geography - Surrounded by lava fields, Khaybar is set in the Harrat Khaybar - a five-million-year-old geological structure. Harrats are lava flows in Saudi Arabia,(comparable to those in Hawaii, Iceland or Sicily) that results in a desolate landscape. To the town's southeast are the 'Black & White Volcanos', with dark Basalt cones contrasting with ones of creamy Comendite. West of these volcanos are lava tubes - where liquid lava flowed and created now hollow passage within an already-hardened lava flow.

A brief history - Khaybar is surrounded by a dense area of Bronze Age, and later, structures. These include graves and 'funerary avenues', Kites & Mustatils. Research has also identified 15km of "rampart walls" including almost 6km, with bastions, that enclosed part of the oasis. It's been dated to around 1980BC.

In pre-Islamic times, the last neo-Babylonian ruler Nabonidus mentioned 'Khibra' in his Harran inscription, this is generally assumed to be Khaybar. Khaybar was inhabited by Jewish tribes – possibly arriving after the various battles involving Babylon in the Levant – and the later Persian conquest of Babylon after the Battle of Opis in 539BC when captive Jews were permitted to leave Mesopotamia. More must have arrived after the destruction of temples in Jerusalem by Rome in AD70. The Jews built up profitable date and orchard farms, making Khaybar a prosperous trading centre. Archaeological remains indicate effective irrigation systems were developed to support the agriculture.

Khaybar became prominent in conflicts with the Prophet Mohammed, with the Battle of Khaybar in AD628. This followed the Battle of the Trench in 627 – instigated by some of Khaybar's population. Khaybar, at this time, may have had over a dozen fortified settlements – which did not save the town.

In the decade after the death of the Prophet Mohammed – much of the Jewish population of Khaybar was exiled to Iraq and the Levant by the Caliph Umar.

However, a population of Jews remained. They paid the Jizya tax, levied on free resident non-Muslims, a form of tribute and exemption payment to the government. Under the early Caliphs, Khaybar continued to flourish as an agricultural colony working to supply dates, fruit and vegetables to the growing Empire. The irrigation systems were expanded, and new settlers from Arabia and Persia arrived and the settlement provided with administration buildings.

Khaybar oasis & fortified settlement

A Jewish population was noted around AD1173, by Benjamin of Tudela, a Jewish traveller. In the early 16th century, the Ottoman Turks gained control over Khaybar, along with the west of Arabia.

Charles Doughty, from his 1876-88 journey through northwest Arabia, thought that it might be a conquest target of the Al Rashid rulers in Hail. The forces of Sharif Hussein of Makkah, with T.E. Lawrence, raided Khaybar in 1916 during the Arab Revolt against the Ottomans. Lawrence remarked on the impressive ancient ruins of the oasis.

The Ottoman Empire finally lost Khaybar in 1917 when troops loyal to Sharif Hussein actually captured the town. Just a few years later, in 1925, Khaybar voluntarily joined the new Kingdom of Saudi Arabia under King AbdulAziz without resistance. This allowed Khaybar to escape Saudi conquest campaigns directed at other Hijaz oases, like Taif.

In modern Saudi Arabia, Khaybar again became a productive agricultural centre benefiting from modern technology and investment. Archaeological work also increased, uncovering Khaybar's ancient canals, irrigation systems and fortress ruins. Some parts have been restored as tourist attractions.

What's in Khaybar - The modern town of Khaybar is strung along Highway 15 (M45) - with services set back on, appropriately, service roads. The main places of interest are to the town's north.

The area of **Historic Khaybar** is accessed from its car park GPS 25.753719, 39.252600 - with very poor directional signage and through a modern residential area. The drive from the coffee shops in modern Khaybar is around 15km. Historic Khaybar, like AlUla - is a paid 'guided' experience or with audio guide (each option separately included in cost),- seasonal October - April SAR95 or coach from AlUla SAR215. It is essential to check at AlUla regarding openings or www.experiencealula.com. Visits are by timed visiting slot (arrive about 20mins before) – are from the car park it's another drive, in Historic Khaybar's vehicle, to the reception area, which has small snacks as in AlUla. Ask about any other places around the Khaybar area that are open - and how to get to them.

An escorted walk (or self-guided with audio guide) from the reception area leads down, on a narrow, rough footpath to the valley floor. Here is an oasis of **date plantations** (not as verdant as those in AlUla) & **fortified villages** set on mesas – at the time of researching this book these were not possible to enter. As with AlUla Old Town, restrictions are placed on where it's possible to explore. Much of this area is being developed for tourism, so options are likely to expand.

In the general area around the north of Khaybar are numerous **prehistoric stone structures**, 'Kites', 'Mustatils' (oblong in shape) and others - small examples are a couple of hundred meters east of the entrance drive from the ticket office to the reception of the paid attraction. These structures are built from natural stone taken from the immediate local. The stones are around 50cm in diameter each, certainly a size managed by a single person, perhaps 2 or 3 courses high - and a wall could be 500m long or more. The Kites are hunting traps to direct and herd animals into a constricted area for slaughter. These permanent traps suggest a settled population in the area in which they were built. The Mustatils may have a ritual significance. These structures may date back 7,000 years - and unfortunately are not signed, but fortunately are generally not fenced off. Khaybar's appeal will be significantly increased if it opens more of the historical area to paying visitors.

Black & White Volcanos - in Harrat Khaybar

Black & White Volcanos / بركان أسود وأبيض - GPS - 25.750583, 39.973528 These are a collection of volcanic cones of both black lava flows & cream Comendite. Obsidian, associated with the Comendite, was used by Neolithic people (here around 10,000–3,500BC), presumably the people who also created the stone structures around Khaybar. These volcanos are part of the Harrat Khaybar lava fields - and potentially active as tremors still occur. The cones rise about 2-300m above the surrounding lava. Around 20km west (towards Khaybar) of the track to the volcanos is another track - that also leads south - to the **Umm Jirsan lava tubes**.

Getting There The impressive Black & White Volcanos are along a road leading east just before the red & white buildings of Funduq Al Rais Al Abyadh (funduq is the local Arabic for any hotel) at a petrol station a few kilometres before Khaybar - a 72km drive on tarmac - then about 15km to the south on a very rough track. East of the turn to the volcanos - the tarmac road disappears into a poorly maintained sandy track.

CHOICES TO EAT IN - LIKE SO MANY OTHER TOWNS AWAY FROM MAJOR cities, Khaybar would benefit from a greater choice of dining options. As always in this book, local places rather than nationwide chains are highlighted. Try **Kyan*** coffee shop +966920011100 (24 hours) and **Alina** * coffee shop Phone: +966554073957 for light snacks (24 hours). Both are less than 1km apart on the west side of Highway 15 (M45) - less than 15km north of Funduq Al Rais Al Abyadh. A bit farther south on Highway 15 (M45) **Nakhat Al Shuwayat Al Bukhari*** restaurant +966556330408 - meat & rice, apparently Central Asian in style but in reality, so geared towards local taste that it is Saudi.

Accommodation - Hotels are even more scarce than options to eat in - in the petrol station at the junction of Highway 15 (M45) south of central Khaybar town, which leads east to the Black & White Volcanos, is the extremely basic **Funduq Al Rais Al Abyadh*** +966505364271 (red, yellow & grey colour) - if no staff are available in reception, speak to the laundry nearby. South on Highway 15 (M45) is **Thahmad Hotel**** +966557159588, about a 4km drive from the petrol station. About 10km north of the petrol station, also on Highway 15 (M45), is the **Faris Apartments** *

+966597549996. At the Black and White Volcano itself - (turn south 72kms east of the junction with Funduq Al Rais Al Abyadh) is a winter season premium priced **Volcano Camp** **** - that effectively blocks easy access to the volcanos - available through www.experiencealula.com.

Getting there Between Madinah - Khaybar is a 170km drive on Highway 15 (M45) - at least 2 lanes. The road between Tayma and Khaybar is also Highway 15 (M45) - around 260 km. Alternatively, from AlUla it's a cross-country journey on the single-lane Route 375 - of around 230km. Between Al Hait and Khaybar - use the roads via Madinah. Alternative - shorter routes are not tarmacked all the way - and include poorly maintained sandy track. As with cities away from Dammam, Jeddah and Riyadh - there are no local bus services and poor taxi options. SATRANS coach does offer limited connections.

CHAPTER 15
TAYMA

Tayma / تيماء - GPS - 27.635011, 38.553407 **Population** (appx) 37,579 **A Brief History** - Tayma is an ancient oasis city located in northwestern Saudi Arabia. With a long history as a trading post on part of the incense route, Tayma has been inhabited since at least the early Bronze Age. The city saw the rise and fall of various kingdoms and empires over its long history.

One of the earliest known artefacts found in Tayma is a stone inscription of the cartouche of the Egyptian Pharaoh Rameses III, dating to around 1175BC. This indicates Tayma was part of the sphere of trade and possibly influence of the New Kingdom Egyptians during the late Bronze Age. Tayma was enclosed by an 18.2 km long wall of mud brick and sandstone, perhaps dating in origin to as early as the late/mid-2nd millenniumBC (a comparable date to the cartouche of Ramesses III), although it mostly enclosed land which was not built on. Within the exterior walls, more compact walling protected the city and its citadel.

Later, around the 9th centuryBC, Tayma came under the control of the Qedarites. This powerful tribal confederation dominated much of northern Arabia and controlled the trade routes from the south.

Tayma was conquered in the 6th centuryBC, by the Neo-Babylonian king Nabonidus. This was after his conquest of the Levant. Nabonidus made Tayma his residence and principally lived there for around ten years between 552-543BC – the reasons for his stay are unclear. However, a few years after his return to Babylon, the Persians, under Cyrus the Great, overran his Empire. Archaeologists have uncovered some inscriptions and monuments from Nabonidus' stay in Tayma, providing valuable information about this period.

After the fall of the Neo-Babylonian Empire, Tayma faded from prominence for several centuries. However, its fame lingered as Tayma was mentioned in the Biblical books of Jeremiah 25:23, compiled by the final centuries of the 1st millennium and Job

6:19, composed after the Neo-Babylonian period. As with many towns of northwestern Saudi - Tayma was inhabited by a substantial Jewish population.

The city regained attention in the early Islamic period because it supported a branch route of the Syrian Hajj Road between Damascus and Makkah. Medieval-era geographers often mentioned Tayma in their descriptions of the Arabian Peninsula.

In AD1181, Raynald of Chatillon, the Crusader lord of Oultrejordain, based at Kerak Castle in modern Jordan, launched a raid on a pilgrim caravan near Tayma. This raid increased the anger against Raynald by the Ayyubid ruler, Saladin. After capturing Raynald a year later, Saladin personally executed him as punishment for his attacks on pilgrims, including the raid near Tayma. This dramatic episode symbolises the widespread clash between the Crusaders and the forces of Islam during the medieval era.

Various Victorian-period travellers visited the town, including Charles Doughty and later Charles Huber. Doughty mapped the area and drew inscriptions found on a stele. Huber later collected the stele. The stele is written in Aramaic with images of warriors, and dated to the 5th centuryBC – another, simple, stele was found & dated to the 6th centuryBC. Both are in the Louvre; the major piece is known as the **Tayma Stele**.

The last historic monument built in Tayma is the Rumman Palace which dates from around AD1919.

Tayma is another paid attraction with a Rawi, SAR95; see www.experiencealula.com for updated visit information. A ticket office & reception in Tayma is next to Haddaj Well (north of the roundabout on Highway 15 (M45)) in the oasis & another to the town's northwest - on Haritha Al Ansari St near Al Hamra Palace. Coach travel and entrance from AlUla is SAR295, again check www.experiencealula.com as it's a seasonal service. During the winter season, Wednesday has some extra events in Tayma - check the website for details.

What's There- Much of the ancient area of Tayma is behind a fence to the west and south of the roundabout near the oasis, the central part of the town. This area includes Qasr Al Ablaq (Ablaq simply refers to its alternating courses of dark & light stone) - dating probably to the Ghassanid period (200BC-638AD). Within the general oasis area and less than a kilometre north of the roundabout (park on the road before the well) is the **Haddaj Well**. This ancient, essential, part of Tayma's infrastructure is a massive, collectively owned stone-lined water well with around 77 pulleys (previously worked by camels) for buckets to haul up irrigation water. It may date to the time of Nabonidus.

To the well's east is **Tayma Fort** - called Rumman Palace after the man who built it around AD1919 - during the Al Rashid period just before that dynasty's defeat by Amir AbdulAziz. The fort is a simple mud-brick structure and is included in the paid tour. Inside the prayer area is a classic regional style with a mihrab (prayer niche) and a mimbar (pulpit) as a niche within the wall.

Haddaj Well

This is rather than a pedestal or wooden pulpit structure as, say, in Cairo or Damascus. **Souq Al Najem** and a scattered date oasis is north of the fort. The reception has bikes available as well as electric chauffeur-driven golf buggies.

Farther east is the small **Al Fajr Heritage Museum**, +966 504768737 (contact before setting out to ensure its open) SAR30, secreted away after a 2km walk on a convoluted route through the date oasis. This is comparable to other privately operated museums, with a plethora of items of interest to the owner, Fahd Saleh Al Fajr. The visit is made more enjoyable if he guides you. West of the oasis, Haritha Al Ansari St passes the closed **Al Radam Palace** (late Iron Age 600-300BC), broadly the period of Nabonidus on the way to **Al Hamra Palace** (under the same entrance ticketing as elsewhere in Tayma). A small information room is next to its car park. Excavations suggest Al Hamra Palace dates to 553-542BC - again, the period of Nabonidus. The building is stone built, probably using material from its immediate location. The **town's walls** are easily seen on the road leading to Al Hamra Palace from the oasis. They are stone built and even today give an impression of their strength. At 18 km in circumference, building the walls must have been an immense task in a sparsely populated desert region. What created the need to do so much work? Perhaps the walls were intended to make any potential enemies feel that a successful attack was impossible. The number of soldiers defending the 18 km walling must have been considerable, even against small armies. Access to the walls is restricted by the metal fencing used throughout Saudi Arabia around historic sites.

Al Hamra Palace

~

RESTAURANTS - THE RESTAURANT OPTIONS IN TAYMA ARE LIMITED - south of Haddaj Well on the Highway 15 (M45) roundabout is **Al Salama Restaurant** * +966554399389 cheap takeaways 24hour, **Broast Al Arabi** * broast in Saudi is a generic term for a KFC clone +966501355853 14:00-01:00 diagonally opposite the petrol station southeast of Haddaj Well on Highway 15 (M45) - behind it is **Restaurant Supply of Meals**! +966507603115 10:00-midnight meat and rice style. However, there is a worthwhile and very convenient place - opposite Haddaj Well is the **Old Town Coffee*** shop. It's a local operation - drop into it and support local enterprise.

Accommodation - Though a bit away from the oasis - consider the relatively new **Jewel Places** ** +966507151807 about 1.5km south of Highway 15 (M45) & Al Ablaq Hotel ** southwest of the Haddaj Well & behind the petrol station on Highway 15(M45).

GETTING THERE, TAYMA IS ABOUT 200KM FROM ALULA VIA HIGHWAYS 70 & 15 (M45) or Route 250 from Khaybar on Highway 15 (M45). If travelling from Tabuk - it's south - on Highway 15 (M45) after about 270 km. As with cities away from Dammam, Jeddah and Riyadh - there are no local bus services and poor taxi options. SATRANS coach does offer limited connections.

Al Hait

< Jabals Al Manjor and Raat

Route 7900

Route 8510 > Hail

Rafef North Apartments

Ⓢ Shopping area

 Al Hait old settlements

< Khaybar

Ⓣ Al Hait walling

Ⓣ Al Hait ancient fields

CHAPTER 16
AL HAIT

A l Hait / الحيط - GPS - 25.979526, 40.475461 **Population** (appx) 8,289 **A quick overview of the geography** - Al Hait is within an igneous landscape of granite & old lava flows - this is comparable to many other areas of the northwest. This stone has been used for the buildings, field terracing and town walls.

A Brief History - The oasis town of Al Hait, also known historically as Fadak, like so many other historic settlements in Saudi Arabia is a collection of small, compact villages. It's set along an ancient north-south trade route in the east of the Hijaz region. There is evidence of the Babylonian ruler King Nabonidus having visited here as its mentioned in the inscriptions of Harran (as Fadak). With its reliable water sources and fertile soil, Al Hait has been inhabited and cultivated since at least the 1st millenniumBC.

In the 7th centuryAD, a Jewish tribe inhabited the oasis. Islamic tradition records that after the Muslim victory at the Battle of Khaybar, the Jews of Al Hait agreed to surrender the oasis to the Prophet Muhammad for some share of the agricultural production. Muhammad then may have gifted Al Hait to his daughter Fatima. After Muhammad's death, the second Caliph, Umar, disputed Fatima's inheritance of Al Hait and took control of the oasis for the state treasury.

In the early Islamic era, Al Hait became a stopping point for pilgrim caravans travelling between Syria and the holy cities of Makkah and Madinah. It was also a base for Muslim armies launching raids against Byzantine territory. For much of the subsequent period control over the oasis town was contested between various Muslim dynasties.

By the 19th century, Al Hait had declined into an inconsequential settlement. In 1830, the Ottoman sultan gifted Al Hait to Mohammed Ali Pasha of Egypt for his services, presumably the battles in Arabia. The area was still inhabited by a small population engaged in agriculture and camel herding when King AbdulAziz conquered the Hijaz in 1925. Today, the town illustrates how state employment, which is by far the primary economic engine in many towns, supports a Saudi town's economy. There is little agriculture, some animal husbandry, and not much industry. Government employment in areas such as teaching, healthcare and government administration underpin private local services such as shops.

What's There The straggling new town of Al Hait is to the north of the original, old settlements. These ancient settlements overlook a shallow wadi where the original agricultural fields can be seen. The old fields are small, walled, and some slightly terraced – however lack of water has devastated the agriculture. Dead date palm trees, collapsing field walling, and abandoned settlements all built from dark igneous stone - create a truly desolate spectacle.

The agriculture and remains of the **old settlements** are surrounded by the original town walls. All these walls are now collapsed down to a couple of meters in height – still giving an excellent impression of their extent. The wall may have been around 7km long and is most complete on the western side. Outside the walls, there are also multitudes of prehistoric stone circles. With some careful curation, the area could be much more enjoyable. This is one town where you may be the only non-resident. For some people, Al Hait is a stepping stone to the UNESCO Rock Art site at Jabals al-Manjor and Raat - west of Shuwaymis.

≈

RESTAURANTS AND ACCOMMODATION - IN THE SOUTH OF HAIT, SOME small restaurants are along the main shopping street - or you can buy snacks in a supermarket. A simple hotel option in the north of the new town is **Rafef North Apartments** * +966506306226. There are two separate large buildings, less than 10 years old) next to each other - ask to see a room in each – the more recent property is on the left.

≈

GETTING THERE AL HAIT IS A STRAIGHTFORWARD DRIVE OF 230KM north of Madinah on Route 356. Madinah is also the best link between Al Hait and Khaybar. Alternative - shorter routes between Al Hait and Khaybar are not tarmacked all the way - and include poorly maintained, little-used, sandy tracks that are not at all suggested.

Jabals Al Manjor and Raat.

CHAPTER 17

JABALS AL MANJOR AND RAAT - SHUWAYMIS

J abals Al Manjor and Raat - Shuwaymis / الشويمس - GPS - 26.132111, 39.902656 **A Quick Overview Of The Geography** - The rock art is on sandstone hills - surrounded by a sandy plain.

A Brief History - Saudi Arabia contains thousands of ancient petroglyphs and rock inscriptions, providing a window into prehistoric cultures. Among the most significant sites are Jabals Al Manjor and Raat at Shuwaymis, rock art complexes in northern Saudi Arabia. These sites only became known to people outside the local area in 2001 - an illustration of how remote the area is. More studies at Jabals al-Manjor and Raat took place in 2002 & 2005.

Jabals al-Manjor and Raat contain over 15,000 petroglyph panels scattered over large rocky sandstone outcrops. For somebody with a casual interest, the rock art site at Jubbah is more accessible, (in all respects) than Jabals Al Manjor and Raat. However, rock art at this isolated site is impressive.

Here are innumerable examples of rock art, spread over a wide sandstone area. These are either on the hillsides overlooking a plain - or on large slabs that have fallen off the hills. Irrespective of the surface the rock art is on - considerable scrambling is needed to get views of it. The often deeply incised carvings depict a variety of human and animal figures, including ibex, leopards, lions, ostriches, cattle and dogs. Many have a fluid and attractive style. Impressive packs of hunting dogs, dancing across the surfaces are a feature; this was a hunter-gatherer society. The dogs appear to be **Canaan Dogs,** on a leash, perhaps the earliest images of domestication of dogs. There are over 18 clusters. Many have been dated to the Neolithic period, approximately 6,000-4,000BC, representing some of the oldest rock art in Arabia.

∾

GETTING THERE JABALS AL-MANJOR AND RAAT ARE NORTHWEST OF Route 7900 at Al Hait, a one-way drive of almost 70km. The phrase, 'Back of Beyond' is more than appropriate here. The route leads through the village of Shuwaymis & scattered livestock operations, to the UNESCO Rock Art site of Jabals al-Manjor and Raat. It is a combination of tarmac, whose construction appears to have been abandoned before reaching its destination, and then poorly maintained sandy road - 4x4 country with 2 vehicles suggested in case of breakdown or getting stuck. There is no signage (or useful services such as petrol) on the route. Shuwaymis is passed 30km away from the UNESCO site. The site is fenced & locked, as with similar remote & not so remote sites in the country. There is a small government building, connected with tourism, opposite the site entrance (just off the track). However they may direct visitors to search for key-holding Bedouin to provide entrance. These Bedouin will lead the way in their 4x4 vehicle - it will be hundreds of SAR, after negotiation.

Human, Dogs on a lead - and maned Lion

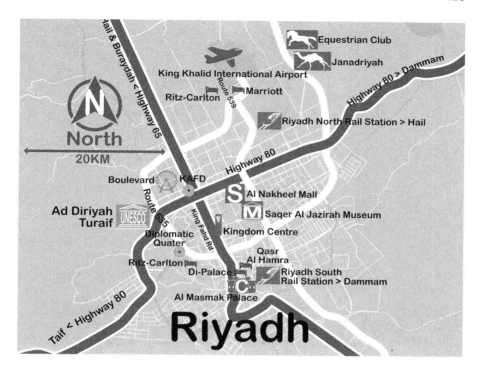

CHAPTER 18
RIYADH

Riyadh / الرياض - GPS - 24.645419, 46.709711 **Population** (appx) 6,924,566
A Quick Overview Of The Geography - Riyadh is in a sedimentary geological area - characterised by the limestone Tuwaiq Escarpment. This runs from Al Qassim in the north - past Riyadh towards the southwest and Wadi Ad Dawasir. The escarpment's edge faces west, rising several hundred meters above lower areas - creating what is called the Edge of the World.

A Brief History - The early history of Riyadh centres around an oasis settlement called Hajr (now in southern Riyadh), located on caravan routes crisscrossing the Arabian Peninsula. It was founded around the 5th centuryAD. The Banu Hanifa tribe inhabited the area by the 6th centuryAD. Several other settlements grew over the following centuries, including Riyadh – which was walled from AD1737.

After the destruction of Diriyah (see below) in the early 19th century by the forces of Egypt's Mohammed Ali Pasha– the subsequent Al Saud rulers of the Second Saudi State settled in Riyadh in 1824 after expelling the Egyptian forces. As the capital of the Second Saudi State, Riyadh grew quickly over the following decades. In 1891, Riyadh fell to the forces of Muhammad Al Rashid from Hail. The Al Rashid rule was short-lived and in 1902, the young AbdulAziz bin Abdulrahman Al Saud (future Amir then King AbdulAziz) recaptured Riyadh and Masmak Fort in January 1902 after a bringing a small force from Kuwait.

From Riyadh, Amir AbdulAziz bin Abdulrahman Al Saud went on to consolidate control over the Arabian Peninsula, finally establishing the modern Kingdom of Saudi Arabia in September 1932 – and including the southwest from 1934. His titles changed between 1902 & 1932 – for simplicity before 1932 Amir is used & after that King. New fortifications, still from mud-brick, at Al Murabba Palace were built in 1936. As the Saudi capital, Riyadh gained new prominence and development.

Growth accelerated significantly from the discovery of oil. The opening of the old Riyadh International Airport in 1946 and the rail line from Dammam, which was opened in 1951 were key elements in supporting growth. King AbdulAziz ordered sections of the old city walls demolished to accommodate urban expansion in 1950. Riyadh was transforming from a traditional desert town into a modern metropolis.

Masmak Palace

Orientation A sprawling, largely low-rise city. The exception is Riyadh's main arterial road, King Fahd Rd, is adjacent to many key places of interest in central Riyadh. This has several skyscrapers leading to King Abdullah Financial District with its own concentration of skyscrapers. The soon-to-open Metro's Blue Line runs along much of the King Fahd Rd central stretch. Beyond the current northern edge of the city at King Salman bin Abdulaziz Rd will be the 'New Murabba'. This is a planned urban complex - with a vast cube 'The Mukaab' at its heart. To the west is Wadi Hanifa and Turaif. One thing Riyadh is not - a walking city. Though the two areas around Al Masmak Palace and King AbdulAziz Historical Center (Al Murabba) are good to walk in – as is Turaif. In most respects it's comparable to a city in the USA, rather than Europe, with limited public transport and wide highways. App called Taxis are ideal to use here – until the Metro opens.

THINGS TO SEE IN RIYADH

In the north of **King Fahd Rd** is **King Abdullah Financial District**. Its **Grand Mosque**, though overshadowed by the financial district's skyscrapers, is a standout building designed by Riyadh-based Basem Al-Shihabi's Omrania. Looking like a futuristic spacecraft, it is apparently inspired by the small gypsum formation, the desert rose. The Mosque is located in the southern area of the KAFD and best accessed by the Metro's Blue, Yellow or Purple lines (when they open) or off the junction of King Fahd Road and Northern Ring Road (exit 4). Not accessible inside for non-Muslims.

In the central section of the King Fahd Rd are two landmark skyscrapers - ideal as visual orientation points. The **Kingdom Centre** (locally known as the 'bottle opener' because of its very distinctive design) www.kingdomcentre.com.sa, with its almost Eye of Sauron-like sky bridge. This includes a high-end, brand-focused mall with Louboutin, Gucci, Channel, Dior, Burberry, and more. It's a place to go to people watch, window shop or shop until you drop. The Four Seasons Hotel and **Sky Bridge** (Sat-Thurs 09:30-23:00 / Fri 16:30- 23:00m Cost SAR 60 & SAR 20 for children 2-10) add to the luxurious attraction. East of the Kingdom Centre is the future development, King Salman Park, with an expected variety of cultural projects. **Al Faisaliah Mall** is easy to spot with its rocket-like skyscraper just south of the Kingdom Centre.

It's a patchy mall, home to British department store Harvey Nichols and many other stores. This is still not as vibrant as other malls. There is another good food court here, a feature of malls in Saudi Arabia. The main draw for visitors has to be the viewing deck, which costs SAR25 and, as it's in a globe, gives a nearly 360-degree view of the city. Saturday to Thursday 9:00 AM – 12:00 AM Friday 13:30 PM - midnight. This entire section of King Fahd Rd has numerous other smaller shopping malls. South of Al Faisaliah Mall is **King Fahd National Library** 08:00-20:00 (closed Fri & Sat) www.kfnl.gov.sa. with a small, landscaped park. Use the King Fahd Library metro station - on the Blue Line. To the far west of Al Faisaliah Mall is the Embassy Area - off the Jeddah Road - about a 5km drive from King Fahd Rd. Here are most embassies from Saudi Arabia's key diplomatic partners.

King Fahd Road swings around the **King AbdulAziz Historical Center** in Riyadh. This is the umbrella phrase for the complex of buildings, and small parks, that includes the National Museum and Al Murabba Historical Palace (part of King AbdulAziz Historical Centre) www.national-museum.org.sa Opening hours for general public visits are 09:00-20:00 Sat-Wed/14:00-22:00 Thurs & Fr (Sun closed). Cost FOC per person during general public hours. This general area may be closed for official visits; though the focus for high profile visitors, and the attendant publicity, is shifting to AlUla and NEOM.

Designed by Canadian architect Raymond Moriyama, the **Saudi National Museum** of Saudi Arabia was opened as part of the King AbdulAziz Historical Center in 1999. This is a key location for official visits - and may be closed while they enter. The museum is intended to be a cultural and civilisation centre to introduce the history of Saudi Arabia.

A secondary purpose, that is increasingly important, is as a hub for tourism in Riyadh and Saudi Arabia in General. The eight halls

Kingdom Centre

are located on two floors. On the Ground Floor - Man and the Universe briefly covers astronomy, geology, and the natural world; Arab Kingdoms - an overview of the small kingdoms that previously occupied Arabia. These are too numerous to mention here but includes Najran in the south and Dumat Al Jandal in the north, Pre-Islamic/Jahiliyya Era Hall - Jahiliyya means the age of ignorance which refers to the Pre-Islamic Era, and this somewhat overlaps with the Arab Kingdoms hall.

Moving upstairs - Prophet's Mission is an overview about the Prophet Mohammed & his life, Islam and the Arabian Peninsula is an overview of the history & development of Arabia following the introduction of Islam. First and Second Saudi States anchors the overview of the initial period of the Al Saud rule. Unification of Saudi Arabia – this is a continuation of the First and Second Saudi

National Museum

States as it covers what is in effect the third, and current Saudi state – under King AbdulAziz; The Hajj and Two Holy Mosques illustrates the Hajj as a pilgrimage & how Makkah & Madinah have been developed. Most halls are single rooms – however the sections covering Islam and the First & Second Saudi States have several rooms each. Temporary exhibitions are held - an added bonus on many visits. There will be an increasing focus on local artists – and live cultural events. The exhibits are well laid out and informative in a spacious building – worth a visit.

National Museum

Al-Murabba Historical Palace is within the King AbdulAziz Historical Centre. Construction for the palace was started in 1936 and completed in 1945. The mud-brick palace must have been out of date before it was occupied because of the rapid changes in Saudi Arabia at the time. Al Murabba Historical Palace replaced Al Masmak Fort as the principal public building for King AbdulAziz. It was created from mud-brick, with ceilings created from raw tree logs, date palm-leaf stalks and mud ceilings/floors, traditional Arabian decorations, and crow step-roof lines. From 1972 through to 1999, the building was gradually opened to the public. Set within a spacious series of courtyards, the main building's plan is an oblong building with a substantial open courtyard. Over 30 rooms, some opening onto the courtyard or a veranda on the First Floor (upper). The Ground Floor was used for security, offices and general services, and the First Floor (upper) was for administration and reception rooms. Displays of traditional clothes, jewellery and furnishings are on display. Occasional temporary exhibits are made within the courtyard. The mud-brick building with columns and traditional timbered ceilings is interesting. The general area has several interlinked landscaped gardens and numerous water features. Opening hours are random, so this is an add-on to the National Museum, not a specific visit. Look for an old car collection at the rear of the museum, including the Rolls-Royce given in 1945 by UK Prime Minister Winston Churchill to King AbdulAziz.

Northeast of King AbdulAziz Historical Centre is **Riyadh Zoo** (entry) 09:00-15:00 (closes at 17:00) Friday 13:00-15:00 (closes at 17:00) on AlAhsa St in Malaz. Ticket prices have varied from FOC to SAR11.25. Here there are various zones including Elephant, Tiger and Monkey. It's a small zoo, under 16 hectares, (slightly larger than London Zoo in Regents park) and much smaller than Bronx Zoo's 107 hectares. The animals are in small pens.

South of the King AbdulAziz Historical Centre is a park and leisure area. Beyond that, to the south, is the Red Palace, which was a museum and will be a hotel. Of more interest is the **King AbdulAziz Public Library** 08:00-20:00 (closed Friday) Adh Dhahirah St. Apart from the expected books, here is a comprehensive collection of Islamic coinage. The library, though relatively new, hasn't kept up with the internet age and research needing laptops - there are limited power sockets & poor wi-fi.

Just east of King Fahd Rd is what little remains of the **'Old Town' of Riyadh**. Qasr Al Hoqm metro on the Blue & Green lines will give access when it opens. This old town is about 1km east to west and no more than 800 metres south to north. North of the metro is a mix of older housing that is now being refurbished, and in the central section is the old **Al Thumairi Souq**. This mixes gold and jewellery shops, souvenirs and handicrafts, perfumes, and general stores. On the corner of Al Thumairi St and Al Batha Road is the reconstruction of one of the gates into Riyadh, **Al Thumairi Gate** - on the eastern edge of the old town.

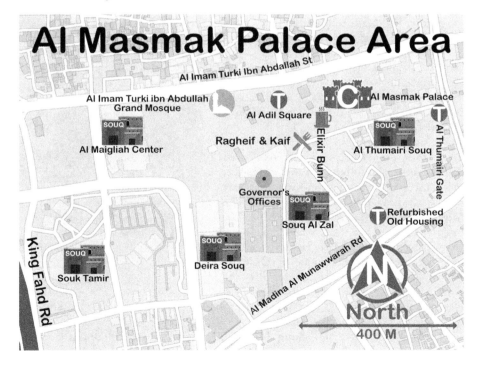

To the west is the **Al Masmak Palace (Fort)**. Opening hours for general public visits are 08:00-20:00 Sun-Thurs, 16:00-20:00 Fri, 09:00-20:00 Sat. Cost No Charge. The metro station Qasr Al Hoqm is a 400-meter walk; alternatively, for taxis, Al

Masmak Palace is off Al Batha St. & Imam Turki bin Abdullah bin Mohammed St. The name 'palace' is at odds with the building's utilitarian castle appearance.

The building was probably completed in 1895 under the Al Rashid dynasty, of Hail. The Al Rashid had occupied Riyadh in 1891 after their victory in the Battle of Mulayda forced Abdul Rahman bin Faisal Al Saud into exile. Al Masmak Palace is the original, now restored, fortification that Amir AbdulAziz bin AbdulRahman Al Saud captured in 1902 at the start of his conquest of Saudi Arabia from Kuwait, the location of his father's exile after the Battle of Mulayda. Though the building was originally within the city walls, these were demolished in the mid-1950s as Riyadh grew in size.

Built of mud bricks, the fort is roughly square with four corner towers just under 20m high. After its capture, it was used as a military arsenal and prison. Entry is by the gate with a small picket gate set inside. Look for the embedded spearhead, in the small picket gate, that is a key part of the story of the fort's capture. The building was restored in 1995. Inside are several courtyards (light wells), off which are a series of rooms. The interior has had the rooms internally connected to provide a continuous walk through the exhibits, starting to the right of the entrance). It includes an overview of historic Riyadh. This is followed by the capture of the fort, portrayed almost as a Hollywood blockbuster, and finally, information again about Riyadh and the fort. This display area is focused on Riyadh in a historic setting.

South of Al Masmak Palace is Al Thumairi St – running west-east. The shops here are focused on Saudi men's clothing and accessories, including glitzy watches. If you are in the hunt for souvenirs or 'antiques' look for the shop with 2 life sized models of camels, 'Kingdom Heritage' 09:00-midday / 16:00-22:30 (Fri afternoon only). Here, so far, are few fridge magnets, and more of an Aladdin's Cave type experience.

From Al Masmak Palace and walking straight ahead, west, you will come to **Al Adil Square** (Justice/Deira Square). This is the site where public executions have been held, on Friday, after mid-day prayers at **Al Imam Turki bin Abdullah Grand Mosque**, (Muslim entry only) with its two prominent minarets, which is next to this square. The Mosque was rebuilt in 1993 in limestone. The building's style is a modern take on an austere central Arabian style. Two covered elevated walkways connect the Mosque to **Qasr Al Hoqm** in the south. Qasr Al Hoqm is the Governor of Riyadh's office complex. It is illegal to take photographs of government buildings and uniformed government officials, such as police and military.

Kingdom Heritage shop

South of Al Adil Square is **Souq Al Zal**. 'Zal' means 'carpet' or 'floor rug'. Souq Al Zal is a traditional market dating to 1901 that has been renovated, selling perfumes and incense, Bisht (a traditional gown for men), swords, unique 'antiques', carpet, men's clothing and shoes. Souq Al Zal focuses on the local consumer and has an appealing atmosphere with casual auctions of older goods. South of Souq Al Zal is an area which has been partially demolished and rebuilt in the style of the early 20th-century town,

Dekhnah Area. West of Qasr Al Hoqm is **Deira Souq** (Wshaiger Souq), which offers a slightly more modern shopping experience. More souqs are further west. You will probably walk less than 5 km around old Riyadh; allow a couple of hours plus the time you spend in the souqs and fortress. An afternoon visit is likely to be more relaxing as government offices will be closed, and there will be less traffic as a result. There are small cafes, including, on Al Adil Square, **Ragheif & Kaif***, 07:00-midday/16:00-22:30 (afternoon only Fri & Sat) & **Elixir Bunn Coffee*** 07:00-22:30 Sun-Thurs 13:00-22:30 Fri & Sat - both have seating outside, enabling people watching.

In Riyadh's northwest (24km from the National Museum) is **Boulevard** 15:00-23:00 (core hours) basic entry FOC on Amir Turki bin Abdulaziz the First. This an evolving leisure and entertainment area - confusingly in two sections in completely separated areas. It's full of neon lighting, and vast video screens with a background of music that would be censored by many public broadcasters in the West, but here is used indiscriminately. Take a pick of the cultural events, activities, shops and restaurants. Wander through **Boulevard World from** SAR29 - where famous locations (Pyramids, Eiffel Tower etc) are reimagined for visitors. The area is also a hub for **Riyadh Season** www.RiyadhSeason.com. During holidays, this will be packed - even if you have a car, use Uber so you can get in and out easily.

Saqer-Al Jazirah Royal Saudi Air Force Aviation Museum +966114922303 09:00-midday 16:00-21:00 SAR10 is in Riyadh's northeast (19km from the National Museum), on the junction of King Abdullah Rd & Eastern Ring Rd (entrance road). Here are a remarkable number of aircraft previously used by the Royal Saudi Air Force. There is reasonable labelling – in English and Arabic. It's an interesting museum for anyone interested in the military. The planes are displayed inside and outside, so it is best to arrive before sunset.

Specialised Retail

Al-Saadawy Arts & Antiques Gallery (Universal Art & Antiques) 12 Abdul-Malik Bin Marwan St. Olaya Riyadh (east of King Fahd Rd), +966-14648182 www.univearts.com is a company specialising in retailing Middle Eastern style interior furnishing and arts. A key part of their offering is Najdi-style products, emphasising quality and authenticity. They also provide an interior design service. With easy parking, **Nakheel Mall** www.arabiancentres.com is just a block south of junction eight on the Northern Ring Road. The mall has a good mix of local (Arabian peninsula brands) and mid-price western franchises like Marks & Spencer. The food court offers an excellent variety of places to eat. Sat-Thurs 08:00-12:0023:00 / Fri 16:00-23:30.

In northwest Riyadh, at the junction of Route 535 and Prince Mohammed bin Salman bin Abdulaziz Road in The Residence Mall, is **Personage**, a fashionable complex, almost a modern take on a department store, which offers Saudi designers retail space. Fashion is the predominant theme here, with a Cafe to help you linger longer. Find it behind **Farzi Café** www.farzicafe.com midday-03:00. Here the slightly Indian/Arabian interior, and outdoor dining make a comfortable option for a range of cuisine, centred around good North Indian dishes. For something lighter, try coffee & cake.

Al Othmain Mall www.othaimmalls.com hours Sat-Thurs 10:00-23:00 (Fri 14:00-midnight) is on the junction of the Eastern Ring Road and Abi Dhar Al Ghaffari Rd is This is a popular destination with a broad selection of mid-price stores, including

Mothercare, Yves Rocher, The Body Shop, and innumerable local brands. However, its vast children's entertainment area and 'Snow City' must be the biggest draw, as the long queues and SAR120 basic entry cost show.

Souq Al Zal - Riyadh

Northeast of Riyadh

On Route 550 (50 km drive from the National Museum) is the **Janadriyah Cultural & Heritage Festival** Venue www. moc.gov.sa. Currently FOC. This does exactly what it says and offers culture in the form of traditional music, cultural dances and camel racing, Different regions in Saudi Arabia have their culture highlighted, and there is also international participation. It usually takes place at the end of December for almost a month. From 11:00-23:00. There have been specific days for men, women and families, so do check in local media or ask your tour company or hotel for details.

If you are a horse racing fan – visit the **Equestrian Club** www.frusiya.com just north of Janadriyah. The race season starts in winter from 3rd week in October through to March. Located northeast of Riyadh - 52km from the National Museum - on Route 550 to King Khalid Royal Wildlife Sanctuary (Thumamah National Park) and after Janadriyah Cultural & Heritage Festival Venue. This is flat racing, with guaranteed sun, landscaped gardens and no betting. It does make a great day out, especially if booked into the excellent restaurant with its grandstand view. There are permissions needed for 'professional' photography. Schedule as per the racing calendar.

King Khalid Royal Wildlife Sanctuary (Thumamah National Park) is located northeast of Riyadh on Route 550, about 75km from the National Museum. This is an area of Sand Dunes and limestone escarpments, and a 4x4 is essential to go off-road.

The **Camel Souq** is just north of this park, but open daily, just off junction of Routes 553 & 550 after some 110 km from the National Museum. Here, potential buyers will find thousands of camels available for sale. Butchers are dealing with young Camel meat - selling by the kilo.

King AbdulAziz Camel Festival www.alaibilfestival.com (Al Aibil is a local word for a camel) is held in the entire month of January. Located northeast of Riyadh, about 50km after the Camel Souq on Routes 550 & 5318. Alternatively on Route 5318, off Highway 80 (M50) to Dammam - it's about 160km to drive – its northeast of King Khalid Royal Wildlife Sanctuary. This major event has Camel Racing, Camel Beauty contests (yes and incredibly competitive they are) and over 20,000 camels to see!

Camels in a Beauty Contest

South of Riyadh

Towards & around the **Al Kharj** area, south & southeast of Riyadh, are some places of minor interest. A collection of small parks, lakes and agriculture are along the southern area of Wadi Hanifa – on the southern outskirts of Riyadh. These are formed by the confluence of Wadi Hanifa with some natural and man-made grey-water streams. South of Arafat Rd is the start of these with the park at **Wadi Hanifa Lake**; passing date gardens, the watercourse is joined by the treated outflow from Riyadh's southern sewage system. The watercourse continues into **Al Hair**, **Riyadh Wetlands** and finally Al Kharj. From the Wadi Hanifa Lake, the convoluted course is around 70kms - and is full of birdwatching opportunities. Almost 60km southeast of Riyadh, off Highway 65 (M35) to Al Kharj, is **Ain Heet Cave**. Exit Highway 65 (M35) and drive northeast across a small wadi. Follow this wadi south for around 1500m, and the cave is north up the hill. After about a 2km walk/4x4 drive, you arrive at Ain Heet. This is a small cave with a water pool within. Some scrambling inside is needed, and suitable safety precautions should be taken based on individual abilities.

Carrying on south Highway 65 (M35) for 40km exit south at Al Jeathen Trading complex and less than 2km south is **Ain Farazan**. This is a falaj/qanat (a man-made water system that evolved thousands of years ago). Here, the excavation shafts can be seen; these allow light and air into the horizontal passage and also serve to remove debris. Historically, they serve to direct water from a source to a fertile agricultural area. West of the junction of Highways 65 (M35) & 10 (M90), after a 6.5km drive on Highway 10 (M90) (south of Lulu Hypermarket), are the twin sinkholes (**Ain Dhila & Ain Samah**) of Al Kharj / As Siah - about 100km from the National Museum. These are popularly ascribed to meteorite impact. Access to these, taking a cautious view from the top down to the water, is sometimes restricted. These were a historical water source and amply illustrate the volume of underground water as the area's aquifer is heavily pumped for the fields around. Around 10km west and east of the junction of Routes 65 & 10, are the milk cattle farms that supply milk for Saudi Arabia and throughout the peninsula. They may be the largest milk farms in the world.

Southwest of Riyadh,

Off Highway 80 (M50), and driving north is the Qiddiya area with the future (under construction) **Formula 1** track and **Six Flags** theme-style park. The theme park will have, of course, record breaking rides – including Falcon's Flight roller coaster which plunges off a 200m high cliff. It is one of the planned 2034 FIFA World Cup bid locations. Qiddiya is a 60km drive to the area. East of Highway 80 (M50) on Route 505 is **Dirab Golf** https://dirabgolf.com/ - traditional greens surrounded by desolate landscape - found after driving 70 km from the National Museum.

West of the city centre (about a 9km drive from the National Museum), between Prince Faisal bin Fahd bin Abdulaziz Road and Wadi Hanifa Road, is the **King Fahd Cultural** Centre www.kfcc.gov.sa. This holds mainly Arab music events but occasionally does host major Western concerts.

Edge of the World - from below

The **Edge of the World** GPS 24.944557, 45.993270 is to the west of Riyadh - it's a lengthy escarpment, here over 30km long, facing west and over an arid landscape. It may represent the edge of the cultivated world and an actual edge. From the National Museum, this is about 110km drive towards the town of Sadus via the King Fahd Road. The way uses Route 5762 (off Route 535) and passes through Sadus - where just to the west of the settlement, next to a date plantation, is a west turn to the Edge of the World. The rough track leads past a water dam - for 27kms - a 4x4 needed for ground clearance. The government might be working towards making this a paid-for guided experience - rather than free to enjoy - apparently due to the possible dangers when driving on a rough road.

The Edge of the World is an extremely barren escarpment within the Tuwaiq Escarpment range. The drop is up to several hundred meters down the talus (scree slope), with views (on clear days) to the west. Sunset is a great time to visit as the sun sets opposite the escarpment - care is needed to drive the unlit track back. Northeast of this escarpment - is the Gazelle reintroduction area at Huraymila - you may be lucky and see these beautiful animals in the wild.

Festivals in Riyadh's region.

Riyadh Season www.riyadhseason.sa. Is a city-wide winter season event, in a multitude of event locations, with a wide range of themes from traditional to modern including traditional cuisine and clothing to music and dance. This runs from December-February. **Al Janadriyah** is a festival held over several weeks by the Ministry of Culture https://moc.gov.sa/en in December. It will typically have Camel, Horse, Handicrafts and Cuisine events. Look in the press for details and find it along Route 550 northeast of Riyadh. **King AbdulAziz Festival for Camels** held at the start of January. Held off Route 550. This covers the world of Camels, including racing, milking events, camel beauty events and more. **Saudi Falcons Club** hold events and exhibitions in October. In late November through to December, they hold the King AbdulAziz Falconry Festival. These various Falcon events are held at Malham (off Highway 65/M35) https://sfc.org.sa. **Diriyah Season**, cultural & sports events citywide - but focused on Diriyah. It's around 3 months – sometime between Oct-Feb www.diriyahseason.sa. **Riyadh Art** - https://riyadhart.sa/ has periodic large-scale art exhibitions especially in December, which includes lights shows (Noor Riyadh). **Misk Art** https://miskartinstitute.org/ also holds events - many held in Prince Faisal Bin Fahd Arts Hall on King Saud Rd. **SoundStorm** is a music festival in the winter in Riyadh; check https://mdlbeast.com/ for event dates in the winter.

As an add-on to many major events (National Day etc) in Saudi Arabia might be a flying show by the '**Saudi Hawks**' an acrobatic team from the Saudi Royal Air Force https://saudihawks.net.

The government hopes to hold the 2030 World Expo and 2034 World Cup in Riyadh.

≈

RIYADH RESTAURANTS AND ACCOMMODATION

Some Places To Consider Eating In - For the more upmarket options, the 5* hotels had the market cornered until recently. Try **Al Orjouan** ***** in the Ritz Carlton or, for the best views, **The Globe** ***** in the Faisaliah Tower on King Fahd Road. However at **VIA Riyadh** www.viariyadh.com a modern building has over a dozen good dining options that make this well worth searching out. Though none are themselves Michelin stared, a couple are operations whose international outlets do have that coveted star. There is also a variety of premium shops in the same building. For a visitor, it's away from the typical sights, on the Jeddah Road in the northwest, with St Regis hotel in the same building and the Ritz Carlton near.

Most lower-cost restaurants open from around 07:00-23:00, and the food is freshly prepared, though the decor is likely basic. Just south of the eastern area of Al Sinaiyah, the industrial area is restaurants catering to the residents and workers. On Al Ounouz St is **Mataem Shatti Mukalla*** 10:00-23:00. This is authentically Yemeni, with rice-based fish, meat and chicken dishes. Unfortunately, it's a bit off the beaten track. **Hommos Al Nakaa** * near the junction of Al Kharj Road and Al Madinah Al Munawwarah Road. This is extremely popular throughout the day, 05:00-23:00. It offers vegetarian plates including hummus, falafel and mutable. **Saravanaa Bhavan** ** www.saravanabhavan.com inside Riyadh Avenue Mall on the junction of Prince Faisal bin Turki bin Abdullah Road and King Faisal Road. Saravanaa Bhavan is part of a well-known, low-cost Indian chain of vegetarian restaurants. **Ragheif & Kaif*** on the western end of Al Thumairi Street, near Masmak Fortress, has indoor and outdoor seating with an attractive ambience. With some great teas, Arabic coffee with dates, and a good selection of fast food, including some excellent halloumi, this is good for a visit to the area around the fortress. **Lavesh** *** (one of two branches in Riyadh) +966595942949 on Prince Turki bin Abdulaziz Al Awwal (13:00-midnight) is a stylish Levant restaurant; choose a table on the upper floor by the windows. **Najd Village** ****, http://najdvillage.com/ on Al Takhassousi St. west of King Fahd Rd - traditional Saudi food in a themed Najd-style building - with on-floor cushioned seating in small private cubicles. **Lusin***** (one of two in Riyadh) www.lusinrestaurant.com inside Centria Mall on Olaya Street (just north of the Al Faisaliah Mall) is a beautiful decor and well-presented food, let down slightly by minor points like drinks offered in cans. (13:00-midnight), is a stylish levant restaurant. **Mama Noura** * www.mamanoura.com.sa 06:00-02:00 – is a Riyadh-based chain of Shawarma fast food restaurants with a good choice of snacks and freshly made Shawarma. The branches are out of the main 'tourist' areas; however, try the one on King Abdulla Road near the Takhassusi St junction or Prince Fahd bin Saud bin Abdulrahman St & Prince Abdulaziz bin Musaid bin Jalawi Street (2.5km west of Al Faisaliah Mall) **Uskudar Steak House***** 13:00-midnight +966534488722 On the Northern Ring Road southern service road (west of KAFD), a Turkish-style restaurant with indoor and outdoor seating. In the city's northwest is **Boulevard** on Prince Turki Bin Abdulaziz Al Awwal Road. This area has leisure activities, primarily focused on popular entertainment, food & and a good range of restaurants.

A Selection Of Accommodation - Riyadh is full of hotels of all types to suit a wide range of pockets. The original 5-star option of the **InterContinental** *** with its excellent facilities is still open; of course, there is the **Ritz Carlton** *****. However, the new **voco*****, www.ihg.com, off the northern section of King Fahd Rd, offers a good alternative. The **Al Faisaliah Hotel******* is being refurbished, undoubtedly making it a good choice when reopened. Lower down the price scale is the **Grand Plaza Dhabab Hotel** *** www.ewaahotels.com, just north of the National Museum. The **Hotel Di-Palace** www.di-palace.com/ ** is centrally located south of the National Museum. **Qasr Al Hamra*** +966114094097 on Al Bathaa Rd - (there are two entrances – the rear entrance leads onto an area of low-cost shopping). The hotel is near the National Museum Blue/Green Line Metro when they open. Near the King Khalid International Airport are a couple of hotels: **Marriott***** www.marriott.com & **Radisson***** www.radissonhotels.com

≈

GETTING AROUND RIYADH

Riyadh is a substantial, low-density city. Broadly speaking, it is bounded by major highways and bisected south-north by another highway. The older centre, focused around Masmak Fort and the National Museum, has a random street layout that is divided by the King Fahd Road (Highway 65/M35), which runs from south to north. This is the major three-lane arterial road and forms part of the more modern city's grid layout. King Fahd Road intersects in the north with the Makkah Al Mukarramah Road (Highway 40/M80), which runs west-east and leads to Diplomatic City and farther to the west to Makkah and east to Dammam.

North of the Makkah Al Mukarramah Road, the King Fahd Road has two of Riyadh's very useful skyscrapers to use as navigation aids: Al Faisaliah Centre, with its distinctive apex holding a globe and Kingdom Centre, with the more iconic sky bridge. These two towers are in Al Olaya District, the premium shopping district of Riyadh.

A northern junction of King Fahd Road is a substantial junction with the Northern Ring Road (four lanes) that crosses west-east and is also part of Highways 80 (M50) and 40 (M80) from Jeddah to Dammam. This junction (junction 4 on the Northern Ring road) is overlooked by the skyscrapers of the King Abdullah Financial District. The district is intended to have a 6-station, looped monorail system that will have a station interchange with the Riyadh Metro lines 1 Blue, 4 Yellow and 6 Violet; the junction station is a Zaha Hadid design. The Northern Ring Road, which runs west-east, has numerous ramped interchanges with a substantial 'clover leaf' complex at junction 8. This is the Eastern Ring Road (four lanes now enveloped by the city, hence the outer Second Ring Road), which leads north, past Imam Muhammad bin Saud Islamic University, to King Khalid International Airport and south to Makkah Al Mukarramah Road. Makkah Road links to the west with the King Khalid Road (four lanes), which forms the principal north-south route on the west of the city. The King Khalid Road leads north from the area of Diplomatic City to the Northern Ring. There are occasional pedestrian bridges across King Fahd Road; the others only have the option of road bridges from the ramped exits. Beyond the general built-up area is a 2nd ring road that will take through traffic. In general, Riyadh is not a walking city.

As most of the central areas of the city have a block system, driving navigation is relatively easy, and the major connecting roads will allow turns to easily make your way around.

Internal Transport

Riyadh has a limited **Local Bus System**. These focus on the southern central area of the city with extensions to the northwest (bus route 9), northeast (bus route 10), southeast (bus route 17) and southwest (bus route 16). Services are at least every 15 minutes; however, as the routes travel through congested traffic, take these as optimal timings. Buses are yet to reach the airport or Diriyah. Payment is through a plastic tap-and-go type card. This card is purchased for SAR10 on the bus or at a hub - and is then topped up on the bus for the fare. Fares are SAR3.45 per ride. Unfortunately, although the company, SAPTCO, operates in other towns and uses the same system in each, the cards are currently not interchangeable.

Intended to open in 2024, is a 6-line **Metro Service** (this has been delayed for some years), a mix of underground and overground sections. The airport is served by line 4 (yellow). However, the most useful for internal travel is line 1 (blue), which runs parallel to the King Fahd Road. This has interchanges with the other lines and usefully Faisaliah Towers, National Museum and Al Masmak Palace. There are 3 consortiums – each building 3/2/1 lines. Each consortium will use different rolling stock. Expect feeder bus services, as in use for the Doha Metro, that will offer a route within say a kilometre or two of a Metro station.

In Riyadh, there is a wide range of **Car Rental** options, both from the airport and the city. There are international brands such as Avis, Budget, and Hertz and local brands include Abu Diyab https://rent.abudiyab.com.sa, Yelo www.iyelo.com.

Road infrastructure & Major Buildings.

Riyadh's general infrastructure is good, with well-lit streets, generally well-maintained surfaces and, on major routes, substantial safety features. Road signage is mainly in both Arabic and English; be prepared for slight variations in the spelling of English places and for signs to be occasionally poorly placed. The traffic volume during working hours mitigates against extremely hazardous driving; however, 'defensive driving' techniques are always advisable. Haphazard, signalled (or non-signalled) lane changes by other drivers are often made, both overtaking and undertaking, and tailgating is normal though not usually intended to be aggressive. In most of the city, a missed turn on a highway can be rectified by turning off a main route and doubling back, as there are frequent exits to service roads even on major routes.

Most government offices will open from 07:30 -14:30. Private businesses usually work from 08:00 –midday prayer time (around 11:30-midday) then reopen from 16:00-19:00. Retail banks open from 09:30 -16:30 pm with, typically, an extended midday break over prayer time. Shops and markets open from 09:00/10:00 until 22:00 or later, depending on the management's preferences. Shops and public offices might close during prayer times (there are 4 during working hours). Prayer timings are dependent on the sun's location and so do vary by up to an hour during the year. Irrespective of actual closure of a business, staff within any establishment may stop work to pray, as is their right.

The area between the Al Faisaliah Centre and Kingdom Centre, both of which are set between the King Fahd Road and Al Olaya Street, includes several shopping malls that make it the most convenient location to have some retail therapy. Shopping, or just window shopping, is a significant leisure activity in Saudi Arabia. The original malls in Riyadh are the Al Akaria complexes that date from the mid-1970s on Al Olaya St, which runs parallel and to the east of King Fahd Road for much of its length. They have a reasonable mix of shops, primarily local tastes in focus, at a medium cost. Centria, also on Olaya St, is decidedly more upmarket, as are the malls in Al Faisaliah Centre and Kingdom Centre, again accessed from Al Olaya St. On the west of King Fahd Road is the Panorama Mall with a mid-price selection, including Marks & Spencer and a children's entertainment area. However, the most popular shopping mall in Riyadh is the Nakheel Mall. It is accessed southwest of the interchange of the Northern Ring Road and Eastern Ring Road, with a medium-price focus.

While Ministries are scattered throughout the city, the greatest proportions are south of the Makkah Al Mukarramah Road and within 3km of the National Museum. About 8km northwest of the National Museum is the complex of crucial government offices focused on Al Yamama Palace, the official palace of the ruler. Grouped next to the palace are key administrative bodies, including the Majlis ash-Shura (Consultative Council) and the Royal Diwan (the executive body for the ruler and his various advisers' office). Not directly associated with the palace but with added usefulness because of their immediate adjacency are the King AbdulAziz International Conference Centre and the Ritz Carlton Hotel with its various restaurants and meeting rooms.

The Diplomatic Quarter, less than 10km from the National Museum, is immediately north of Al Yamama Palace (though separated by the Makkah Al Mukarramah Road). Many embassies functioning in Saudi Arabia are here, including the British Embassy, German Embassy, and USA Embassy. Some of these embassies are also responsible for other states in the Arabian Peninsula; for example, the Australian Embassy in Riyadh looks after Oman and the Canadian Embassy in Riyadh is responsible for Canada's relations with Bahrain.

GETTING TO RIYADH – AIR, ROAD, RAIL, SEA AND AIR

Arrivals into Riyadh from outside the Kingdom will arrive by air into King Khalid International Airport (RUH). The airport is served by numerous carriers, including:- Air France; Air India; British Airways; Emirates; Etihad Airways; Gulf Air; Lufthansa; Oman Air; Saudia; Turkish Airlines and relatively low-cost Air Arabia; flyadeal (low-cost) Saudi domestic, flydubai (low cost) and flynas (low cost). The new airline, Riyadh Air, will join them.

There are several Terminals:- Terminal 1 is used for most international airlines, and Terminal 2 is for international flights by Saudia, Air France, Flynas & Middle East Airlines. Terminal 5 is only for domestic flights by Saudia & Flynas. Each terminal has a complimentary regular shuttle bus service between them, which will be necessary if transferring from a domestic to an international flight.

Currently, there are no bus services from the airport. King Khaled International Airport will be served by the metro Line 4 - Yellow Line serving the airport, and it gives direct interchange onto 2 other lines: Line 1 Blue Line and Line 6 Purple Line. Taking a taxi into town will take up to an hour (using Masmak Fort as the standard central reference point for Riyadh in this guide) with a negotiated cost of not more than SAR200 (53US$ / 40GBP) or if using UBER around SAR110 (30US$/22GBP).

Train

A train line runs between **Riyadh & Dammam** www.sar.com.sa with stations at Dammam, Abqaiq and Hofuf into Riyadh with several departures daily. Between Dammam and Riyadh, the fare is from 105SAR(28US$ / 23GBP). Advance booking is suggested. Email and local mobile phone number are needed on all train bookings. Travel in all Saudi trains is by assigned seating (or bed) only, with no subsequent self-selection of seat. The staff may reallocate seating if needed, perhaps for social reasons. You will need your passport (or local ID) to make the booking and journey and should leave time for security procedures. A limited food service should be available. Take note of sex-segregated areas when required. The journey time from Dammam to Riyadh is up to 5 hours, with most services now using a more modern rolling stock taking 3 hours 40mins.

The station is centrally located in Riyadh, and a Taxi will cost around SAR100 (27US$ / 20GBP) negotiated fare and UBER up to 95SAR(25US$ / 19GBP) for a 6km 20minute journey to/from, for example, Masmak Fort. The bus route 10 passes west of the station.

Between **Riyadh & Hail**, www.sar.com.sa have a single train daily in either direction. Hail departs around 15:45, and from Riyadh departs at 09:30 (extra service on the weekend). The journey is 4 hours 40mins the fare is from 160SAR(43US$ / 35GBP). The same line has services to **Buraydah** and **Qurayyat.** Advance booking is suggested with email and local mobile phone number needed. You will need your passport (or local ID) to make the journey and should leave time for security procedures. A limited food service should be available. Take note of sex-segregated areas when required. The station is in the north of Riyadh. A Taxi will cost around SAR100 (27US$ / 20GBP) after a negotiated fare, and a UBER up to 95SAR(25US$ / 19GBP) for a 6km 20minute journey between it and, say, Masmak Fort.

Coach services by SATRANS coach https://satrans.com.sa/ a joint venture with

SAPTCO (previously SAPTCO ran all public bus services) run from most larger towns to Riyadh. Bookings can be made online or at a bus station - a passport is required. Longer routes make refreshment stops.

Road

By road from the Hijaz using Highway 40 (M80) from Jeddah via Taif, this will take around 10 hours for about 960kms into Riyadh. From the north, Highway 65 (M35) from Haql border with Jordan via Hail and Buraydah will take 15 hours for 1550kms - Hail is around half way. From Al Khobar in the east, the journey to Riyadh is just under 5 hours over 440kms again using the cross-country Highway 40 (M80). From Najran, the journey is some 950 km, which will take some 9 hours via Wadi Ad Dawasir using Highway 10 (M90). In general, in Saudi, avoid travel after sunset due to less-than-ideal road surface & lighting conditions.

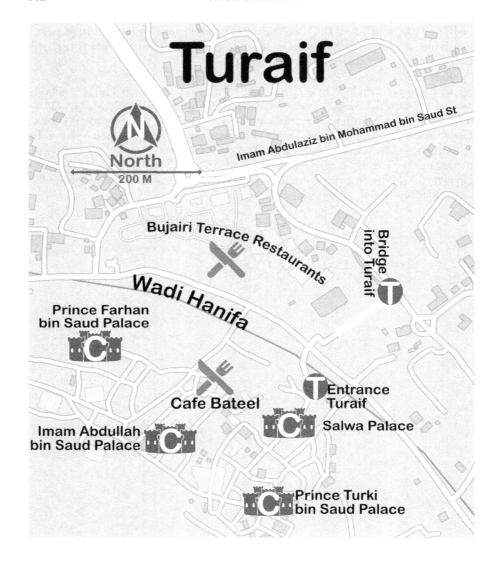

CHAPTER 19
DIRIYAH/TURAIF

Diriyah / Turaif / الطريف / الدرعية - GPS - 24.734334, 46.575957 **Population** (appx) 61,609 **A Brief History** - Turaif (correctly At Turaif) which is a core component of the greater Diriyah area, is an ancient town located in the Najd region in the heart of Saudi Arabia, on the side of Wadi Hanifah. The town was founded between 1446 and 1447 by Mani Al Muraydi, who built the first houses and walls in the area.

The rise to prominence for Turaif began in the early 18th century with Muhammad bin Saud, who became the Amir (ruler) of the town in 1727. Amir Muhammad bin Saud entered into a pact with Sheikh Mohammad bin Abdul Wahhab, who arrived around 1744 after convincing Muhammad bin Saud to implement Islamic law throughout his domains.

By 1765, the Al Saud family controlled large areas of the eastern Arabian peninsula through warfare, using surprisingly small numbers of men, and political alliances. Over the following decades Turaif prospered as the capital of the First Saudi State with the state's expansion towards Iraq and the Hijaz. Impressive multi-story palaces and mosques were constructed using mud-brick in the iconic Najdi architectural style.

After the Al Saud occupation of Makkah in 1803 – the Ottoman Empire, through Egypt's Mohammed Ali Pasha, laid siege to Diriyah in April 1818. After battles and sieges, Turaif was captured in September 1818, leading to the end of the First Saudi State.

Much of Diriyah, including Turaif, was destroyed during the Ottoman siege, with much of the population relocating elsewhere, especially to Riyadh. Turaif was then little more than a squatter's settlement.

In 1902, Amir AbdulAziz bin Abdulrahman Al Saud captured Riyadh, following which he became Amir and leader of the Al Saud family, instead of his father who died later in 1928. This capture began the rise of the modern Saudi state. Turaif remained abandoned until the 1970s, when efforts began to restore the old town. Archaeological work uncovered remains of the substantial mud-brick palaces and fortifications that once dominated Turaif. Many publications call Amir AbdulAziz bin Abdulrahman Al Saud – 'Ibn Saud'; however as other members of the family have also been called Ibn Saud, in this book he is called AbdulAziz –with his title Amir or King (he was on various dates Sheikh, Amir, Sultan & finally King – depending on the date as he rapidly grew his territory).

Wadi Hanifah

Today Diriyah is a sprawling northwestern suburb of Riyadh (26km from the National Museum), with Wadi Hanifah winding through from North-South. On the west bank of Wadi Hanifah is Turaif, the original Al Saud settlement and a growing development of tourist infrastructure.

Following some studies, buildings in Turaif were structurally consolidated after 1982, and in 2010 Turaif was listed under UNESCO for its outstanding universal value as an influential centre of the First Saudi State. Ongoing restoration efforts have focused on preserving the traditional Najdi architectural style while at the same time the broader Diriyah area developed into a modern town. Some key sites in Turaif have been restored, including the Salwa Palace compound, initially constructed by the founder Mani Al-Muraydi in the 15th century.

Today, Diriyah/Turaif has both historic and modern sections and is promoted by the government as a tourist destination. The historic town of Turaif retains much of its traditional character with winding alleyways, mosques, fortifications and old homes built from mud-brick and stone. Just outside the historic district is a new luxurious development called the Diriyah Gate project www.dgda.gov.sa. As well as housing aimed at upscale residents – it will have hotels as well as other cultural & leisure infrastructure including a planned 'Royal Diriyah Opera House', a marked change from the time music was an anathema to the ruling family. A Diriyah version of the Champs-Elysees is intended to connect the general area around Al Bujari Terrace with King Saud University, 4km southeast. To the southwest another project, Wadi Safar, is being developed, again with a focus on leisure, to include golf and more.

Mannequin Abdullah bin Saud Al Saud - Turaif

General Entrance Al Bujairi Terrace and Turaif SAR50 (guided tours booked at the Turaif information office from SAR100) www.diriyah.sa 10:00-midnight Fri 14:00-midnight only (last entrance 23:00). From 1ˢᵗ October 2023 advance booking is required for both Turaif and Al Bujairi Terrace. This might change during less busy summer months.

Restaurants (there are 13) www.bujairi.sa/dine will deduct this entrance charge from their bill on presentation of the ticket. There is paid parking near the entrance, though its better with the area having congestion if a taxi is used. Note your own car registration as it may be needed for exit.

Turaif District (the old mud-brick district), This was listed in 2010 as a UNESCO World Heritage Site is an increasing focus for tourism in the Riyadh area. A small ticket office at **Al Bujairi** area is in the first general area you enter. Al Bujairi has the substantial Sheikh Mohammad bin Abdul Wahhab Mosque (no entry to non-Muslims). In this general area are shops and pleasant restaurants scattered among landscaped grounds. Events such as E-Prix are held immediately north of the Turaif site, next to Al Bujairi. Cultural events under the 'Layali Diriyah' banner are held from late January.

The remains of Turaif is reached by pedestrian bridge, over a landscaped section of **Wadi Hanifah** - this landscaped area is worth strolling along - to the east (turn left). The west (right turn) has palaces in a security area. The wall surrounding the settlement forms a backdrop to the wadi - and there are small pavilions to sit in along the way – look for Bait Mubark a small house on the north side of the wadi. The pleasant walk is about 1500m one way.

A small information office is at the end of the bridge into Turaif – get a map here.

After entering Turaif from the bridge over the wadi there are designated walkways that take you through the built areas - though much of the original settlement still needs to be included. The initial building is the **Salwa Palace**, the residence and first home of the Al Saud Amirs and Imams (the two titles are often used for the same person) during the First Saudi State. Al Salwa Palace also has an information centre and museum, Diriyah Gallery) about the area and the Al Saud family. Rising four stories high - it is the largest palace on the site. It was probably built by Abdulaziz bin Muhammad bin Saud (1803 to 1814) and residence for two subsequent rulers. Today, there are several sections - and it is the focus for sound & light shows. Check the website, with your hotel or with Saudi Tourism for events during the winter. East of Al Salwa Palace is **Sablat Modhi Mosque** (Imam Mohammad bin Saud Mosque), a mosque built during the reign of Imam Mohammad bin Saud. Sheikh Mohammad bin Abdul Wahhab was the preacher at this Mosque. Several buildings are in the northeast corner of Turaif, **Bait Al Mal** (the treasury) and Sablat Modhi (Modhi's reception room). These have the Trade and Monetary Museum with coinage and products of trade. Walking on the main path (southwest) from Salwa Palace, you will pass a couple of small palaces for the brothers Ibrahim and Fahd, and then comes **Imam Abdullah bin Saud's Palace**. Abdulla bin Saud, the last ruler of the First Saudi State, was defeated by Mohammed Ali Pasha and executed in Constantinople in 1818.

Turaif - UNESCO Site

The **Arabian Horse Museum** follows; unfortunately, horses may not be in it. Opposite the horse museum is a military museum. At this junction is **Bait Al-Ardah** (Al Ardah is a performance dance), which occasionally may have traditional Saudi dance & music. Turning west – and then north there are several small galleries about traditional architecture & daily life. There are toilets in this old area.

In the northwest, overlooking the wadi, is the **Amir Omar Bin Saud Palace**. This substantial building is just beyond Bateel Café, and marks the limit of the redeveloped area.

Eating Options

Where to eat - Turaif is rapidly becoming a leisure centre, with the UNESCO site as a branding focus, though restaurants and entertainment are the key element now. The **Bujairi Terrace** has numerous choices to eat in - most are ***+ in cost. Inside the Turaif UNESCO site is **Cafe Bateel***** https://bateel.com/en/cafe - it overlooks the landscaped wadi and is overlooked by the settlement. There are other Cafe Bateel outlets in Saudi - each is worth dropping into if convenient. Immediately next to Bateel is a small **gift shop**. Look at the hotels in Riyadh for accommodation.

GETTING THERE AD DIRIYAH ABOUT A 23KM DRIVE NORTHWEST FROM THE National Museum on Wadi Hanifah. Use Route 40 (M80).

CHAPTER 20
USHAIGER AND SHAQRA

U shaiger/ أشيقر - GPS - 25.339330, 45.193322 **A Brief History** - Ushaiger and Shaqra are almost twins in their modern-day appeal. Ushaiger was home to the modern rulers of Qatar, the Al Thani, in the 17thcentury, before they relocated to Yabrin, then Qatar. The settlements general history is comparable as small farming settlements - with attacks by the Egyptian forces arriving to attack Turaif and the Al Saud rulers. Shaqra is reputed to have dug substantial defences.

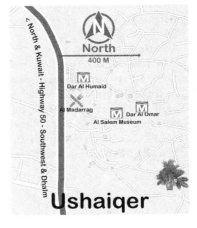

Ushaiger is a scattered town between the arms of the Ad Dahna desert. The traditional mud housing was abandoned several decades ago in favour of a modern settlement to the west. Some old housing has now been renovated and used as heritage museums. The overall impact is not quite as polished as Shaqra, making this a more authentic experience. Several individual buildings within the area can be visited. These include **Dar Al Humaid** 14:00 – 21:00 and **Al Salam Museum** SAR10 09:00 - midday / 16:00 – 21:00, and **Dar Al Oma** 16:00- 21 00r. They have similar collections of cultural artefacts, household equipment, weapons and early to mid-20th-century technology. Each museum is the owner's work, as is typical throughout the country. Also, as typical, they have little information, even less in English. Ushaiger is worth strolling around to see more old mud-brick houses; the agriculture is now suffering from drought.

Al Madarrag**, a restaurant, is available on weekends only 12:00-16:00. The hours are a demand related decision – so check during holiday periods. This is very traditional

– with seating in a shaded outside area around a garden. Check carefully how the meals are charged; it's typically a buffet sold by weight. The village makes a good stop if you drive north to Buraydah using Route 505 to the west of Ushaiger or a day out from Riyadh. North of the old settlement, a short, tarmacked road leads up a **low hill** - that gives a broad overview of Ushaiger.

Shaqra / شقراء - GPS - 25.256133, 45.257401 **Population** (appx) 32,215

Ushaiger

North of much of modern Shaqra is the old settlement. Around 10 hectares, it's a compact area of old mud-brick housing, with date plantations to the northwest. The old wall was probably built in 1816 after the Egyptian's campaign, and a new defence in 1901 to deal with the Al Rashid. There are sections of the wall remaining, and several old mud-brick houses, mosques and souqs have been restored. There are a good dozen restored buildings. To the east (through the **Al Talha Gate** – where the town wall stretches south) is the **Shaqra**

Museum (09:00-22:00 Mon-Thurs / 16:00-22:00 Fri & Sat) & **Hilewah Heritage Souq**. This is the largest museum, with various artefacts on display – this also has an open courtyard and a small refreshment facility with snacks and drinks. North of this is the **Majlis Al Muhanna** (majlis is a sitting area or reception room), a smaller building without artefacts. A walk of less than a kilometre southwest leads to **Al Subaie Historic Palace**, a three-floor building Thurs-Sat 08:00-18:00. Dating from around 1940 it was used to accommodate King AbdulAziz and restored in 2000. Palace, as used in so many places in Saudi Arabia, is used to infer home of an important person, government administrative centre or military fort - rather than always a substantial home of a ruler. North of Al Subaie Historic Palace, in the centre of the old settlement, are **Al Issa House** and **Bait Al Joumah**. The restored houses have a comparable age to Al Subaie Palace. A small, pleasant hotel, **Bait Sulaimani** ** +966509337410 uses a restored house in the centre of the old housing. Just outside the core of the old town is **'Heritage Guest-House'*** +966503194520 – a charming, slightly more rustic design. **Le Park Hotel** ** +966116280014 is a modern take on the traditional properties. Ushaiger and Shaqra don't have much to choose between them. Shaqra has the hotels, while Ushaiger has Al Madarrag restaurant. However, Ushaiger's date plantations mixed among the housing are nice. Shaqra is about 20km from Ushaiger - if you have time, they are easy to combine.

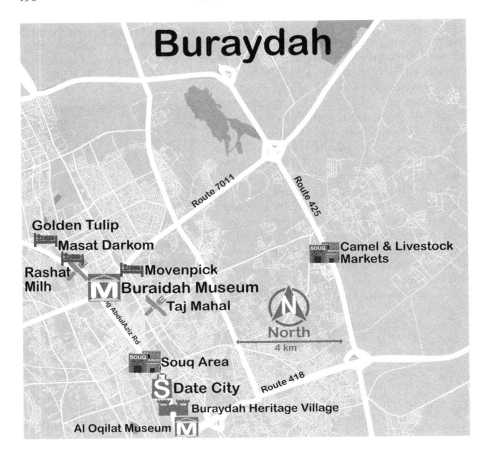

CHAPTER 21
BURAYDAH

Buraydah (Qassim is the name for the general region) / بريدة - GPS - 26.350009, 43.956979 **Population** (appx) 571,169 **A Brief History** Though dominated by nomadic tribes, the Banu Tamim tribe transformed Buraydah into a centre of trade, agriculture, and camel breeding. Various families took power: Al Duraibi from AD1577, Al Abu Alyan from around 1776, and Aba Al-Khail from 1874. They were occasionally independent – and at other times confirmed in power by the Al Rashid of Hail or Al Saud.

In the late 19th century, Qassim became caught up in the power struggles between the Al Saud family and the Rashidi dynasty based in Hail, to the north. The Rashidis conquered Qassim in 1875 as they expanded their domain. Rashidi rule ushered in an era of instability with heavy taxation that angered many Najdi tribes. This continued until the final defeat of the Al Rashid by Amir AbdulAziz bin Abdulrahman Al Saud in 1921.

The main places of interest in Buraydah (Buraidah) are a couple of museums. **Buraidah Museum** 08:00-14:00 Sun-Thurs no charge entry +966163231700 on King AbdulAziz St. The exterior is impressive. Inside are displays of cultural artefacts and agricultural equipment. They are displayed in a style you will be familiar with from local museums scattered around Saudi Arabia. A section is devoted to weaponry. Information about the reign of King AbdulAziz and a 1950s white Cadillac used by the king.

The other main museum is **Al Oqilat Museum** www.aloqilat.com 08:30-midday & 16:00-19:00 currently FOC - south of Buraidah Museum, about 600m west off the King AbdulAziz Rd interchange. Its exterior is a more curvaceous version of the Buraidah Museum - having the appearance of a traditional house. The interior, with its courtyard-style appearance, is overflowing with displayed items. With its photo gallery of notables - this museum exemplifies the possible purpose of many private museums:

to elevate the prestige of the owner, family and tribe. Of these two museums - the Al Oqilat Museum is more engaging – and probably more welcoming.

Buraydah Museum

Buraidah's original souq area is west of King AbdulAziz Rd, about 4km drive south of the Buraydah Museum. The main King Fahd Mosque, with its two minarets, is just north of the souq. As there is a new food market area less than 2km to the south, this older food market may be discontinued. In this general souq area is the date market in the car-park area! Nearby is the meat, fruit, and vegetables souq. Just to the east & south of these food markets, is the older shopping area of Buraydah. In the south of this market area is yet another modern replica of a fort, a museum structure, though closed. Early morning is the best time to visit these markets. In these markets, be respectful regarding photography, and note in Qassim generally - that some foreign governments have travel warnings Page22. Farther south on King AbdulAziz Rd is the new main date market, '**Date City**' - also with fruit and vegetables. Here is held an annual date event, in August & September. East of the city - on the Ring Road Route 425 (southbound lane) is the **Camel Souq**, which has other livestock and wild animals for sale. The camel souq itself is in the north of the large area of over a kilometre in length and is almost certainly the largest camel market in the world. Here, most of the animals are sold for meat. Tucked away is a bird market.

Southwest of Buraidah, off Route 414, is **Souq Al Musakif** 16:00-21:00 - GPS 26.0980187,43.8676119 - it's around 35kms drive from Buraydah Museum. This is a replica, built in 2007, of a previous souq demolished in 1974. It's laid out in the style of a traditional Najd fortified house. A large central courtyard has rooms off it. Here also are small shops selling 'antiques' and heritage items, along with small places serving local cuisine. Within the same complex is **Al Bassam House** 09:00-21:00 - Fridays 16:00-22:00, a small museum again in the style of a traditional Najd House. The displays are quite attractive, focused on local culture up to modern times.

North from Buraydah (off Highway 85/M25) is the **Imam Turki bin Abdullah Royal Nature Reserve** (https://itba.gov.sa/en) a vast 91,000 sq. km area stretching through the Nafud Desert toward the Iraqi & Kuwaiti borders. The settlements of Laynah and Rafha are a focus as are the **Zabbala** castle and pools on the Darb Zubaydah pilgrimage route from Iraq. Here are various leisure activities, eco-tourism, bird watching, hiking, experiencing nature and cultural experiences with the local Bedouin communities, learning about their traditional way of life and enjoying authentic cuisine. This is the first of the reserves to offer activities - email tourism@itba.gov.sa to know more.

To the west of Buraydah and south of the vast expanse of pivot fields is the small town of **Al Bukayriyah**, just north of Highway 60/M70), the expressway to Madinah. Here on the edge of the town, and within its own date oasis - is the **Al Swailem Palace** 15:00-18:00 - a museum. It's a mud-brick structure - in origin from the early 19th century and restored lastly in 2023. The interior is simple - however, the attraction here is that it's the focus for celebrations at Eid and other occasions. Off Highway 65/M35), about 40km northwest of Buraydah, toward Hail is **Ayun Al Jawa**. In the northwest of the town is the old settlement. This has had some restoration in 2000, and now makes an interesting stop on the road with the old school, souq, houses and so on. It is less than 5km drive from Highway 65 (M35).

~

A Selection Of Restaurants & Accommodation - There is an extensive selection of simple local-style restaurants in Buraydah; try the more expensive hotels for better ones. The cheap snack offering from **Rashat Milh** * +966 57 066 8000 on King AbdulAziz Road is good for takeaway food. 06:00-midday / 16:00-02:00. Al **The Taj Mahal Restaurant** ** on At Tarafiyyah Road (near Carrefour) +966 16 382 9993 give a good range of Indian food 12:30-15:00/18:30-01:00.

A Selection of Accommodation - A surprising range of hotels makes this an easy place to stay between Riyadh and the north. Consider **Masat Darkom** * +966 55 414 0066 on King Fahd Road (there are a few other lower cost options here); **Golden Tulip** ** on King AbdulAziz Road or **Movenpick** **** www.movenpick.com on the junction of King Abdullah Road and King Fahd Road. A search should provide options to stay in farms in the broader surrounding region such as **Ghudai** **- https://ghudai.com about 40km drive northwest of Buraidah Museum.

~

Getting There - Buraydah is served by Prince Naif bin Abdulaziz International Airport - with flights to Dammam, Jeddah and Riyadh, several Egyptian airports, Istanbul, Pakistan and a few others. By road, Riyadh is about 370km on Highway 65 (M35). Hail, also on Highway 65 (M35), is about 280km. Jeddah is about 1,000kms - via Madinah. An alternative to driving is to use the train from Riyadh or take the SATRANS coach. As with many cities away from Dammam, Jeddah and Riyadh - there are no local bus services and poor taxi options - though Uber is available.

CHAPTER 22

FAID

Faid (also Fayd) / فيد - GPS - 27.120238, 42.523747 **A Brief History** - Faid is a crucial location on the historic Darb Zubaydah, a series of caravansaries between the relatively new city of Baghdad (founded 762) and Makkah. Zubaydah bint Jafar (765 – 831), granddaughter of an earlier Caliph, the wife of the Caliph Harun Al Rashid and mother of another - financed the improvement of the route. This family ushered in the pinnacle of the Abbasid dynasty's rule. Work along the route included levelling the ground and creating a series of fortifications, along with water and general services supplies. Ibn Battuta wrote that "all reservoir, cistern or well on this road which goes from Baghdad to Makkah is due to her generosity". Faid is about halfway between Baghdad and Makkah. This pilgrimage route continued as an organised structure until the mid-13th century, when it gradually lost its importance as other routes became used.

A small **Faid Visitor Centre Museum** 10:00-18:00 Sat-Thurs / Fri 14:00-18:00 FOC, greets visitors to modern-day Faid. The visitor centre has information about the site along with some artefacts. A landscaped garden is adjacent. Hundreds of years ago, it was a barricaded town- with walling of around a kilometre that surrounded **Kharash**, a substantial castle/caravanserai. Today, part of the town's southern wall and fortified centre is restored - notably the bastions - as are what may be storage rooms. All are built from igneous stone.

The remains of a columned mosque is in the site's southwest. From almost 700km away - it's perfectly aligned to Makkah. In the north of the site is a **cistern** - this was a key draw on a cross-desert pilgrimage. A couple of kilometres drive south (beyond modern Faid) is another **cistern**.

Faid citadel - Kharash

An area of ruins, most almost decayed to the ground, is to the west and north of the main site. A small date plantation 300m to the north is separated from Kharash by a cemetery. Beyond the date area is a small, abandoned **mud-brick village**.

Faid is a remarkable aspect of the Abbasid Empire and the hardships involved in undertaking the Hajj. It however, by itself, does not have the interest for a dedicated visit. However – its on Highway 65 connecting Riyadh and Dumat Al Jandal – with Jubbah, Hail and Buraydah on the way. Therefore, take an hour to have a look if you intend to drive past.

About a kilometre southwest of the museum, there is simple accommodation. Opposite the museum is a very basic restaurant.

Getting to Faid The settlement is just west of Highway 65 (M35)- after driving northwest for around 530kms from Riyadh (via Qassim). It's around 110 km southeast from Hail - using Highway 65 (M35).

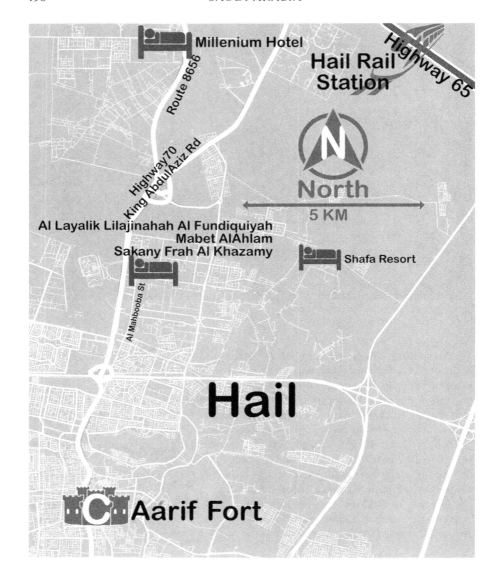

CHAPTER 23
HAIL

H ail / حائل - GPS - 27.516421, 41.702234 **Population** (appx) 448,623 **A Quick Overview Of The Geography** Hail is surrounded by volcanic rock and a large outcrop of granite mountain farther west. 20km to the east is sandstone. The Nafud sand desert sweeps from the north, where it encircles Jubbah, down towards the southeast towards Riyadh. The remains of Paleolakes are found throughout this desert, notably at Jubbah.

A Brief History - Hail's origins trace back to an oasis settlement that grew up around its plentiful water springs. The area was within the tribal area of the Shammar tribe. This tribe today spreads from Jordan, Syria, Iraq, Kuwait and Saudi. The Sheikhs of the tribe had, almost, automatic support from its population - as they were from the tribe. The Al Ali subgroup of the Shammar tribe gained control over Hail as early as around 1500AD. Over the 17th and 18th centuries, the oasis became an essential stop for caravan trade routes crossing the Najd region. But it was still just a modest fortified village clustered around a fort.

That changed in 1836 when Abdullah bin Ali Al Rashid, also part of the Shammar tribe, conquered Hail, with the support of the Al Saud in Riyadh, and made it the capital of the Al Rashid emirate. He built high mud-brick walls around the city, constructed a palace, and established a permanent local military. Hail entered a golden era as the Al Rashids expanded their domain across northern Arabia, sometimes reaching into Syria and down to Riyadh. Despite their military successes and being allied with the Ottomans, the Rashidis were weakened by regular conflict and power struggles within the family; several rulers were killed by other family members. Internal strife characterised much of the dynasty's history.

European travellers who visited Hail in the late 19th century provided descriptions of the city as, remarkably, it prospered under Al Rashid rule. Accounts described a city dominated by the towering Rashid fortresses made of mud-brick and stone. The city was protected by rings of high walls and watchtowers. British traveller William Gifford

Palgrave visited in 1865, detailing Hail's bustling markets, thriving agriculture, and multi-story mud-brick houses. Explorer Lady Anne Blunt stayed in 1881, being received at the court of Amir Mohammed bin Abdulla. Adventurer Charles Montagu Doughty lived in Hail in 1888. In 1914 Gertrude Bell, the British multifaceted Arabist, passed through.

Aarif Fort

Date groves and wheat fields surrounded Hail, supporting its growing population that peaked at over 60,000 in the early 20th century.

After playing off the rival Ottoman and Saudi powers for decades, the Al Rashidi finally collided with the rising Saudi state under Amir AbdulAziz bin Abdulrahman Al Saud. In 1921, Amir AbdulAziz bin Abdulrahman Al Saud besieged and conquered Hail, marking the end of the Rashidi dynasty after their being in power for nearly a century.

What's in Hail - Much of Hail's architectural heritage from the Al Rashid era has been demolished or neglected. The grand mud-brick palaces of the Al Rashid dynasty with their decorative facades have vanished - apart from a couple of towers. The town is a regional administrative centre, though giving the impression of a less important place.

North
1 KM

Ghattat St

Barzan Palace
North Tower

Barzan Mosque

SOUQ Date &
General Souqs

Old Housing

Qishlah Fort

Riyadh St

Aarif Fort

Route 70 King Abdulaziz Rd

Hail

Overlooking the core of Hail is the **Aarif Fort**. This sits on a small hill on Prince Mirqin bin Abdulaziz Rd - it's intended to be open 09:00-17:00. Probably an early fortification was built here by 1790 by Issa bin Ali bin Saleh Al Ali. The more modern fort was completed around 1844 under the Amir Abdullah bin Ali Al Rashid and enlarged later, it has a commanding location over the city. Modern restoration was undertaken in 2001. With limited accommodation - the thin rectangular design of the fort, matching the hill's outline, appears to have been created as a canon platform to bombard attackers rather than a stronghold for troops.

North of Aarif Fort is an area of older housing, in a very dilapidated state. This leads to a couple of **Towers**. These are all that remain from the Barzan Palace a massive complex built in the 19thc from 1801 onward and visited by those Victorian and Edwardian explorers. They are in the square opposite the green-domed Barzan Mosque. A collection of mud-brick houses has been built over part of the site.

Southwest, across a road junction, from the Barzan Towers is a **modern souq area**, with an area for dates. Here, from summer onwards, fresh dates are sold. It's a popular place at the weekends.

Crossing Highway 70, King AbdulAziz Rd, is the **Qishlah Fort** - a two-story barracks surrounding an open courtyard. It was finished in 1941 under Abdulaziz bin Musaed Al Jalawi Al Saud, the governor of Hail - it looks far older. Inexplicably, given the historical animosity, it may have taken the name from a Turkish word for an army barrack. It became a prison - and soon will be a tourist attraction. This is currently closed for renovation. 500m east of Qishlah Fort - towards Aarif Fort is a small remnant of the **city wall**. It's just north of a school and east of a 7 floor building for the Governor of Hail.

Qishlah Fort

Getting There Hail's airport connects with Dammam, Jeddah and Riyadh - with a few flights to Cairo & UAE. Hail is a 360km drive south of Dumat Al Jandal - the express road Highway 65 (M35) cuts through the golden sand dunes (quartz sands with iron oxide coating giving the colour) of the Nafud Desert along almost the entire route. What is missing are petrol stations and other services - fill your tank before leaving & bring refreshments. The town is 630 km northwest of Riyadh, along Highway 65 (M35) via Buraydah. An alternative to driving is to use the train from Riyadh or take the SATRANS coach (this service was run by SAPTCO). The rail line is visible along most of Highway 65 (M35) north of Buraydah. As with many cities away from Dammam, Jeddah and Riyadh - there are no local bus services and poor taxi options - though Uber is available.

~

A Selection Of Restaurants & Accommodation - Hail has a surprising need for restaurants with good local or other cuisine. Look for one of the local chains' Page27. To the north of the town centre, several reasonable-value hotels are almost adjacent to each other, just east of Highway 70. **Al Layalik Lilajinahah Al Fundiquiyah*** +966165333959, **Mabet Al Ahlam*** +966165318835 & **Sakany Frah Al Khazamy** * +966501595888 are on Al Mahbooba St. They are broadly comparable, and more hotels may spring up here. Far out of town, the **Millenium** *** www.millenniumhotels.com is an option off Highway 65 (M35) & towards Jubbah. For something a bit different, **Sharfa Resort** ** +966505571919 is northeast of the town. Set within a date farm, with some livestock, its ambience is rustic, though the accommodation is modern. **Nisnas** *** http://alboraq.com.sa/nisnas is a fixed camp about 65km north of Hail - and 100km east of Jubbah. This is in a semi-desert setting.

CHAPTER 24
JUBBAH

Jubbah / جبة - GPS - 28.029420, 40.919016 **Population** (appx) 5,622 **A Brief History** - The site at Jubbah is based on a paleolake that may have formed in two periods firstly 36,000-17,000 ago & then 9,000-6,000 years ago. Near the summit of Jabal Umm Sinman (west of the settlement) is a pre-historic stone tool quarry site.

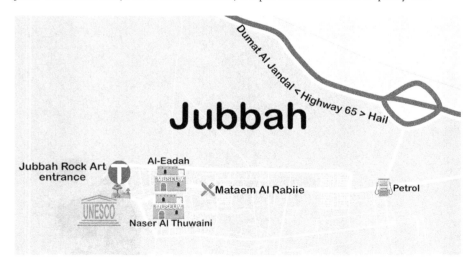

This is from the Mousterian (160,000 to 40,000) period, and here stone working assemblages have been found. Below the summit, rock art was created on sandstone rock. Other evidence of humans has been found 200kms west. At another paleolake, 150km southwest, a human finger-bone, dated around 85,000 years ago, has been found. Semi-nomadic herders probably travelled through the region, taking shelter in the rock formations. Approximately 7,000 years ago (dating's have been made by radiocarbon analysis, micro erosion, optically stimulated luminescence and colourimetry), people began decorating the sandstone outcrops with intricately carved images of wildlife and themselves - creating the rock art we see today. Exfoliation of the rock surfaces and collapse of some rock faces have been going on for millennia, there must have been a greater concentration of rock art thousands of years ago.At Jubbah, the population may have used the water associated with the paleolake (where the village and agriculture now are), to obtain water in a period of desertification. This would allow permanent settlement and agriculture.

Around 700BC, the Thamud civilisation emerged, creating some of Jubbah's most prominent rock art. Thamudic inscriptions, written in a script unique to this civilisation, adorn the sandstone cliffs, as does the later Kufic Arabic.

Jubbah oasis was visited by several European travellers and historians in the late 19th and early 20th century, including by the Blunts in 1879, Doughty 1888, Huber 1899, Euting and also Musil in 1914, Philby 1952. They wrote brief accounts of the site. Lady Ann Blunt mentioned only 80 houses and Sinaitic script, but none of the travellers mentioned rock art in the area.

Chariot & Horses - Jubbah - UNESCO site

Jubbah's rock art remained largely unknown to the outside world until a team of European archaeologists visited in 1945. In 1976 & 1970, reports were made. But full-scale studies did not begin until 1986, 2002 & most comprehensively in 2011. In 2017, the UN cultural agency UNESCO inscribed Jubbah on its World Heritage List.

Jubbah is a sprawling settlement - with housing scattered in the date and general agricultural plantations. Agriculture, especially the pivot fields, relies on pumped fossil groundwater to irrigate the crops. The main attraction here, however, is not the agriculture; it's the UNESCO Rock Art site. This is paired on the UNESCO listing with Jabals al-Manjor and Raat - about 400km drive southwest. Jubbah is far more accessible in all respects. To west of Jubbah's scattered housing is a sandstone hill with a small public park at its northeast. Here are the offices that allow entry to the fenced area that encloses the site Sun-Thurs 09:00-17:00 weekends are generally closed. Toilets are in the park's south. The entrance is currently FOC.

Gravel paths - and, in most cases, metal staircases lead to clusters of rock art which can be seen over 5km of the western hill area. The area below the hill is devoid of vegetation allowing sight of many of the stairs, and allowing a decision to be made how far to walk. The hill on which the rock art is located rises around 300m above the surrounding area - and the rock art is in the lower area of this hill. Erosion has created a mass of surfaces in the sandstone where the art has been created. Most of the art is not immediately visible from the general surroundings - so a climb up the staircases will be needed. The art includes human figures and domesticated animals - camel, cattle, dog, donkey, horse and also wild gazelle, ibex, lion, oryx, ostrich. There may well be more than 10,000 separate workings in the general Jubbah area - a small fraction is easy to see. Apart from animals and people - early Arabic script has been found - it's an excellent site.

Naser Al Thuwaini Museum

In Jubbah village itself are a couple of small private museums. The collections are comparable to other small private museums in Saudi. **Naser Al Thuwaini Heritage Museum** +966540889895 SAR20 displays include camel equipment. household goods, **Al-Eadah for National Heritage & Tourism** +966506184514, currently FOC, is more of an experience-based operation. They are about a kilometre apart in the western area of Jubbah.

~

RESTAURANTS & ACCOMMODATION

There are few places to eat in Jubbah - and the supermarkets only offer a limited food selection. Look for **Mataem Al Rabiie*** (cream and maroon sign board) +966165411011 - it serves a wide range of fresh fruit juices and cooked food, geared, of course, to local taste. It's on the south side of the principal road on the northern edge of Jubbah.

Consider accommodation with the **Al-Eadah Museum** who offer desert camps - otherwise, Hail offers accommodation options.

~

GETTING THERE

Jubbah is on Highway 65 (M35), 250km south of Dumat Al Jandal and 120km north of Hail. This section of Highway 65 (M35) between Dumat Al Jandal and Hail currently has no petrol stations - there are some in Jubbah. From Highway 65 (M35), take the Jubbah exit south, then drive west towards the rust coloured Jabal Umm Sinman – it dominates the area. All streets in Jubbah terminate in the west, on a road that runs parallel with this rugged hill. Jubbah, though small, does have ATMs & petrol stations. The petrol stations are good to use as Highway 65 (M35) doesn't offer any nearby – Radifah's in the north is 250kms away & Hail's are over 70km away.

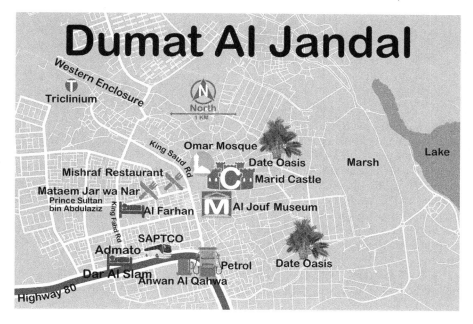

CHAPTER 25

DUMAT AL JANDAL

Dumat Al Jandal / دومة الجندل - GPS - 29.811147, 39.866051
   A Quick Overview Of The Geography - Dumat Al Jandal is set north of the Nafud Desert - in a complicated mix of sedimentary rock formations, including Sandstone to its east and limestone plateau to the north. It lies in a significant depression within the landscape. Until the 20th century animals worked shallow wells, drawing water to irrigate the oasis. This is now impossible as the water table has dropped. A modern artificial lake to the east above the date oasis is a modern supply for the oasis and Sakkaka. To this lake's east is what was a paleolake. Though Dumat Al Jandal is the more historical settlement - it's Sakaka that is the area centre for government.

   A Brief History - With evidence of human occupation of the oasis area in the 6th millenniumBC, Dumat Al Jandal has an impressive period of human occupation. Geography has largely favoured the town on caravan trails - as the sand dunes of the Nafud Desert are less than 10 km to the south.

   The first mention of a fortification here was in the 8thcBC. The town was within the sphere of Qedar, the northwest Arabian kingdom, between the 10th-1st centuriesBC. Known to the civilisations in Mesopotamia as Adummatu, Dumat Al Jandal was conquered by the Neo-Assyrian ruler Sennacherib (705–681BC) and his son Esarhaddon (681-669BC). Slightly later, the Neo-Babylonian ruler, Nabonidus, may have conquered the town during his campaigns towards the Mediterranean and down to Tayma.

   During the late 1st millenniumBC, the town was subsumed within the Nabataean (4th century BC-AD106) sphere. The town was mentioned in a dedicatory text of 45BC under King Malichos II. An attack by Queen Zenobia (died AD 274) of Palmyra, 600km to the north, due to the town's fortifications suggests that the origins of Marid Castle may date before then. The castle's foundations have Nabataean evidence in them.

   Later Dumat Al Jandal was part of the Kinda kingdom, a constituent of the

Christian Ghassanid federation that acted as a buffer for the Byzantines against the Sasanian Empire. After the occupation by Khalid ibn Al Walid (died AD642), the population were early converts to Islam. A church next to Marid Castle was developed into the Mosque as was commonly done with churches elsewhere. This mosque has been attributed by some Saudi authorities to Umar bin Al Kattab (AD634-644).

Over the following centuries, Dumat Al Jandal was contested by various empires and tribes seeking control over northern Arabia. In the mid 19th century the town came under the rule of the Al Rashid dynasty as they expanded their domains from Hail. The sheikh of the principal tribe in the area, the Al Ruwallah, Amir Nuri Al Shalan (who was part of the Arab Revolt), used it as one residence.

Today - 10km north of the oasis is Saudi Arabia's largest wind-farm with a planned 99 turbines.

Marid Castle

What to see

In **Dumat al Jandal**, the places of interest in the town are relatively close to each other. The **Al-Jouf Regional Museum** (Al Jouf Museum of Archaeology and Ethnography) King Saud Road (in the west of the date oasis) 014 622 2151 was opened in 2020. This museum should, ideally, be the first place you visit in the town, it's immediately next to the historic area. Unfortunately, it is currently closed, but check if it has opened.

Immediately next to and north of the museum is **Marid Castle** currently FOC 08:00-16:00, is perched on a low rocky outcrop. The castle has two main sections. The castle's keep, with its 5 distinctive pinnacles, is made of dressed stone, with the upper parts & parapets of mud brick. A remarkable water well plunges into bedrock - presumably, the water source was a reason for the citadel's location. A larger, more recent part of the castle to the south encloses a large courtyard. A series of walls may have surrounded Marid Castle. These are in any case ploughed over and obscured by the farms of the oasis.

Omar bin Al Khattab Mosque

. . .

OMAR BIN AL KHATTAB MOSQUE IS LOCATED IMMEDIATELY NORTH OF the castle. Its 12.7m stone-built minaret is next to the entrance. The mosque's appearance is claimed to be as originally built. A columned, stone walled, prayer room has an undecorated Mihrab (prayer niche) - and a recessed Minbar (pulpit) for the Imam to give a sermon from. It's a very authentic, atmospheric space. Do dress appropriately for mosques in Saudi - and of course, footwear should be removed. It's best to visit 08:00-11:00 Sun-Thurs and therefore avoid prayer times.

To the north of the mosque is an abandoned village, **Al Dari**, that has had some modern consolidation for tourism - it was abandoned in the mid-1970s. This is a tiny remnant of what will have been numerous small settlements throughout the oasis. In the village excavations in 2023 have found Assyrian 8th centuryBC pottery and Nabataean occupation evidence. The date oasis is beyond the village. Several other archaeological sites (all enclosed by the metal grid fencing you will be familiar with from travelling through Saudi Arabia) are west of the oasis, including the 'Western Enclosure', which is about 2km long from east to west and over 300m from north to south. This enclosure was a natural valley, whose boundaries were improved by walling. These walls are visible in places and may have been over 4m high. Today, the area is principally agriculture. A Nabataean open-air **triclinium** is to the south of this area, immediately overlooking the plain, dated as being used between the 1st centuryBC and 2nd centuryAD.

An ancient well is to the west of the triclinium. Originally many wells were in the oasis - their shafts lined with stone plunging up to 30m down below the surface. A series of ancient falaj/qanats, the man-made water channels found in Arabia, are north of the old town area. These channels focus on **Dumat Al Jandal Lake** to the east of the town - now developed as a leisure area - busy at the weekends and evenings. The lake (about the 4th largest in Saudi at less than 2 sq km) has landscaping on its western (town) side. Below it, towards the town, is a marshy area in which the volume of water fluctuates considerably over the months & years - this was the first artificial lake.

～

RESTAURANTS & ACCOMMODATION OPTIONS - OPPOSITE MARID CASTLE is **Mishraf Restaurant** ** 07:00-midnight - offering good views, coffee cakes & and reasonable food. **Mataem Jar wa Nar*** (Jar and Fire Restaurant – such a nice name) +966537113454 05:00-midday & 16:00-midnight (closed Fridays) Prince Sultan bin Abdulaziz Street (opposite the museum) offering a buffet-style selection. The small coffee shop **Anwan Al Qahwa** (Coffee Address)* almost 24 hours (closed midday prayer on Friday and dawn prayers daily) in the petrol station at the roundabout on Highway 80 (M50) is convenient & good.

Al Farhan ** +966146223622 is one of a small chain of hotels in Saudi - King Fahd Rd. The following two hotels are adjacent to each other - **Admato Hotel** * +966146226228 - entrance off King Fahd Rd & **Dar Al Slam Furnished Apartments** * +966146223111 - on Highway 80 ((M50 - King AbdulAziz Rd) - ask to see the choice of rooms in Dar Al Slam they are different.

≈

How to get there DUMAT AL JANDAL IS 360KM NORTH OF HAIL VIA Highway 65 (M35) – linking to Highway 80 (M50) into town. The expressway has no services on the road beyond Hail. An alternative is the train, whose station is on Highway 65 (M35), a drive of 20km away. The SATRANS coach station is on Highway 80 (M50), south of the town centre. As with many cities away from Dammam, Jeddah and Riyadh - there are no local bus services and poor taxi options.

CHAPTER 26

SAKAKA

S akaka / سكاكا - GPS - 29.993529, 40.200249 **Population** (appx) 204,174 **A Brief History** - Sakaka's close proximity to Dumat Al Jandal may mean it has a similar historical background.

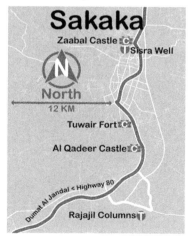

What's in Sakaka - East of Dumat al Jandal, Sakaka has few outstanding attractions. These are made difficult to find by the road layout and absent signage. Unique are the **Rajajil Columns** 08:00-14:00 Sat-Thurs currently FOC. Rajajil is the Arabic for men. These are narrow oblong stones - up to 3 meters high; usually, they are in groups, placed in an upright position - there are several dozen groups spread over a broad area in the far south of Sakaka. Many have petroglyphs on their surface. The Rajajil Columns might date back 6000 years and may be associated with religious practices. There is a visitor centre from 08:00-14:00 (closed weekends). This is a reasonable display and information centre. If the site is not open when you visit, the inevitable metal mesh fence doesn't stop seeing the stones.

The northern area of the town is where **Zaabal Castle** sits on its rock outcrop of around 50m high. There is no real infrastructure inside - simply a curtain wall connecting four towers. The towers are either merely originally decorative, or to add even more elevation as lookouts. The Zaabal Castle may have an origin in the Nabataean period - with rebuilds 900 years ago and in its current form 400 years ago. The nearby **Sisra Well** (the local English spelling) shares a name with the Biblical

Canaanite general Sisera (around 1,400BC) mentioned in the Bible book of Judges 4:2. In which case the well is perhaps dated to 1100BC, or earlier. There are other small fortifications in Sakaka - **Al Qadeer** (behind a fence) & **Tuwair Fort** within a private farm. They are almost impossible to locate. Both are placed on small hills - and have an appearance of some antiquity.

Rajajil Columns

Getting there - Sakaka is 45km northeast of Dumat Al Jandal on Highway 80.

CHAPTER 27
QURIYYAT TRAIN

Q **uriyyat Train**/ سكة قريات - GPS - 31.419564, 37.288375
    What's there - In the far north of Saudi - the rail line that extends north from Riyadh through Buraydah and Hail terminates at Quriyyat near the Jordanian border. It's about a 1,200km journey through steppe, low hills and sand desert. Occasionally, an overnight, sleeper service train operates - the only one in Arabia, hence its inclusion in the book - www.sar.com.sa. Fortunately, having arrived there are a few hotels in town. The return could be by plane from Qurayyat Airport or SATRANS coach.

Of course - what does one do having arrived! There are a couple of sites to the east – on Highway 85.

Kaaf Palace

Kaaf Palace (Qasser Kaff) 09:00-14:00 Sun-Thurs currently FOC is an unexpectedly large fort in a remote area. Built by 1918, by the Amir Nawaf bin Nouri Al Shaalan, - the grandfather of a wife of Crown Prince Mohamed bin Salman and son of the famous Al Ruwallah Tribe's Sheikh the Amir Nouri Al Shaalan. Several other members of the Al Saud family married other females of Nawaf's family, including King AbdulAziz - an illustration of the power of large tribes and the alliances made by marriage. The fort is a mix of stone and mud brick construction. To its northwest is a substantial **mountaintop Citadel,** having a kilometre long wall, with bastions. South is a small abandoned mud village - with its Date oasis. Evaporation pans in the southwest still seem to be worked for salts. However, just north of Kaaf Palace, an amusement ground looks abandoned. The reason for the location of these two surprising fortifications in a remote area, is that this is the original route through the broad Wadi Sirhan from the Mediterranean, Jordan and Syria to the Arabian Gulf.

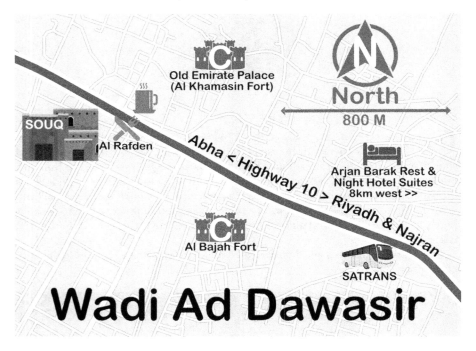

CHAPTER 28
WADI AD DAWASIR

Wadi Ad Dawasir / وادي الدواسر - GPS - 20.474189, 44.790970 **Population** (appx) 77,433 **A Quick Overview Of The Geography** - Wadi Ad Dawasir is set on a broad sandy valley that runs north-south. To the west are the foothills of the southern Hijaz Mountains, and to the east is the Tuwaiq Escarpment's southern end.

A Brief History - Wadi Ad Dawasir is an oasis valley in central Saudi Arabia that has been inhabited since ancient times due to its reliable water sources. The area was settled as early as the 4th centuryBC. One of the chief settlements of the area was Qaryat Al Faw, which thrived from the 4th centuryBC and continued as an important settlement until the 4th centuryAD. This time span is comparable to other trading towns that relied on the land-caravan trade from southern Arabia through to the Mediterranean. A critical caravan stop on the incense route through the desert. Qaryat al-Faw was a wealthy and highly developed city, used by the Mineans (Yemen), Lihyanites (from Dedan), Nabataeans – and Graco-Romans. The town flourished with residential areas, souqs, temples, and a necropolis, with elaborate architecture and an advanced irrigation system that allowed extensive agriculture and date palm cultivation in the arid climate.

Wadi Ad Dawasir continued to be an important settlement after the coming of Islam in the 7th century due to its location on caravan routes. The Old Emirate Palace, also known as Al Khamasin Palace, was finished in 1916 as the seat of the governorate for Amir AbdulAziz bin Abdulrahman Al Saud.

What's in the Area - In **Wadi Ad Dawasir** itself, there are a couple of forts. To the north of Highway 10 (M90) is the **Old Emirate Palace** (Al Khamasin Fort). This was built early in the period of expansion of Amir AbdulAziz bin Abdulrahman Al Saud's state and was built between 1911-1916. The Fort was improved in 1942 and again in 1958 before being abandoned as a seat of administration in 1978. The other, smaller, fort is **Al Bajah Fort** - south of Highway 10 (M90). This dates to the period of the Second Saudi State - probably under Amir Faisal bin Turki Al Saud (1834-1838). It is in a state of almost total collapse, used as a dump for rubbish. One of these forts may have been where, at 'Dam', Wilfred Thesiger was imprisoned - as recounted in his book 'Arabian Sands'. Both are next to Al Lidam village - and in the local Arabic, the emphasis is on the second syllable, 'dam'. About 600m west of Al Bahja Fort is the general **Wadi Al Dawasir Souq** area - with fruits & vegetables, including dates. Around Wadi Ad Dawasir are vast areas of pivot fields - crops grown are typically fodder for animals and grain (wheat). To the north of the town, an attempt to halt encroaching sand has been made since 2005 with a tree barrier.

Emirate Palace

Southeast of the town is **Uruq Bani Maarid Reserve**, Saudi Arabia's first UNESCO Natural Heritage Site. Here in the southwestern dunes of the Rub Al Khali desert is a reintroduced population of Arabian Oryx. See more - www.ncw.gov.sa - and to organise a visit, contact through https://eservices.ncw.gov.sa/ServiceCatalog for a "Protected Area Visit Permit" - allow at least 2 weeks for the process to work through.

Qaryat Al Faw, 120km southwest of Wadi Ad Dawasir along Route 177 and adjacent (east) to a small petrol station & other services 19.789, 45.133. It's one of the more celebrated archaeological sites in Saudi Arabia, with excavated pieces in the National Museum.

The site is on an ancient trade route from southern Arabia to Iraq and elsewhere. It grew during a wetter climate and may have sat on a river embankment, beneath an escarpment. Flint workings from the Holocene have been found, and the escarpment's plateau have scattered funerary structures including cairn tombs. There is ample rock art associated with the escarpment. In the plain is an ancient trading settlement of some 40,000sq m. Qaryat Al Faw at its peak dates to around 4th century BC - 4th century AD. Nearby is a fort and caravansaries.

Unfortunately, as the site was nominated in January 2023 for inclusion on UNESCO's World Heritage list, Qaryat Al Faw (also Qurat Al Faw) is well within a fenced area to the east of the petrol station, and not currently open. Hopefully it will not just be a trophy addition to a UNESCO collection of sites.

Getting to Wadi Ad Dawasir - the town is spread along Highway 10. It's about 600km between Riyadh and the town, while between Abha, to the west, & Wadi Ad Dawasir its about 420km. To the far southwest is Najran, around 415km using Route 177.

$\approx$

A SELECTION OF RESTAURANTS & ACCOMMODATION - THERE ARE restaurants along the Wadi Ad Dawasir through road Highway 10 (M90). Around McDonald's & Dominos are a collection - including **Al Rafden**** +966117840137 midday-01:00 and opposite several coffee shops including **Panama** +966557597914 16:00-01:00 & **OneZone** 05:00-14:00/16:00-01:00 (Friday closed morning) +966532055354.

For a key through route, Wadi Ad Dawasir has few worthwhile hotels - check out **Arjan Barak**** https://arjanpark.sa on Highway 10 (M90) and **Rest Night Hotel Suites**** www.restnight.com.sa also on Highway 10.

CHAPTER 29
ḤIMA

Ḥima / حمى - GPS - 18.250238, 44.451711 The Cultural Rock Art in Ḥima, Najran is the core area of one of the largest rock art concentrations in the world – including many anthropomorphic examples. At its heart is a collection of water wells – an isolated source about 100km northeast of Najran & Wadi Ad Dawasir, which is over 250 km to the north. They were critical for trade caravan between south & north Arabia - the key trade route before the Red Sea ocean route after the Roman occupation of Egypt & Northern Arabia. Listed as a UNESCO site – the rock art is believed to have a span of 7,000 years – from near the present day back in time. Evidence of human activity dates back 1.8 million years, in the form of stone tools.

Hima is a spread-out UNESCO-registered area. It's noted for rock art, comparable to the sites at Jubbah and Jabals al-Manjor and Raat. As with other key historical sites in Saudi, there is metal mesh fencing around the archaeology - with little possibility of getting entry at most places. The central location at Hima is actually not rock art but is the Hima Wells. This is a grouping of water wells close to the village of Hima. The wells still appear to be used - as the entrance gate to them is open. The five stone-built wells are linked by water channels that would allow livestock to drink from them. 1600 meters before the water wells, on the local road leading to them, is a small hill - with rock art. There is around 14km between some locations of this UNESCO listing.

Hima is a considerable drive from larger towns. Wadi Ad Dawasir is about 380km to the north, along Route 177. It's a featureless drive. Najran is to the south - again using Route 177. It's around 119km - with little of interest except Najran's outskirts. There are no reasonable restaurant options in the small settlement of Hima. As it's a long drive – bring snacks and mineral water - and ensure you have enough petrol.

Hima Wells - UNESCO site

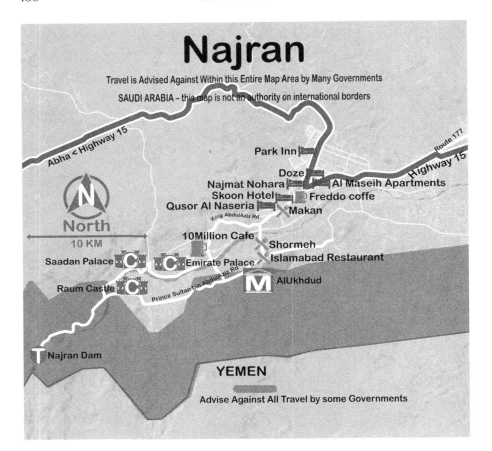

Najran

Travel is Advised Against Within this Entire Map Area by Many Governments

SAUDI ARABIA – this map is not an authority on international borders

Abha < Highway 15

Route 177

Highway 15

Park Inn

Doze

Najmat Nohara   Al Maseih Apartments

Skoon Hotel   Freddo coffe

Qusor Al Naseria   Makan

King AbdulAziz Rd

North

10 KM

10Million Cafe

Shormeh

Saadan Palace   Islamabad Restaurant

Emirate Palace

Prince Sultan bin AbdulAziz Rd

Raum Castle   AlUkhdud

Najran Dam

YEMEN

Advise Against All Travel by some Governments

CHAPTER 30
NAJRAN

Najran / نجران - GPS - 17.481058, 44.177347 **Population** (appx) 381,431 **A Quick Overview Of Najran's Geography** - The town of Najran runs within an expansive valley - from east to west, overlooked by mountains rising to nearly 2,000m above sea level - 6 or 700m above the valley floor. The eastern part of the valley opens out into the southwest dunes of the Rub Al Khali desert.

A Brief History - One of the earliest known events in Najran's history was its conquest, around 685BC, by the Sabaen King Karibil Watar I, who was the Mukarrib, King, of Yemen. The Sabaens were an ancient civilisation controlling much of the southern Arabian Peninsula during this period. Under Sabaen rule, Najran likely began to be fortified at Al Ukhdud, a substantial stone citadel dating back to the 6th centuryBC and continuing in use to at least the 3rd centuryAD.

In 25BC, the Roman prefect of Egypt, Aelius Gallus, battled near Najran as part of Rome's attempt to control the incense trade routes of southern Arabia. However, Rome was unable to gain control over the region.

Najran had become a significant centre of Arabian Christianity in the 4th centuryAD. However, it was attacked in AD328 by the Lakhmid king Imru Al Qays bin Amqu, a Yemeni Christian ally of the Persians. Imru al-Qays pillaged Najran but spared the lives of its Christians.

Around AD523, the city was attacked again - this time by the Jewish king Dhu Nuwas, ruler of the Himyarite kingdom in Yemen. He massacred many of the Christians in Najran who refused to give up their religion and convert to Judaism. The Axumite Kingdom of Ethiopia, as a result, responded by invading and defeating Dhu Nuwas in AD525, giving the Christians of Najran protection.

Najran continued to be a leading centre of Arabian Christianity in the following decades, with a cathedral, monastery, and bishop mentioned in accounts from the era. The region came under Muslim control after the death of the Prophet Muhammad in AD632 and the subsequent Ridda wars and Muslim conquests.

Rock Art - Al Ukhdud

During the reign of the Rashidun Caliph Umar bin al-Khattab between 634-644AD, the Christian community of Najran was encouraged to convert to Islam or leave Arabia. Many did convert, some left, although a community of Christians persisted in the oasis over the subsequent centuries. A mosque found with the walls is dated 8thcAD.

In the 9th century, the Christians and Jews of Najran were said to have made a pact with the Zaydi Imam al-Hadi Ila l-Haqq Yahya bin al-Hussain, who ruled northern Yemen from 897-911AD. The Imam agreed to provide security to the Christians and Jews of Najran in exchange for Jizya tax payments.

Najran and the surrounding region were ultimately incorporated into the Kingdom of Saudi Arabia after it was acquired through the Treaty of Taif by King AbdulAziz Al Saud in 1934. At this time, there was a community of around 600 Jews remaining in Najran. After Saudi rule, many of these Jews emigrated to the Yemeni city of Sanaa.

What's in the Area - Najran is in Saudi Arabia's southwest. When considering visiting, check your government's warnings Page22 due to its proximity to Yemen; the border is within sight of the town. The old town is in the west of the valley. Increasingly, the eastern areas of Najran have modern residential and commercial areas – the town is the regional administrative centre. This modernity is especially noticeable east of where Highway 15 (M45) makes a sharp right angle at traffic lights.

The oldest building we know of in Najran is **Al Ukhdud**, a 'citadel'. This is entered via a small Visitor Centre (Sat-Thurs 10:00-18:00 - Fri 13:30-18:00) Currently FOC on Prince Sultan bin Abdulaziz St (route 1002 that runs west-east) – its 11km southwest of the sharp turn on Highway 15 (M45) traffic lights - the entrance is signed.

The reception cum information centre for Al Ukhdud is well laid out - with Arabic & English text providing a nice overview of the site. The staff will probably be delighted to have your visit. To see the citadel and other places within the site - a walk of between 3 and 4 km is needed from the information centre; this is all in the sun.

Al Ukhdud's citadel is square with impressive exterior stone walls of around 235 metres long on each side and up to 150 cm thick. The remaining stones' substantial size suggests they could carry the weight of a very high wall. It is worth walking around the entire length of the walls - but if that's too much, the gateways into the town are in the west and east - with a direct walk through the centre. A maze of collapsed buildings is inside the citadel, and bushes and trees have taken root.

Al Ukhdud - UNESCO site

On the exterior walls and on the main street inside, there are a few interesting examples of rock art. Look for rock art of lions, camels, snakes and more, and Himyaritic inscriptions on major walls. The site awaits thorough excavations. Finds to date include coinage from the Sabaean 1200BC-AD275, Himyarite 110BC-525AD and Qataban appx 450BC- AD50 Yemeni dynasties. Additionally, glass wear, ceramic & stone Incense Burners have been found. A mosque is to the citadel's northeast - though its orientation to Makkah is poor. The **Najran Museum** is yet to open - its immediately west of Al Ukhdud via Prince Sultan bin Abdulaziz St (Route 1002).

North of Al Ukhdud is an area of farmland that extends for 20+ kms with scattered Date Palms, and some impressive **mud-brick tower housing**, a few are occupied. The farms are following the west-east course of the wadi. The wadi itself is usually dry – the dam upstream blocks most floods – and after all, it hardly ever rains.

In the west of Najran towards the end of King AbdulAziz Rd, on the other side of the wadi and agriculture from Al Ukhdud, is the **Emirate Palace** / Najran Fort nominal hours 09:00-15:00 Sun-Thurs - +966175421060 - it does close for state celebrations.

This fort was finished in about 1943 and has a traditional mixed Najd/ Najran style. The central residential building is surrounded by a curtain wall and is topped with a white crow-stepped gable and 'brides lace' design. The rooms are furnished, and have displays of crafts, including palm basketwork. Historic photos of Amir AbdulAziz dating back to 1916, meeting with regional leaders are standouts. However, it's the attractive and maze-like layout that makes this such an appealing place to visit; don't miss the easy climb to the roof.

Around the Emirate Palace are some fairly **Traditional Souqs** - especially to the south.

Emirate Palace

About 500m South of the Emirate Palace and King AbdulAziz Rd. is the Fruit and Vegetable Souq, which is busiest at the weekend, especially on Friday. A Bird Souq on Friday is west of the Emirate Palace; northwest is a collection of traditional men's clothing shops with an extraordinary variety of products. Do bargain and to avoid disappointment ask specifically where the 'old' item is made - India is a frequent source of artificially antiqued products, and China may be a source of other items, the same as in the rest of Saudi and the world over. The genuine old daggers (Janbiya & Khanjar) may have animal horns, such as from Rhinoceros, & ivory, which is prohibited in many Western countries.

Even further to the west of Najran's town centre, on Prince Naif bin Abdulaziz Street, just east of a small petrol station, is **Saadan Palace** - also known as Al Makrama Palace after the family who build it and Al Aan Palace - nominal hours 16:00-20:00 Wed-Sat currently FOC. Originally built around 1689, this is a fortified building over 3 or 4 floors, surrounded by a curtain wall with an attractive gatehouse. The parapet is a 'brides lace' design. Renovations were carried out between 1988-2019. Take a guided tour if offered.

Located on the west of the city off Prince Sultan bin Abdulaziz (Route 1002) and less than 2km away to the southwest of Saadan Palace is **Raum Castle**, on a hill south of Prince Naif bin Abdulaziz Street. It was built by Yemeni forces between the Saudi occupation of Abha in 1922 and the Treaty of Taif in 1934. Raum Castle was in use for Saudi security until 1953. There are a few rooms within its simple stone structure. The climb up around 200m from the plain to the fort is over almost a kilometre and is via a steep zig-zag path from its southeast that has been stepped in places and largely improved. To the north, in the distance, the Saadan Palace can be seen. Below the fort to the immediate northeast & east are fields and old **mud-brick tower housing** scattered in them.

Men of Najran with their Arabian Horses

To the south is the Yemen border, running through the mountains 7 km away. **Najran Dam** is about 26kms west of Najran City beyond Prince Nayif bin Abdulaziz

(Route 1020) with possible security checks (it is essential infrastructure) just before the 1st tunnel that may turn back tourists unaccompanied by a Saudi national. The road passes through 2 single-lane tunnels (the longest is 1.5 km), with occasional pull-ins to allow wide vehicles to pass, unlined roofs are of natural rock that looks crumbly & loose. Alternatively, there is a track a track along Wadi Najran. The dam, along with its surroundings, is an excursion if you have time. However, it is unlikely to have much water and is not especially rewarding.

In the east of Najran City is the **Animal Souq** south of King AbdulAziz Road, about 2.5km east of the Emirate Palace, not far from the Hospitals & in the shadow of Burj Najran water tower (to the east of the Animal Souq). Camel sales (and Slaughterhouse), and animal fodder are here, again busiest at the weekend.

~

A SELECTION OF RESTAURANTS & ACCOMMODATION

Convenient restaurant choices include **Islamabad Restaurant*** - 09:00 midnight +966558814061 for Pakistani style on Prince Sultan bin Abdulaziz St (Route 1002) 1500m east of Al Ukhdud; **Al Sufrah Arabic Restaurant***, 11:00-02:00 +966175425984 next to Islamabad Restaurant. To the North of Islamabad Restaurant on Al Husain St that leads north are numerous restaurants, including for **Shormeh*** +966175436664 16:00-02:00 for shawarma and similar quick meals. At the western end of King Faisal Road on Abu Bakr Al Siddiq (opposite Qusor An Naseria Hotel) is what might be the best option in Najran - **Makan** **, 13:00 -midnight +966505727776 a north Indian style of food in an attractive setting. Less than a kilometre east of Emirate Palace / Najran Fort on King AbdulAziz Rd (next to a petrol station) is the tiny **10Million Cafe*** 07:00-02:00 Fri 14:00-02:00. The larger **Freddo Coffee** * 06:-13:00/16:00-midnight is on King Salman bin Abdulaziz Rd (just north of King AbdulAziz Rd).

Najran's hotels are mainly clustered around the junction of Highway 15 (M45) and Route 177, in the more modern part of the town. **Doze** * https://doze-hotel. business.site +966175291555 300m east of Highway 15. **Qusor An Naseria** ** +966175228000/554551533 Abu Bakr Al Siddiq, south of King Faisal Rd.; **Park Inn** *** https://www.radissonhotels.com on Highway 15 (M45), **Najmat Nohara** ** njmtnwarh@gmail.com, a few streets west of the junction of Highway 15 (M45) & King AbdulAziz Road; **Al Maseih** for Furnished Apartments* +966175291115 King AbdulAziz Road by the pedestrian bridge. **Skoon Hotel** ** +966175458555 just south of King Faisal Rd.

~

GETTING TO NAJRAN

Najran Airport has flights from Dammam, Jeddah & Riyadh. The road from any city, into Najran, as with many roads in Saudi, is poorly lit at night and, especially after the tedious drive, is best used in daylight. Najran is almost as far south as you can get in Saudi Arabia - from Riyadh, it's almost 1,000km on Highway 10 (M90) & Route 177.

From Jeddah, Highway 15 (M45) swings through the mountains via Taif and Abha. Alternatively, use Highway 10 (M90) onto Jizan and then through the mountains and Dhahran Al Janoub. Either way - it's also approaching 1,000kms. Abha is about 270kms, and Jizan is about 350kms. Route 177 runs between Wadi Ad Dawasir and Najran - it's a tedious drive of around 415km - with only Hima Wells of any interest en-route. SATRANS coach https://satrans.com.sa/ has services from Riyadh, Abha, Jizan (Jazan) via Abha, Jeddah via Taif/Abha check services carefully as this company was established in 2023 and took over from SAPTCO who now are a joint partner – so routes may change. Car Hire companies include Yelo & Theeb. As with many cities away from Dammam, Jeddah and Riyadh - there are no local bus services and poor taxi options.

CHAPTER 31
DHAHRAN AL JANUB

Dhahran Al Janoub / ظهران الجنوب - GPS - 17.663497, 43.507967 **Population** (appx) 24,134

A Brief History - Dhahran Al Janoub was a crucial crossroads along ancient trade routes that connected the southern Arabian Peninsula with neighbouring regions.Before AD430, a Yemeni Jewish king named Abu Karib Asad al-Kamil led an army from Yemen through Dhahran Al Janoub towards Makkah. This was likely part of a broader campaign to control trade routes across the peninsula. In the year AD570, according to Islamic tradition, the Yemeni Christian ruler or viceroy for Aksum, in the Horn of Africa, Abraha bin Al-Sabah Al-Habashi led an expedition from Yemen

northwards to Makkah. His intention was to destroy the pre-Islamic Kaaba and divert Arabian pilgrimage traffic towards the Christian churches he had built in Sana'a and other Yemeni cities. To intimidate potential foes, Abraha's army included several elephants. Tradition is that Abraha likely marched his troops along the western coastal route past Dhahran Al Janoub on this campaign.

Today, Dhahran Al Janoub is often overlooked - or considered a town to drive through. However, west of Highway 15 (M45) - in the centre of the town (south of the main mosque) is the **Al Houza** settlement - picturesquely overlooking small agricultural fields. The fields run along the banks of the wadi that snakes through the town. Car parking is in a spacious area immediately north of these old houses. The mud-brick houses form a cohesive settlement - about 250m in length. While some of the 3 or 4-floor houses have collapsed - others have been maintained. It makes a worthwhile stop.

There are a few other smaller mud-brick villages within a few kilometres - as satellites of this larger settlement. As its set at over 2,000m it has a relatively moderate climate.

~

GETTING TO DHAHRAN AL JANOUB IS ON HIGHWAY 15 (M45), ABOUT 115 km northwest of Najran and 154km southeast of Abha. It makes a good break from driving. Driving from Jizan - it's about 230km using the expressway Highway 5 (M55) and Route 2002.

Al Houza

RESTAURANTS & ACCOMMODATION ON HIGHWAY 15 (M45) - MOVING from north to south - is **Mashahawi Al Sultan**, ** +966581395055 11:00-02:00 serving a broad interpretation of Levantine food. South of this, on Highway 15 (M45) is **Mataem Anaqed**** +966500044861 11:00-midnight with rice & meat dishes, along with less filling shawarma and other 'fast food'. In the southern part of Dhahran Al Janoub is **Lucknow** * midday-midnight +966545258929, with North Indian cuisine. For a light break, try **Qasr Al Ron** ** coffee shop - +966530003814 midday-midnight & along with coffee & cake - it does offer light cooked food. ACCOMMODATION - There are hotels along Highway 15 (M45) - check out **LayLay Hotel** ** +966545868538 in the south next to the hospital.

CHAPTER 32
RIJAL AL MAA

R ijal Al Maa / رجال المع - GPS - 18.212418, 42.273431
     A Quick Overview Of The Geography – in the General Area - The
Hijaz Mountains' height increases from around 600 meters above the sea in the
Madinah region - to 3,000 around Abha. They form the eastern side of the Red Sea Rift
- an active spreading zone within the earth's crust. To this ridge's southwest is a
continuation in the form of the East African Rift - and to the north is the Gulf of Suez
and Dead Sea Rift. Volcanos are associated with the Red Sea Rift - with numerous
examples from the Khaybar area south to Jizan. They include the Black & White
Volcanos east of Khaybar, the Harrat Rahat field just south of Madinah - whose last
eruption was in 1256 and Jabal Yar east of Jazan city, its last eruption around 1810.
Some spectacular mountain escarpments face towards the distant Red Sea, especially
south of Taif. Valleys plunge down from the plateau - reaching the valley floor 2,000
meters below at Abha. The mountains are mainly igneous in origin - with large areas of
basalt flows, granites, and clastic (conglomerate).

A Brief History - Rijal Al Maa is believed to be at least 900 years old. It's in the
upper reaches of the Wadi Hali and was the capital of the tiny Emirate of Hali - that
itself dates from around AD1000. The Emirate's other main centre was at Hali Bin
Yaqoub - where the Wadi Hali has its exit into the Red Sea. Ibn Battuta visited this in
1330 after crossing from Sudan.

The old town of **Rijal Al Maa** entrance SAR20 09:00-21:00 daily – (it's a village-
owned co-operative) is a compact settlement that rises on the slopes of a small hill. Built
with cleaved dark-coloured stones decorated with white quartz stones, the village has a
very cohesive appearance. A small museum includes traditional weapons and silver
jewellery. The small plaza in front of the village has cultural events in June & August
and on special occasions such as Eid.

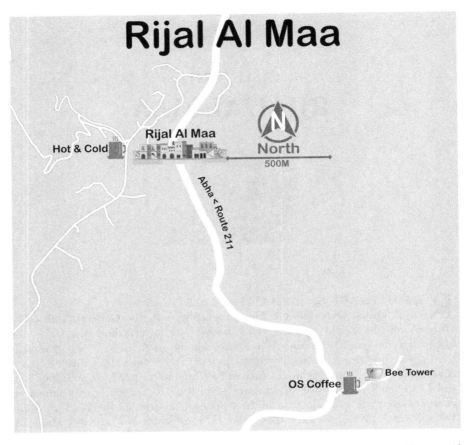

Some rooms are decorated in bright, traditional geometric patterns, Al Qatt Al Asiri. This style of interior domestic decoration is traditionally done by women in mountainous regions of southwest Arabia. They might be a tradition going back several hundred years. In the early mid-20th century, foreign visitors noted them.

Just south of the housing is a man-made channel for water runoff. It has Sidr trees growing in it. Look for African Grey Hornbill birds and Hamadryas Baboons - feeding on the small fruits of the Sidr.

Though much of the old village is no longer lived in, indeed take care when walking around as some houses are in poor repair - at the highest reaches of the hill are modernised properties. The drive between Rijal Al Maa and Abha is superb and passes the **lower cable car station** from Soudah. Small engine cars may struggle on the ascent - rising 1700m over a linear distance of 12km; fortunately, the road zigs and zags upwards - (see Page38 for driving hints) and through a **series of tunnels**. More Baboons are on the upper escarpment at Soudah; these are clearly commensal with humans Page281. If you visit the area in the last 2 weeks (appx) of September – enquire about the 'Flowermen Festival'. This is a cultural event whose hub is Rijal Al Maa.

Fortunately this is outside summer school holidays – but still weekends will be busy with increased hotel prices in Abha.

Rijal Al Maa

Restaurants & Accommodation - On the road between Abha & Rijal Al Maa are several small restaurants - about 10km before Rijal Al Maa from Abha - **Redan Manady Restaurant**** +966507419917 07:00-21:00 **Asadaf Fish Restaurant** ** +966502370028 09:00-23:00.

Opposite the old settlement of Rijal Al Maa is the **Hot & Cold** coffee shop 08:00-23:00 (Friday from 13:30) +966598000250. Further down Route 211 (less than 5km drive) in Khrar village is **OS Coffee** 09:00-21:00 +966506966092 in simple surroundings - with splendid views. About 200m away in the same settlement is **Bee Tower** +966508885946 08:00-20:00 - with Bee hives nearby and a variety of honey for sale in a delightful setting, worth the drive.

A drive south of Rijal Al Maa for 3kms offers small restaurants - try **Mlahma Al Janoub** ** +966558095234- for local meat-based dishes.

There is accommodation about 4km south of Rijal Al Maa **Shaqaq Mafrushat Ragia** +966546862242 & **Shaqaq Llijar Al Youmi** (shaqaq is the Arabic for a flat/apartment) +966507195479. More choices are in Souda or Abha.

Getting There Between Abha & Rijal al Maa it's about 50kms drive - Rijal Al Maa is west using Routes 214-2442&211 see Page38 for driving hints.

Al Qatt Al Asiri.

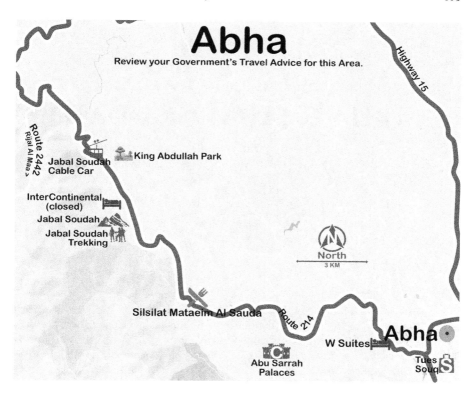

Abha

Review your Government's Travel Advice for this Area.

Route 2442
Rijal Al Maa >

Jabal Soudah
Cable Car

King Abdullah Park

InterContinental
(closed)

Jabal Soudah

Jabal Soudah
Trekking

North
3 KM

Silsilat Mataeim Al Sauda

Route 214

Highway 15

W Suites

Abha

Abu Sarrah
Palaces

Tues
Souq

CHAPTER 33
ABHA & JABAL SOUDAH

Abha / أبها - GPS - 18.214370, 42.496611 **Population** (appx) 334,290 **A Quick History** – The site of Jerash 33kms east of Abha, in Ahad Rafidah, was probably the main political and economic settlement in the earlier history of Abha's region. By the 18th century, it seems power had relocated to the west of Abha with the Bani Maghed family and onto Al Saqa and, finally, Abha. In September AD1834, Egypt's Mohammed Ali Pasha took Abha. After Mohammed Ali Pasha's forces withdrew in 1840 - the area again had several local powers. The Ottomans came in 1872 and eliminated local centres of power. The Ottoman governor Muhyiddin Pasha built the Shamsan Castle in 1912. Hasan bin Ali Al Ayde a local governor for the Ottomans - became an independent ruler after the Turkish defeat in World War One. However, he had little local support - and the local tribes became allied with Amir AbdulAziz bin Abdulrahman Al Saud in Riyadh. Inevitably, Hasan bin Ali Al Ayde was defeated by forces supported by Amir AbdulAziz bin Abdulrahman Al Saud. Muhammad bin Ali Al-Idrisi, of Jizan assumed the governorship. However, his position was shaky, and a conflict occurred with the local population. Finally Amir AbdulAziz bin Abdulrahman Al Saud sent his 16-year-old son, Faisal bin Abdulaziz. as titular head of the army to occupy much of the mountain region. In October 1922, Abha fell, without a fight. After conquering the rest of the region in 1924, the now King AbdulAziz had the Al-Shada Palace built - though the building now only remains as a small tower in the town centre.

What to search out

Abha is a key summer destination in Saudi Arabia and regional capital. It seems to be overlooked now, in favour of developing and publicising AlUla, NEOM and Turaif - but who can ignore its almost 3,000m in height, giving a cool summer climate and year-round appeal. Weekends and holidays, especially the summer school holidays (June, July, August), sees peak demand. As with many of the settlements in these mountains, the scenery conspires to overshadow the towns. In Abha - check out if possible **Asir**

Regional Museum +966172307307. This is a purpose-built government museum with several themed halls, including Saudi Living Hall, Heritage Hall, Antiquities Hall, Pre-Islam Hall, Islamic History Hall, and Contemporary History Hall. Like so many regional museums in Saudi Arabia, this was closed when this book was published - but included as it might reopen.

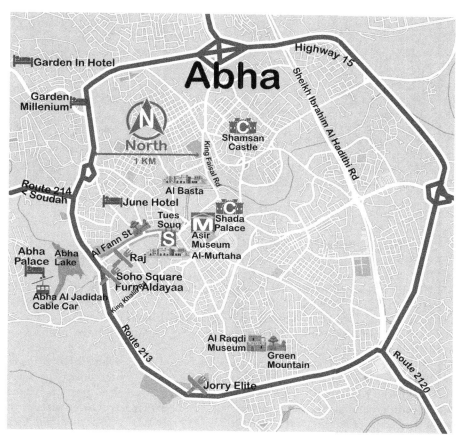

East of the museum, beyond the large King AbdulAziz Grand Mosque, is **Shada Archaeological Palace** - it's about a 10-minute walk. This is, unfortunately, a shadow of its former self and is now simply a single tower rather than a fort cum palace. As with the Asir Regional Museum, this is currently closed. It is located in a modern area of government buildings, and farther east is a **modern shopping area** selling gold, everyday items and some souvenirs. The general area has ample parking – during government working mornings (Sun-Thurs) some may be full, but the others away from buildings might be empty – in the afternoons most are empty.

Tuesday Souq - Abha

The **Tuesday Souq** 'Souq Youm Al Thalatha' (07:00-19:00 individual shops may have slightly different timings) is about 300m west of the Asir Regional Museum and massive flagpole (across a broad road). The market - with stalls & semi-permanent buildings, is hidden behind an oval walled enclosure. It trades throughout the week but has its main day on Tuesday. Look for dates, honey (with comb) and spices, as well as household goods. Woven date palm baskets and other handicrafts create a fascinating area to shop and browse in. There is a separate section only for women. This souq is well worth visiting as it's full of interest.

Al Basta District is about 500km northeast of the Tuesday Market. This is an area with a few, very traditional, older houses. They are gently crumbling away, unfortunately. A distinctive feature is the stone tiling (schist slate) set as horizontal bands protruding from the walls. They are not only decorative but practical as they help stop rain from washing away the mud walling. In other areas of Asir, the mud layers might be lime-plastered and painted in bright, primary colours to emphasise the appearance. Immediately to Al Basta's south is the '**Ottoman Bridge**' that crosses a small wadi.

Al Basta - Abha

Al-Muftaha Village is south of the Tuesday Market. Here is a small complex of traditional-looking buildings. It is now temporally closed, but it was an active hub for arts in Asir - with the Asir Photography Club and a theatre. As with the Asir Regional Museum, it's included as it might reopen - work does appear to be going on.

To the west of Tuesday Souq is a landscaped section of King Khalid Rd which loops around this western area of Abha; locally, this section is called '**Al Fann St**' (The

Art St.). This has a linear park which holds the Abha Festival (August and September) and, in mid-summer, especially, has street decoration along about a kilometre.

The South American tree, the Jacaranda, which is planted here blooms in early summer, adding colour and its sweet and mild fragrance to the street's appeal. There are several places to eat along this stretch, including the **Kaya Cafe*** (daily 06:00-midnight) for light snacks and coffee.

At the western end of Al Fann St (King Khalid Rd) is the **Abha Dam and Lake**. The dam's lake is small, and the public areas are poorly maintained. On the far side of the lake is a cluster of hotels and other accommodations. The lake is a leisure area, with access from the south off Amir Faisal bin Khalid Rd. Next to **Abha Palace Hotel** ***www.abhapalace.com.sa is a terminus of **Abha Al Jadidah Cable Car** SAR100 Daily 14:00-19:00 www.syahya.com.sa SAR100/. This takes you over part of the city, via two re-routing stations, to the **'Green Mountain'** hill in the centre of Abha. The cable car journey is over road, escarpment (resident Baboons might be seen) and town – with great views in clear weather. There are refreshment & dining options at both the termini. **Al Raqdi Museum** Sat-Thurs 16:00-23:00 +966 50 575 3329 SAR20. West (immediately below) the Green Mountain is this an eclectic collection laid out as if a home. This is not a 'must see' – though given how many places in Abha are closed, it becomes a possible visit. It includes agricultural equipment, costumes and a good offering of traditional handicrafts. Opening hours tend to be flexible, as in many other places in Saudi Arabia, so arrive well after opening, and certainly a long time before closing so you have time before it closes. There are local handicraft products for sale.

Al Fann St

On a low hill overlooking the city from the north, **Shamsan Castle** is a dilapidated fort cum barracks that may date from 1912, just before the Ottomans withdrew. A small courtyard and a few rooms that have lost their roofs, and open out onto the courtyard are all that remain. Some 'beautification' of the surroundings has been done. This may, or may not be open, depending on the guard.

Fatima Museum, SAR20 Daily 11:00-20:00 +966505749843 about 7km southeast of central Abha on Route 2120. This charming private museum (off a small courtyard) is focused on women's life & traditional decorative 'Al Qatt Al Aseeri Art' of Abha and Rijal Al Ma. This art is traditional geometric designs on walls created by women of this region of Saudi Arabia. This art is recognised by UNESCO within its 'Intangible Heritage' list. The museum has some traditional costumes and silver jewellery on display. Food is also available, as are souvenirs from a small shop. Compared to all other private museums in Saudi, this is a 'must visit' when you are in Abha. Parking space is limited – there might be places in the local.

Farther southeast, (a 100km drive from Abha) off Route 2110, is the village and **Cable Car** at **Al Habala** 13:30-18:00 SAR80 www.syahya.com.sa. The village and its agriculture are set below a steep cliff - reached today by the cable car, offering extraordinary views on a bright day. The village name mean rope, perhaps ropes were used to either climb down or drop/lift goods. Close to the upper cable car station is a small hotel, the Al Habala Resort, under the same management, with accommodation in chalet-type buildings.

Southwest of Abha (a 21km drive) are the **Abu Sarrah Palaces**, nominal hours 16:00-21:00 SAR35 - Just over a kilometre south of Route 214 to Soudah. This is a grouping of historic buildings that date to around 1836. They focus on a 6-floor fortified tower house. The buildings themselves are in excellent condition, though without much in the way of furnishings. A drink from the coffee shop might help ascend their steep stairs. The surrounding valley, with its terraced fields, adds to the reason to visit.

Jabal Al Soudah, to the west of Abha, for many years had claim to be Saudi Arabia's highest place. Recent surveying by non-official visitors, using GPS (against known base stations & using three separate measurements) to find its elevation had a height of 2,999m above sea. The same GPS survey team gave **Jabal Ferwa** 100km to the southeast as 3001.8m, and they expressed absolute confidence in the greater height of Jabal Ferwa. Nonetheless, Jabal Soudah is more accessible than Jabal Ferwa and will retain its popular appeal for greater height. The mountain is not a noticeable peak, simply the highest place on a gradually ascending plateau.

Jabal Al Soudah – trekking path is a walk about 1,200m southwest of the southern buildings of the closed **InterContinental Hotel**, which leads to a path, which is not especially well maintained. It follows a ridge line through the escarpment woodland (Juniper etc). The best length is around 10km – and the descent is about 1km. It ends up about halfway towards Al Shabain - return on the same path. This should not be attempted if it means a walk after sunset or if the cloud cover drops and covers the route. Baboons might be in the area, see Page281. Mountain rescue in Saudi Arabia is difficult to organise & of course, it's important to ensure your insurance (whether international or Saudi) covers you.

View down Wadi Kasan towards Rijal Al Maa

Al Soudah National Park (King Abdullah Park) is on the plateau at Al Soudah. Here, there are scattered Juniper trees, and in summer, the rain and mist enable other vegetation to grow. There are other paths through the area and views from the escarpment edge down southwest towards Rijal Al Ma. Route 214 meanders around the plateau, eventually joining Highway 15 (M45) north of Abha.

Within Al Soudah National Park is a **Cable Car** station 09:30-17:00 www.syahya.com.sa as a seasonal operation - its currently closed for repairs. This is immediately next to Route 214. The cars descend to near Route 2442, a great journey down a valley from the escarpment –from 2717m down to 1334m (1534descent) over 3km. Unfortunately, having reached the bottom – there isn't much to see in the immediate local, so enjoy the ascent (if it reopens). Soudah is an area intended to be redeveloped under the Saudi Vision2030. This means that key areas will change - including, presumably, the InterContinental Hotel and Cable Car.

Male Hamadryas Baboons

RESTAURANTS & ACCOMMODATION IN ABHA

Abha has a broad selection of dining options. **Raj Indian Restaurant** ** https://raj.com.sa 13:00-02:00 West end of King Khalid Rd – offers north Indian style food – and Indian style Chinese; **Soho Square** *** +966503007506 08:0002:00 -

13:30-02:00 Fri King AbdulAziz Rd opposite Abha Dam – a general western menu style.

It is one of several meal options along this stretch of road. **Furn Al Dayaa** ** www.furnaldayaa.com.sa/ 07:00-01:00 / 07:00-11:00-13:00-01:00 Fri - next to Soho Square) King AbdulAziz Rd opposite Abha Dam – an interpretation of Italian / Mediterranean food; **Jorry Elite** *** +966172285588 Daily 07:00-11:00 12:30-midnight King AbdulAziz Rd in southern Abha southwest of the Green Mountain – in a large villa style setting with other dining brands. Here, the cuisine is broadly Mediterranean. Towards Al Souda, there is a choice of local restaurants, with distinctly local food. Many are small and might even operate only seasonally - check out

Cable Car - Soudah

Silsilat Mataeim Al Sauda * -11:00-22:00 an operation in a small, converted shipping container for takeaways.

Hotel June (Apartments) **+966172255523 Al Bahrain St (east of King AbdulAziz Rd); **Garden In Hotel Apartments** **+966172500007 On Route 2528 running out of town (above a medical laboratory); **Garden Millenium** (not the brand Millenium) ***+966567101800 King AbdulAziz Rd less than 3km north of Abha Dam; **W Suites** (not the W brand) ***+966500200580 Al Soudah Rd. Al Soudah has numerous rented private apartments – often only 1 or 2 in each building. Their target clients are families. If staying in Abha town doesn't appeal – during the off-season winter months, it is worth searching out a property here. If the InterContinental site does reopen – this might be considered - the location is excellent, and the InterContinental chain is well established in Arabia.

~

GETTING TO ABHA FLIGHTS CONNECT ABHA INTERNATIONAL AIRPORT with Dammam, Jeddah, Riyadh and several other Saudi airports - there are international flights to Egypt & UAE. Having had missile attacks into the airport from Yemen, it is worth reviewing your country's travel advice for this airport. It's about 270km between Abha and Najran on Highway 15 (M45) via Dhahran Al Janoub. Also, using Highway 15 (M45) - it's around 330kms between Abha and Al Bahah. From the coast and Jizan, it's around 200km using Highways 10 (M90) & 5 (M55). SATRANS coach offers services from Jeddah, Riyadh via Khamis Mushait, Najran, Jizan (Jazan) (previously SAPTCO ran these). As with other towns in the southwest - there are no local bus services & limited taxi services.

CHAPTER 34
KHAMIS MUSHAIT

Khamis Mushait/ خميس مشيط - GPS - 18.276306, 42.742453 **Population** (appx) 535,065 (out of Asir's around 2million). **A Short History** - Khamis Mushait was a trading town in the highlands on trade routes both north-south and west - east. Its name 'Khamis' indicates that its market was held on a Thursday - and Mushait was a governor's name. The town's size was small - in the thousands until the Khamis Mushait Air Base was built in 1960. The population has exploded since - to more than the regional capital, Abha. Indeed, urban sprawl means the two cities are a single conurbation.

Khamis Mushait has little of interest to a visiting tourist - apart from **Al Mushait Palace,** southeast of the junction of Highway 15 (M45) and Prince Sultan Rd. Currently under restoration. This residence was built by Sheikh Abdulaziz bin Hussein bin Mushait around 1870, when the region was largely autonomous. With the ascent of Amir AbdulAziz bin Abdulrahman Al Saud, the successors to Sheikh Abdulaziz bin Hussein bin Mushait - Sheikh Saeed bin Mushait and his son Sheikh Abdullah bin Saeed, supported Amir AbdulAziz bin Abdulrahman Al Saud in his conquest of southwest Saudi Arabia. It is from this time that the town grew - expanding greatly after the airbase was built in 1960 & the King Faisal Military City in 1971.

Al Mushait Palace

HOW TO GET TO KHAMIS MUSHAIT THE TOWN IS ON HIGHWAY 10 (M90) almost 1,000km southwest of Riyadh via Wadi Ad Dawasir which is around 400kms away. Abha is only 40 km to the west.

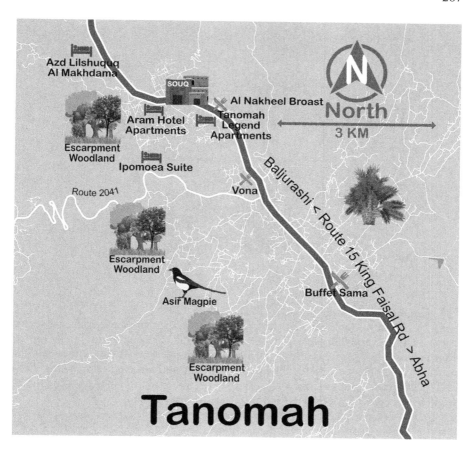

CHAPTER 35
TANOMAH & AL NAMAS

anomah & Al Namas / النماص تنومة - GPS 19.120401, 42.129680
What to look for - At **Tanomah**, in between Namas and Abha are several parks on the escarpment west of Highway 15 (M45). These are fairly rocky on the plateau, but over the edge, a cascade of trees drops away below. There are roads leading west from the highway towards the escarpment, best options about 2km south of the SATRANS coach station from opposite the petrol station. Here is also Husaak www.husaak.com who, if contacted in advance, may offer trekking.

African Paradise Flycatcher

This woodland is a draw for birds. Expect birds in winter to include Abyssinian White-eye, African Paradise Flycatcher, African Pipit, Arabian Green Bee-eater, Arabian Partridge, Arabian Scops Owl, Arabian Waxbill, Arabian Wheatear, Brown Woodland-Warbler, Fan-tailed Raven, Graceful Prinia, Hamerkop, Laughing Dove, Long-billed Pipit, Olive-rumped Serin, Palestine Sunbird, Philby's Partridge, Rufous-capped Lark, Scrub Warbler, White-spectacled Bulbul, Yemen Linnet, Yemen Serin, Yemen Thrush, Yemen Warbler.

If you look hard and are very lucky - Arabia's most sought-after endemic, the rare **Asir Magpie**, is here. In the areas below – an Arabian Leopard has been sighted in 2023.

If you arrive on a weekend - check out the small **Saturday Souq** just 500m south of Highway 15 (M45) (southwest of the small SATRANS coach office). The souq is a spread-out area made up of small shops selling an extraordinary variety of products for the local population – key day is Saturday but drop in if passing on another day. The drive on Highway 15 (M45) is through some great scenery.

Tharban Palace Museum

At **Al Namas**, there is a scattering of ancient settlements and, to the west, dramatic scenery from the escarpments down to the volcano cone near Al Majaradah in the west, towards the Red Sea. The plateau area on which Al Namas is located is full of sprawling villages and a patchwork of small agricultural fields, best seen when crops are grown after the monsoon rains.

Tharban Palace Museum +966118808855 09:00-17:00 Currently FOC - but a change might happen simply because of the economics of providing a free facility that has a cost of provision. Its immediately on Highway 15 (M45) (here named King Faisal Rd) in Al Namas. The museum is set directly on the road (the entrance is through a passageway on the right). This is a restored traditional fortified house (rather than a palace) over several floors, complete with mosque; check about entering the mosque with the usual dress required for mosques. Here, there are limited displays of cultural objects and the expected lack of information. However – the museum is so convenient on the road that a visit at least offers a break along Highway 15 (M45).

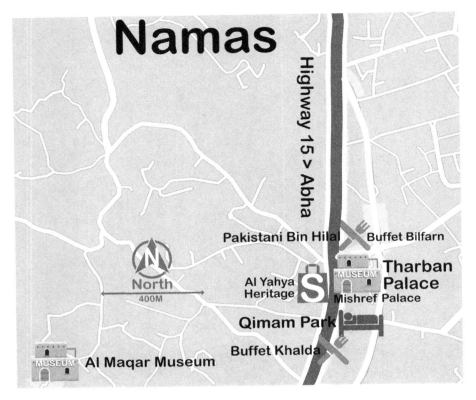

Mishref Palace - Sun-Thurs 09:00-17:00 This is adjacent to Tharban Palace. Entrance from the street to the left of Tharban Palace Museum or Abu Bakr al-Siddiq Street behind. This building is unrestored. Inside are traditional clothing, agricultural equipment, and silver jewellery. Palace, as used in so many places in Saudi Arabia, is used to infer home of an important person, government administrative centre or military fort. **Al Yahya Heritage Museum** Sat-Thurs 08:00-20:00 SAR10 Highway 15 (M45), diagonally southwest of Tharban Palace Museum on the other side of the road. Al Yahya has recently refurbished display area in a relatively modern building with an entrance between the shop fronts on the main road. Here, there are a range of artefacts, including taxidermized animals. There are enough weapons for an army – along with local clothing. There is some information in Arabic, along with staff to try and help. In essence though - it's a retail store with newly manufactured traditional accessories. **Al Maqar Museum** (also sometimes called Namas Museum & Palace of Islamic Civilizations) Daily 08:00-19:00 SAR20 west of Highway 15 (M45) – take a street from near the museums on the road – easiest is from the petrol station. This is a whimsical confection of a Yemeni & Mogul palace created by Mohammed Al Shari. The building, which overlooks the escarpment, and its surrounds are still in need of work, so take care when visiting. There are exposed metal rebars and possibly nails & screws on the paths. The style of the building itself and the views, on a clear day, have to be the main attraction here. The exhibits include furnishings, household goods and documents;

unfortunately, they are without information. Terraced gardens and a coffee shop are outside. The Tharban Palace is a quicker visit, though without the views.

~

SOME RESTAURANTS & ACCOMMODATION IN TANOMAH & AL NAMAS
Tanomah has dining options along the main highway, Highway 15 (M45). **Buffet Sama** * +966172835981 09:00-midnight On Highway 15 (M45) (King Faisal Rd) – Shawarma and 'Broast' – this is principally a takeaway. **Al Nakheel Restaurant and Broast** * +966172826744 Daily 08:00-02:00 On Highway 15 (M45) (King Faisal Rd) in central Tanomah west of pedestrian crossings. **Vona** ** +966562726461 16:00-midnight On Highway 15 (M45) (King Faisal Rd) in Tanomah. A surprising option here – offering Italian-style food – in pleasant surroundings. Al Namas – there is a clustering of restaurants near the Tharban Palace – all are relatively basic. **Pakistani Bin Hilal Restaurant** * +966590537943 04:40-midnight Off Highway 15 (M45) (King Faisal Rd) – on the street to the left of Tharban Palace Museum – Pakistani style – meat and rice-based. Here also is **Buffet Bilfarn** * +966506828810 09:30-midnight Off Highway 15 (M45) (King Faisal Rd) – on the street to the left of Tharban Palace Museum – fast food – Indian style with a good range of options cooked to suit you. **Buffet Khalda** * - 24 hours +966558455043 - On Highway 15 (M45) (King Faisal Rd) – 200m south of museums – simple choice of Indian/Saudi quick food & fruit juices.

Al Namas has **Danat Layalina Apartments** **+966595762266 East of town (about 3km) on Al Namas-Al Faraah Rd./Al Mazan roundabout. Tanomah **Aram Hotel Apartments** **+966172739010 Immediately on Highway 15 (M45) (King Faisal Rd). In the central area of Tanomah, the charming **Ipomoea Suite** *** www.ipomoeasuite.com is southwest of Highway 15 (M45) in an isolated area. **Tanomah Legend for Furnished Apartments** *+966172826505 on Highway 15 (M45) (King Faisal Rd) west of the pedestrian crossing. In north Tanomah **Azd Lilshuquq Al Makhdama** ** +966502799090 On Highway 15 (M45) (King Faisal Rd). In Namas - directly on Highway 15 (M45) is **Qimam Park**** www.qimamparkhotels.com, one of a small chain around Abha; all are comparable.

~

GETTING TO THESE PLACES BOTH TOWNS ARE ON HIGHWAY 15 (M45). Tanomah is about 120km north of Abha & Namas is 150km. Namas is almost 200km south of Al Bahah.

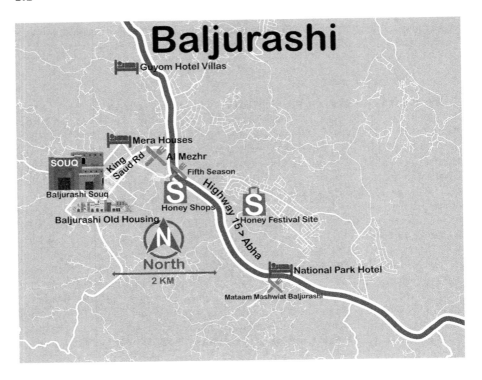

CHAPTER 36
BALJURASHI

B aljurashi / ببلجرشي - GPS - 19.860229, 41.559980 **Population** (appx) 35,985

Bee Hives - Hijaz

Baljurashi was the local capital until Al Bahah was developed. The scenery is very similar to the entire region between Taif and Dhahran Al Jaboub.

What's there - Baljurashi is a spread-out town - in reality, a conglomeration of small villages. About halfway (250-300km) between Abha and Taif, it is a convenient resting place if driving.

Just west of Highway 15 (M45) - a couple of hundred meters from Fifth Season restaurant - there is a collection of shops selling highly prized **local honey**. In the second half of July an '**International Honey Festival**' is held at a dedicated site in Baljurashi 2km, south of the shops, on Highway 15 (M45) (turn leads north near the petrol station).

~

FARTHER WEST FROM HIGHWAY 15 (M45), ALONG KING SAUD ST – A 2KM walk, or drive, southwest from the honey shops to the **Zubaida district**. This area (bordered by roads named after so many Kings – Khalid, Faisal, Fahd_ is what may have been the largest of these small settlements in Baljurashi. Some of the older stone houses have been rebuilt, but many are on the verge of collapsing. Take care when wandering through. There is a market in this older section which is quite active at weekends - with a general offering of products that are sold in local shops. This area also holds fairs on holidays, selling locally crafted products and handicrafts. It's worth the detour - especially as there is that mix of old housing and souq.

Restaurants and Accommodation to Consider - **Al Mezhr Restaurant** ** +966177228717 11:30-23:00 King Saud Rd – Saudi cum Yemeni food (meat & rice). **Fifth Season** ** +966177530444 13:00-midnight is on Highway 15 (M45) in the town centre – market by overhead direction road sign – a mix of Levantine & Indian style cuisine made to Saudi taste. Also, farther east on Highway 15 (M45) next to Panda supermarket – opposite National Park Hotel - **Mataam Mashwiat Baljurashi** ** +966509612569 Midday-midnight. – a mix of Levantine, Indian and Gulf cuisine.

National Park Hotel *** http://www.nationalparkgroup.com/ Highway 15 (M45), just east of the town centre, opposite Panda supermarket. **Guyom Hotel Villas** ***+966508255464 Behind Baljurashi Mall on Highway 15 (M45), just before the town. **Mera Houses** **+966581900882 West of Highway 15 (M45) – on King Khalid Rd from King Saud Rd (exit at Al Raji ATM).

Getting There Baljurashi is on Highway 15 (M45) - 300km north of Abha & less than 40 south of Al Bahah. Between Taif and Baljurashi, its 250km.

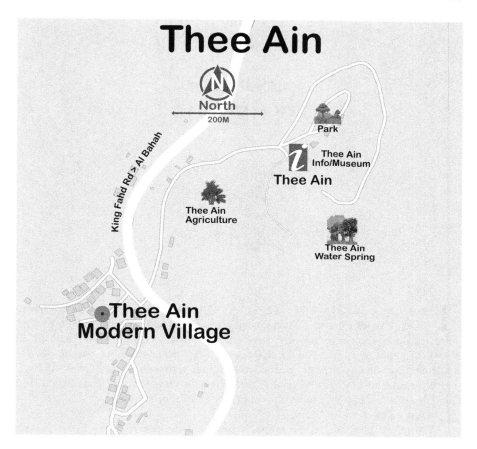

CHAPTER 37

THEE AIN

Thee Ain / ذي عين - GPS - 19.931791, 41.442455 09:00-17:00 daily Currently FOC **A Brief History** - Thee Ain may date from the 16th century. According to local legends - some fighting men were later involved in defeating Mohammed Ali Pasha's army at Qunfudhah, on the Red Sea coast, in May 1814. It's a common claim by settlements in the southwest, demonstrating long-term allegiance to the Al Saud. Largely abandoned by the end of the 20th century - Thee Ain was rehabilitated from 2009 under a government project as a tourism-focused centre.

What's There

A small parking area has a **modern information centre** that's worth looking around. It provides details about the culture of the region and is well laid out. The entire village is no longer lived in. About 4 dozen houses rise up a small hill - to a separate citadel at the top. The houses, built from natural stone - vary from one to four floors and have been restored since 2009. Though a similar layout to Rijal Al Maa - here there isn't (so far) a house with traditional artefacts laid out. The town overlooks agriculture to its west - and, most interestingly, to the south. The southern area that can be walked through leads to a **water spring** - from which the village takes its name - Ain/Ayn is the Gulf Arabic for water spring.

The village is used for government events and filming - during which it closes. Though currently free - Thee Ain is such a compact site that it would be easy to create a paid-for entry - in a comparable way to the locations attached to AlUla - perhaps this will happen.

∾

WHERE TO EAT AND ACCOMMODATION - THE NEAREST PLACE TO EAT IS A small roadside coffee shop, **'On the Road'** on King Fahd Rd 400m opposite Thee Ain. Father away, Mindi & Mazba Sarawat and Buffet Al Ikhwan Al Jaw are about 6km south of Thee Ain - each on a different side of King Fahd Rd. Beyond these 20km from Thee Ain is Al Makhwah with a small market, busiest on Tuesdays. This small village has a collection of simple restaurants along the King Fahd Rd, non are standouts – but they offer a wide choice.

Check the hotels in Al Bahah for places to stay in.

~

GETTING THERE THEE AIN IS A 30KM DRIVE FOLLOWING THE KING FAHD Rd down from Al Bahah - it's a spectacular drive as the road plunges west, down from the plateau. The route cuts through tunnels in the mountain slopes as it descends about 1400m. It's not quite such a slog back up as the route between Rijal Al Maa and Soudah – all part of the visit experience (see Page 38 for driving hints).

Thee Ain

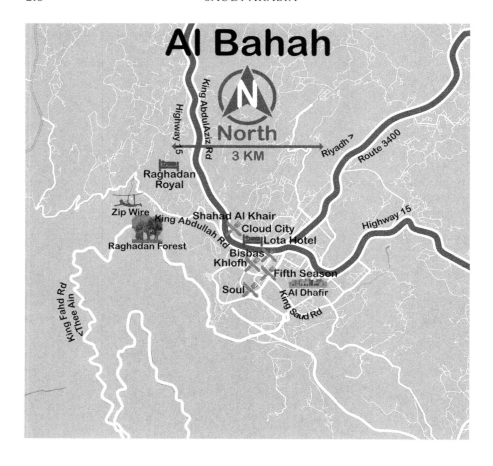

CHAPTER 38
AL BAHAH

A l Bahah / الباحة - GPS - 20.023220, 41.451198 **Population** (appx) 90,515
What to look for - The main attraction in **Al Bahah** is its nature - and the infrastructure built around it. **Raghadan Forest Park**, west of the town, is a leisure area on the edge of the wooded escarpment at 2200+m. There is, however, a focus on man-made attractions, notably **Al Baha Zi-Line**, a kilometre-long zipline midday-21:00 SAR120 (40-120kg) +966583380576, which spans a valley in the area. A bus transports you from just off King Abdullah bin Abdulaziz Rd to departures. From there, you swoop over abandoned terraced fields, woodland and roads. In Raghadan Forest Park, there are walkways through the general area, along with restaurants etc. As with most areas in these mountains, the peak season is during Saudi school holidays - mid-June to late August. For much of the year, away from weekends, there will be fewer people.

Also at Al Bahah Raghadan Forest will be a planned open-top bus service that will operate to several destinations in the area.

Much of the centre of town is relatively modern - with little of note. Perhaps the most extensive area of **older housing** is to the east of the modern centre - south of Highway 15 (M45), King AbdulAziz Rd, and north of King Saud Rd, at Al Dhafir. Even here, the buildings are not especially interesting. On Highway 15, about 10km north of Al Bahah's Cloud City Hotel, is '**Ben Rakosh Palace**', an old stone complex of buildings that is partially restored.

∼

RESTAURANT & ACCOMMODATION OPTIONS
Al Bahah's restaurants' cluster along Highway 15 (M45) – with many near Cloud City Hotel or, perhaps more interestingly, in the older part of town south of Highway 15 (M45).Al Bahah. **Fifth Season**** +966177240444 13:00-midnight King Saud Rd –

junction of Highway 15 (M45) & King Fahd Rd a mix of Levantine & Indian style cuisine made to Saudi taste. – it's also in Baljurashi. **Bisbas Restaurant** * +966530272704 08:00-midnight (Fri afternoons only) 100m a bit hidden near the junction of Highway 15 (M45) (King AbdulAziz Rd) & King Khalid Rd – cuisine from the Horn of Africa - its spicy and meat and rice-based.

Shahad Al Khair* +966509967281 10:00-23:00 (Friday 14:00-23:00) Highway 15 (M45) in centre of town - a simple buffet style – curried meat & rice. **Khlofh** * +966535512223 05:30-11:00/17:00-22:00 in the older part of Al Bahah 300m south of Highway 15 (M45). Al Quds Rd west of King Khalid Rd – snacks – based on beans Ful (Fava) & Lentils. **Soul** *** www.sggroup-ksa.com/soulalbaha Daily 07:00-midnight southern end of King Fahd Rd looking like a European Alpine Schloss – about 1km south of Highway 15 (M45). International cuisine.

Some hotels - **Cloud City Hotel** ***+966177230330 immediately on Highway 15 (M45) in the town - **Lota Hotel** ** +966507654055 on Highway 15 (M45) east of Cloud City - to Al Bahah's west **Raghadan Royal** ** +966503776802 is south of Highway 15 (M45) towards the Raghadan Forest.

Various units of simple Cave accommodation at Jabal Shada Al Asfal. Its reached from Al Bahah by King Fahd Rd on a combination of tarmac and very rough mountain track - overall about 70km southwest. Advance booking needed - contact +966501152935/+966503783161. These are all individually owned by different families of the Al Shadawi tribe - so if one is full they will be able to suggest an alternative. This is probably the most northerly area, in Saudi, that grows coffee.

~

GETTING TO AL BAHAH - KING SAUD BIN ABDULAZIZ AIRPORT SERVES AL Bahah - flights to Dammam, Jeddah and Riyadh. Between Al Bahah and Abha, it is around 330kms on Highway 15 (M45) and between Taif and Al Bahah, it's 220 km appx. SATRANS coach offers services to Taif & Abha and other cities via Taif & Abha. As with many cities away from Dammam, Jeddah and Riyadh - there are no local bus services and poor taxi options.

Shahad Al Khair

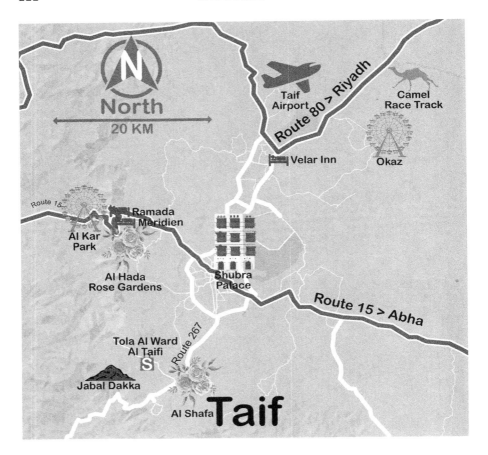

CHAPTER 39
TAIF - AL HADA & ASH SHAFA

Taif / الطائف - GPS - 21.286333, 40.414833 **Population** (appx) 563,282 **A short insight to the Geography** - The high plateau from Taif south to beyond Abha is a complicated mix of granites and metamorphic rock, granite, greenschist, etc. With so many minerals, these are potentially fertile, hence the innumerable small villages on the western escarpment area. Many valley areas where water flows after rain are intensively farmed. The western escarpment area is stunning - especially on days with low humidity - as this allows extensive views west.

A Brief History - Taif is an important city in western Saudi Arabia located in the Hijaz region about 50 miles southeast of Makkah. In pre-Islamic times, Taif was a religious centre that housed the idol of the goddess Lat, who was one of the three chief goddesses of Makkah, along with Uzza and Manat. As a pilgrimage site, Taif drew worshippers from across Arabia to the temple of Lat. The city was also known for its agricultural bounty from the vineyards and fruit orchards in the surrounding fertile lands - its elevation allowed for a greater range of plants to be grown.

In AD630, the Prophet Muhammad led a Muslim army to attack and besiege the city of Taif after the failed negotiations with the Banu Thaqif tribe that controlled the city. The two-week siege was unsuccessful, but the event marked a critical moment in the ongoing conflict between the new Islamic movement and the pagan tribes of Arabia. Though the siege failed, Taif submitted to Muslim rule by AD631 without further bloodshed after realising the futility of resisting the tide of Islam. The idol of Lat was destroyed in the city.

Taif remained an important city in the Hijaz under Muslim rule, . In the 8th century, the Mosque of Abdullah bin Abbas was built in Taif at the site where the companion of the Prophet was buried. It remains the main mosque in Taif today. Over the centuries, Taif was controlled by various Muslim dynasties, including the Abbasids, Fatimids, and Ayyubids.

From 1517, Taif fell under the control of the Ottoman Empire along with the rest of the Hijaz region. The Ottomans valued Taif for its strategic location near Makkah, on the route to Baghdad. Agricultural production, especially fruits, continued to thrive in Taif and served to supply Ottoman troops stationed in the region. It's from this date that the rose (Rosa × damascena) may have been introduced from the Bulgarian area that was also part of the Ottoman Empire.

In 1802, Taif was conquered by the Saudi forces for Abdulaziz bin Muhammad bin Saud, who removed Ottoman control. However, in 1813, the Ottoman viceroy Muhammad Ali Pasha of Egypt retook Taif for the Ottomans. The Swiss traveller Johann Ludwig Burckhardt visited Taif during August & September 1814 during Ottoman control and left an early Western account of the city. He described its orchards, vineyards, and Rose gardens.

Over the next century, Taif remained under nominal Ottoman control – they finished the small Ottoman Fort in 1834. Eventually, in 1916, Taif became part of the short-lived Kingdom of the Hijaz. In 1924, the emerging power of Amir AbdulAziz bin Abdulrahman Al Saud decisively retook Taif, bringing the city under Saudi control.

Under Saudi rule in the 20th century, Taif continued to develop as an important city in the kingdom. In the 1970s, Taif was chosen as the site for summer government activities due to its milder climate compared to Riyadh. This was much as the British Raj relocated from Calcutta, Delhi & Bombay to spend summer in Simla in the mountains of northern India. Both King AbdulAziz and King Khalid died at Taif – and were buried in Riyadh. Today, the city serves as a cultural and economic centre in western Saudi Arabia.

What to look for

Taif, with its proximity to the substantial populations in Jeddah and Makkah, is a very popular weekend and summer destination. Though the city itself is just under 1,700m above sea - the difference in climate and attractive open countryside is a draw, as even from Jeddah it's only a couple of hours drive. The attractions in the city itself are yet to be developed for many foreign tourists - potential ones are, unfortunately, not open. Ash Shafa and Al Hada (on the road from Jeddah) are local areas that grow Roses.

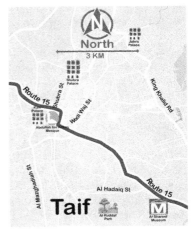

There are several old palaces in central Taif. Built outside the original city walls, they date from the late 19th century to the 20th century. Though, currently, none are open, they indicate the wealth that was available in the area. Most were influenced by buildings in Istanbul, with a touch of Red Sea Roshan. After the government relocated its ministries into Riyadh from Jeddah, foreign embassies followed, around 1984, and Taif reduced in importance. Many major trading families relocated their operations to remain close to the government's operations.

Shubra Palace Regional Museum

The old palaces include the **Shubra Palace Regional Museum** (currently closed). This was built in 1905 by Sharif Ali bin Abdullah bin Muhammad bin Abdulmoein. He was the governor of Makkah under the Ottomans from 1905-1908, when he was replaced (by the Young Turks) and went into exile in British administered Cairo. After King AbdulAziz captured the Hijaz, this became his residence; later, it was King Faisal's when he visited Taif. The palace later became the headquarters of the Ministry of Defense and Aviation. In 1986, the palace was converted into a public museum with household goods, and archaeological displays. The building and its attractive interiors were possibly more appealing than the limited items on display. However, this may change with any reopening. Shubra Palace is north of central Taif on Shubra St just south of Al Jaish St.

Other palaces have not been open – but are probably owned by the state as they have been used by the government – so the increasing focus on tourism may make their opening possible. Their exteriors, which may be crumbling away, are visible. There are a few in a central location - **Kaki Palace** - on the roundabout on Souad bin Hamam St and Al Salamah Road in central Taif – west of the large Abdullah bin Abbas Mosque. This was built just before World War Two for the local Kaki family. West of Kaki Palace is - **Al Katab Palace**, Al Salamah St – west of Salamah Roundabout. This dates from the end of the 19th century & was for the secretary to one of the Sharifs. Later it was used by King Faisal and last used in 1968. North of Al Katab Palace is - **Al Dehlawi Palace**, set in a garden was built at the end on the 19th century by the Dehlawi brothers. West of Al Jaish Rd on Bin Al Nafis Rd. Slightly northwest of Al Dehlawi Palace is - **Mohammed Suroor Al Sabban Palace**, west of Al Jaish Rd on Bin Al Nafis Rd. This was built for the then Minister of Finance in 1927 using iron girders. It may open as a public property as there are moves to acquire it. In northeast Taif is **Jabra Palace** from the early 20th century & was used by King Saud in the mid-20th century. It's a drive of about 6km north-east from central Taif. northeast of Taif on Wadi Waj Rd – west of Airport Rd Route 267.

Abdullah bin Al Abbas Mosque. This mosque (no entry for non-Muslims), clad in cream brickwork, contains the grave of Abdullah bin Abbas (died AD687), a widely respected Islamic scholar. He was a cousin and companion of the Prophet Mohammed and ancestor of the Abbasid Caliphs. Several other graves of notable early Islamic personages are also within the mosque, including, it is said, a grandson of Prophet Mohammed - Mohammed bin Ali bin Abi Talib. There are other claimants to the location of his grave, including in Madinah 's cemetery next to the Prophets Mosque. Note that interest or veneration of specific graves is proscribed in Saudi Arabia. This mosque is in central Taif, on the junction of Abu Bakr As Siddiq and As Salamah roads.

North of the Abdullah bin Al Abbas Mosque is a pedestrian area of older shops and, above them apartments. This is Al Balad, a warren of small streets and alleyways. and during festivals these are decorated, drawing in the crowds. There are shops selling spices and traditional medicines, gold (in the northeast area). This is easy to explore as its, at most, only 500m end-to-end.

Tucked away off Highway 15 (M45) southeast of Taif (a 10km drive from Shubra Palace) is the small **Al Shareef Museum** +966555700008 16:00-22:00 SAR20. Founded at the turn of the millennium - in a recreated old house, this is among the nicer private museums in Saudi - though still a collection of quantity rather than quality and unsurprisingly without information. Here, there are old cars, weapons, carpets and cultural collections.

Damask Roses

In the south of Taif is **Al Ruddaf Park** Mon-Sat 16:00-01:00 – a 10km drive south of Taif east of Route 267 on Al Ruddaf St. This is an ornamental garden with a wide variety of areas to relax on the grass and picnic. The 'Season of Roses' previously Taif Rose Festival is held here from mid-March to mid-April.

The main town between Jeddah and Taif is **Al Hada**. – it's on Highway 80 (M50) 20km west of Taif. Here are a scattering of small family-run farms which grow Damask roses. The oil extracted from rose flowers creates a range of perfumed products. The roses flower in Al Hada and south of Taif at Ash Shafa areas from around late March to mid-April up to 50 days – it's a heat dependent harvest – the season is shorter with more heat. During the season when roses flower, the flower petals are collected at dawn and often late afternoon, before the fragrance has evaporated in the heat of the sun. There are over 900 small farms growing Damask roses. Some of these farms have shops - some have seasonally operating demonstrations and explanations perhaps – there are however around 70 operations that utilise & distil the flowers. The perfume oil is extracted after some 12 hours in a sealed steamer, a further process might be undertaken. The end result are 3 concentrates. rose water, concentrated rose water known as "brides water," and the most intense 'rose attar' oil.

Ahmed Al Sakhry Rose Factory +966505717999 is immediately south of Highway 15 (M45) in Al Hada, just east of the western Al Hada Ring Rd flyover. Sat-Thurs 09:00-21:00 – Fri closed - currently FOC - do buy a product. **Rashed Al Qurashi Factory** https://alqurashei.net Sat-Thurs 09:00-20:00 – Fri 14:00-21:00 from SAR50 in southern Al Hada just before the escarpment.

Al Kar Water Park www.TaifSama.com.sa Daily 10:30-21:30 This is a compact leisure area in Al Kar Tourist Village off the Al Kar-Al Hada Rd Highway 15 (M45), around 50km west of Taif (just before the ascent from Jeddah up to Taif). There are restaurants, various amusement arcades, sound & light, entertainment, cable cars, and water slides. The '**Telefric**' cable car 13:00-23:00 (over about 4kms long) SAR85 (it has been SAR110) ascends between here and the Ramada by Wyndham *** 1000meters above on the mountain escarpment. Tickets available in both locations at Al Hada in the car park in front of Ramada by Wyndham. The 4km is over the Jeddah-Taif highway, a rather disjointed trekking path & rugged mountains escarpment. The Al Kar Water Park has many special entrance offers, so check if one fits your requirements. Do review the health & safety of any activity you undertake – to see if it meets your expected standards.

Souq Okaz, to the north of Taif east of Highway 80 (M50) from Taif to Riyadh after about 50km drive. This has a substantial entertainment and cultural park. This area was a historic major market for 200 years from the beginning of the 6th centuryAD. Today, in what is said to be the same location, a 50-hectare festival is held annually for around 15 days from the end of June, open 16:00-23:00. Camel and Horse events are held along with historical re-enactments, poetry, Saudi restaurants, and general markets. Currently, a major development is being constructed at the site. About 10km drive south of Souq Okaz (on the service road immediately adjacent to it) is the ruined castle **Marwan Palace**. Possibly built by Othman bin Abdul Rahman Al-Madayfi during the First Saudi State (before 1818). It's an impressive, single story, stone built fortification, with accommodation inside for either soldiers or the ruler's family.

Robot Jockeys on Camels

In the same general area is **Taif Camel Racetrack**. Around 25km north of Souq Okaz off Highway 80 (M50) east on Route 4410 is where the Crown Prince Camel Festival is held from the middle of August to the end of September (generally with a break at the start of September) – check media for exact dates in the current year. Competitive events in various categories, special breeds, good looks and speed are held. The camel racetrack is north of Souq Okaz – east of the interchange of Highway 80 (M50) Taif-Riyadh & Routes 4410/4420 – some 55km from Taif.

~

ASH SHAFA / الشفا - GPS - 21.138322, 40.283103 - - IT'S A 40KM DRIVE ON Route 267 to the south of Shubra Palace. Ash Shafa is known, along with other areas around Taif, for Damask Rose cultivation - principally used for Rose Oil. The Damask Rose (Rosa damascena) is believed to have originated near the city of Damascus in Syria.

Roses may have first been grown in the area following the incorporation of Taif into the Ottoman Empire - the local variety is comparable to the Bulgarian "kazanlik" strain. When Swiss traveller Johann Ludwig Burckhardt visited in 1814, he noted "rose-buds, brought from the gardens of Taif. The people of the Hedjaz, especially the ladies, steep them in water, which they afterwards use for their ablutions; they also boil these roses with sugar, and make a conserve of them." Commercial rose oil distillation likely started in the late 19th or early 20th century as the region separated from the Ottoman's with their much larger production areas. By the 1920s, Taif was exporting rose oil to Europe. When Saudi Arabia formed in the mid 1930s, King AbdulAziz encouraged and supported the rose industry as a source of revenue for the kingdom. Today the extracts are used as perfume oil, rose water to wash in, and drink, as an addition for food flavour and a form of pot-pourri.

What's there - Al Shafa is an area with no significant individual attractions but plenty of appeal from its small agricultural villages - many having small farms growing roses. Some of these farms are open to visitors - they typically will have a retail outlet & distillation factory. It's a charming area to visit. As Al Shafa is not busy (except in the rose season, late March to mid-April and usual Saudi holidays) - a leisurely drive south from Taif is rewarding. Along Route 267 to Al Shafa village, there are side roads off to other smaller settlements, which will have small production & retails outlets for rose products.

Tola Al Ward Al Taifi

For example **Tola Al Ward Al Taifi** 08:00-20:00 daily in Al Qama village, about 35km drive south of Taif, with its picturesque shop in the front and distillation in the rear of the building. There are some excellent coffee shops in the area, making use of the weather & views over the open countryside though few reasonable restaurants. The accommodation in this area carries a premium cost and are generally small-scale. Carry on further south (44km from Shubra Palace) using Route 265, and the road leads to the local area's highest peak **Jabal Dakka** - at over 2550m. Look also for areas where Grapes, Pomegranates and Strawberries are grown.

~

TAIF'S RESTAURANTS & ACCOMMODATION

Taif has an excellent range of **restaurants** - a local dish is *Sleeq* (rice and meat); try at **Al Dakka Madghout** **+966532681988 Hassan Bin Thabit St (Highway 15/M45) 12:30-02:00. **Kinda Restaurant** ** +966920020296 Sat-Thurs 11:00-01:00 Friday 13:00-01:00 Okaz St – north of Central Taif - Levantine/Iraqi food. **Al Hadrami Kitchen and Restaurant** +966552267754 Daily 07:00-midnight Al Salamah St - Yemeni style food. **Khayal Restaurant** *** www.khayalrest.com/ Daily 08:00-11:30/12:30-midnight Tera Mall King Khalid St Levantine food. This is one of a small chain – with 2nd branch in Taif at Valley Centre, and also Jeddah, Yanbu, and Khamis Mushait.

   Taif Hotels in mid-summer have high prices - in winter, prices drop - **Al Wadaq**

Hotel ****+966127444450 Central Taif Al Barma bin Malek south of Wadi Waj Rd & Route 267. **Velar Inn** ***+966127517130 Northeast of Taif – a drive of 25km from the city centre on Airport Rd. **Iridium Hotel** **** https://iridium-hotel.com/ Central Taif south of Wadi Waj Rd east of the junction with Route 267. **Lavender Residential Apartments** ***+966127327070 Northwest central Taif on Al Kateeb Rd southwest of King Khalid Rd junction with Al Nazla St Sadeem Hotel Suites **+966127377777 North of the town centre on the junction of Shubra St. & Al Jaish St. **Ramada by Wyndham** Al Hada ** https://www.wyndhamhotels.com Encircled by a loop of Highway 15 (M45) on the escarpment at Al Hada. **Meridien Al Hada** ** www.marriott.com South of Highway 15 (M45) at Al Hada.

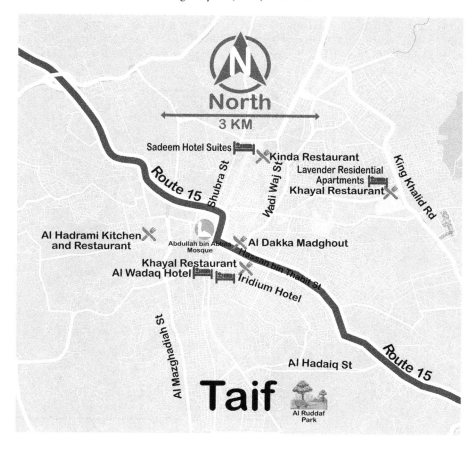

FESTIVALS IN TAIF INCLUDE - THE **CROWN PRINCE CAMEL FESTIVAL** - held in August at the track northeast of Taif off Highway 80 (M50) near Souq Okaz.

This covers the world of Camels, including racing, milking events, camel beauty events and more. **'Season of Roses'** - held here from mid-March to mid-April.

TAIF HAS A **LOCAL BUS SERVICE** OF 9 LINES. THE HUB IS JUST 100M BEHIND (northwest) of Abdullah bin Al Abbas Mosque These bus services extend to Shafa & Al Hada. Payment is through a plastic tap-and-go type card. This card is purchased for SAR10 on the bus or at a hub - and is then topped up on the bus for the fare. Fares are SAR3.45 per ride.

How to Get to Taif - Taif's airport has flights from Dammam, Jeddah, Riyadh and other local airports. Using Highway 80 (M50) from Jeddah, Taif is just under 200km away. Riyadh is around 900km on Highway 80 (M50), and Abha is less than 600km on Highway 15 (M45). SATRANS coach offers services from Jeddah, Riyadh, Madinah (via Jeddah), and Abha. For taxi – check out Uber.

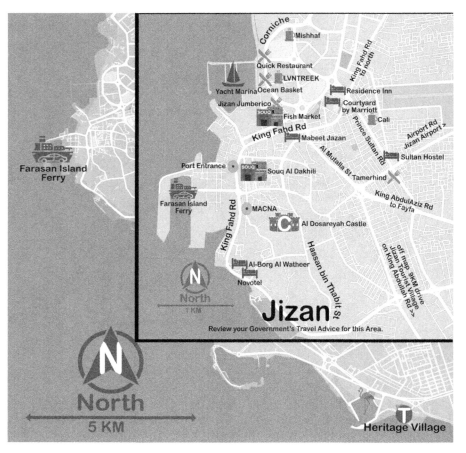

CHAPTER 40
JIZAN

Jizan جازان
16.887635, 42.544828 **Population** (appx) 173,919
A Brief History - For much of Jizan's history, it has been ruled by external powers, early rulers came from Yemen, Sabaeans, Minaeans, and Himyarites. The Aksum Kingdom, a powerful civilisation in present-day Ethiopia and Eritrea, expanded its influence over various regions along the Red Sea, including Jizan from AD525. King Khosrow I - the Sassanid ruler of Persia - sent a couple of sea-born armies at the request of Yemeni subjects of Aksum. The area and Western Yemen became a vassal kingdom from around AD570, though at times it was directly ruled by Persia.

From the death of the Prophet Mohammed, the region was incorporated into the Islamic Empire - though even from the start, it was a tenuous rule. In the turmoil of the Umayyad period Abdullah bin Al Zubayr bin Al Awwam took power over the Hijaz & Jizan, from 683-692AD. The Abbasid Caliph appointed Muhammad bin Ziyad as governor of Zabid in Yemen in 819AD, and his dynasty, the Ziyadid, ruled Jizan till around 1018AD. A series of petty rulers gained power until Egypt's Ayyubids ruled from 1174-1229, followed by Yemen's Rasulids from 1229-1454 and Yemen's Tahrids from 1454-1517 – and the Ottomans after they conquered Mamluk Egypt from 1517. Finally, the Yemeni Qasimids/Zaidis ruled from 1597–1872, after which the Ottomans retook power. In the early 20th century, the Idrisids, a local Arab dynasty, rose to prominence, gaining control over Jizan. The Idrisid rulers established their seat of power in Sabya until Jizan was incorporated into Saudi Arabia in 1934.

~

WHAT'S IN JIZAN – THE MOST SOUTHERLY TOWN IN SAUDI, JIZAN ISN'T full of attractions although it's a regional administrative centre– it's perhaps best to consider visiting it grouped with the Farasan Islands & Jabal Fayfa.

Al Dosariyah Castle Daily 15:00-22:00 FOC Off King Fahd Rd in the south of the city, is a small fort with a commanding location & great views over the sea and town. Explore the two floors and 4 corner gun towers. In origin, this square castle may be from around 1815, during the initial Egyptian campaign from 1811-1811 against the First Saudi State on behalf of the Ottoman Sultan. It was rebuilt in its current form after 1872, during the later 19th century Ottoman rule. Locally, it is also given an age of 500+ years, so may sit on an older building. Its name may come from the Arabic for a division of an army. Substantial repair work was carried out from 2020 in addition to earlier renovations from 2012 - so it's in nice condition. Al Dosariyah Castle is a focus for the Jizan Winter Festival (usually in January) and is largely an entertainment & leisure focus throughout the year for special events. Heritage Village Daily 17:00-23:00 FOC King Abdullah Rd.

Less than 15km southeast of Al Dosariyah Castle is a **Heritage Village**. This is a small area of modern reconstructions of the historic styles of Jizan's architecture. While somewhat glamorising the interiors, they give an idea of what life was like, before oil. There is an indication, in Arabic, of the governorates within the Jizan region and the building styles that were used. Traditional artefacts and costumes are in the houses. If you have time, this does make a good visit. It's quite popular in the evenings and weekends & the small souq adds to the appeal.

Jizan Winter Festival events are also held here. Just to its north & west are salt-water bodies with some mangroves - look for Flamingos, Crab Plovers, Common Snipe, Sandpiper, Indian House Crow, Indian Mynah (both these Indian species have spread around Arabia's coastline) Black Kite, Osprey. and so on.

East of the port in Jizan is **Souq Al Dakhili** - a low-cost general market over several streets, busiest in the evenings, especially at weekends. Here are traditional gold shops, selling elaborate gold jewellery. To see the wealth of Red Sea fish - head for the **fish souq** on the Kurnaysh - near the yacht marina & shopping malls. Here in the modern area, there is an extraordinary variety of fish sold. Among the varieties for sale are shark, tuna, hamour (grouper), parrot fish, crab, lobster and prawns and lots more. Check out the small kitchens - where fish that you have purchased can be cooked to order. Near is the fruit & vegetable market (and meat).

With its proximity to the Farasan Islands, Jizan offers **Scuba Diving** – Rubban Dive www.instagram.com/rubban.dive (+966 500018448) and Jizan Diver +966500660852 are perhaps the most established. However – research here https://swsdf.sa/

Jizan Winter Festival entertainers

JIZAN PLACES TO CONSIDER EATING IN & ACCOMMODATION

While you are in Jizan - see if the restaurant you choose has *Marsa* for dessert. It's a Jizan regional speciality with flour, bananas, honey and ghee (clarified butter) mashed together – a calorie rich dish. **Jumberico** * +966557987035 Daily 11:00-23:00 southwest of Al Jarir Bookstore – next to the Fish Market – Kurnaysh. It's not far from the sea – so the seafood here will, hopefully, be the 'catch of the day'. **Ocean Basket** ** +966173232685 Sat-Thurs 11:00-midnight Fri 13:00-01:00 west of Al Jarir Bookstore - next to the Marina again on the Kurnaysh; **Quick Restaurant** ** +966173170317 Daily 13:00-01:00 Kurnaysh – west of the car showrooms - is another seafood option. **Tamarind** ** https://tamarindjizan.com Tamarind Prince Sultan Rd is a mix of Indian and some Levantine & East Asian cuisine – all cooked Indian style for Saudi taste & hopefully yours. **Happy Hospitality Seafood Restaurant** **** +966557767712 Daily 13:30-midnight King Fahd Rd southern section south of the port. Seafood again – always worth having – immediately by the sea. Jizan also has a remarkable number of good coffee shops - look for **LVNTREEK** +966581887771 - 08:00-15:30/16:00-02:00 (Fri afternoon only), a stylish option with reasonable Pastries. **Cali** is another option (one of many, of course) +966555618494 is just east of Prince Sultan Rd. and is open 24 hours with a casual atmosphere - supposedly of California (a second branch is in the east of the town near the Airport).

Interior Jizan-Farasan Ferry

Mishhaf - +966557182871 Prince Abdullah Al Faisal Rd - not only coffee but also roasted beans - ask for Khawlani Coffee Beans, the UNESCO Intangible Heritage production.

Some Places to Stay In - Jizan has a nice range of hotels that make it a good base for journeys to Fayfa and the Farasan Islands. Check out **Mabeet Jizan** (OYO 295)* +9668008146590 King Fahd Rd; **Al Sultan Hostel** (a hotel) ** +966173111107 on Prince Sultan St, **Novotel** ** https://all.accor.com/ on King Fahd Rd. **Al Borg Al Watheer Hotel** ** http://alborghotel.com King Fahd Rd. **Residence Inn** (Marriott) and also separately **Courtyard by Marriott** *** https://www.marriott.com Prince Mohammed bin Nasser Rd**Getting There** Driving south on the coast from Jeddah - Jizan city is the farthest you can go - take Highway 5 (M55) for 720kms - it's a tedious drive, so take a few breaks. From Abha on Highways 10 (M90) & 5 (M55), it's just less than 220kms. Najran is less than 350km - taking Highway 15 (M45) out of Najran. SATRANS coach has services from Abha, Jeddah. The airport has flights from Dammam, Jeddah, and Riyadh. As with many cities away from Dammam, Jeddah and Riyadh - there are no local bus services and poor taxi options. This is another region where reviewing your country's travel advice is essential.

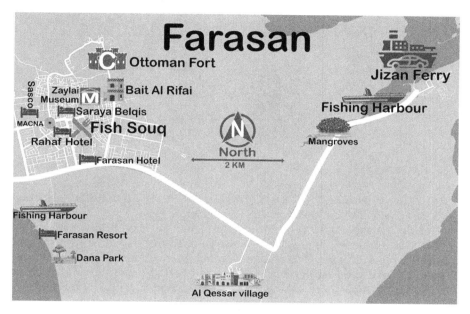

CHAPTER 41

AL FARASAN ISLANDS

A l Farasan Islands / الفرسان - GPS - Ferry 16.894246, 42.540260 - on Island 16.700892, 42.115859 **Population** (appx) 10,118

A Brief History - After the Roman occupation of Egypt & their later annexation of the Nabataean kingdom in AD106, under the Emperor Trajan, trade through the Red Sea increased. Rome typically stationed its military towards the Empire's frontiers. A base was established on the Farasan Islands by AD110 – also during the rule of Trajan. Indeed, various units of the Roman Legio VI Ferrata (6th Iron clad Legion) part of the standing army were deployed to the Farasan Islands before AD139 – probably under Emperor Hadrian (117-138). One important artefact from the islands is a Latin inscription dating from AD144, during the Roman Empire's control of the region. A detachment of Legio II Traiana Fortis (Trajan's 2nd Legion) also served on the islands. Support for this distant outpost might have originated from the port of Berenice in Egypt. In this period, the Roman Army was a professional force with legionaries serving up to 25 years (or longer). With other legions having served in Hegra – Rome was using a broad range of its military in Arabia. The Legio II had been based in the region for several decades - so perhaps the men had spent their careers in the Arab world. This small island outpost of Rome was, by far, the most distant garrisoned one in the entire Empire. The garrison must have monitored trade ships arriving from Southern Arabia & India. The sea route to India was critical as Rome & the Parthian and later Sasanian Empires of Persia were at war on a regular basis, making a land route between Rome & India impossible. An equivalent distance from Rome to the Farasan Islands would have given a Legion on Greenland or Nigeria.

Over a thousand years later, the Ottoman Sultan Selim I gained control of the Farasan Islands in 1517, incorporating them into the Ottoman province of the Hijaz. In 1901 – a coal storage depot was built by the Ottoman government on Qummah Island, off the main Farasan Island. It was intended for the exclusive use of the German Navy & is now known as the German House/Fort. The Ottoman Empire withdrew from the

Farasan Islands in 1916 after losing them to the British during World War One. Along with other areas of Jizan, they came under Idrisi rule until being annexed by Saudi Arabia in 1934.

Bait Al Rifai

What's in the Farasan Islands - The journey to the Farasan Islands by ferry takes around 90 minutes. Unless you wish to take a boat ride around the island and see all the limited number of sites, the time between the morning arrival and afternoon boat departure (say around 5 hours on the island – this schedule may change) is enough to do either boat or land sights - or quickly both. There are always informal 'taxi' services from the port to either take you into the main town (SAR30-45 - do negotiate the price) - or around the island (SAR300+).

In the centre of the main Farasan Island is a whitewashed **Ottoman Fort**, in reality little more than a small house, is on a low hill to the north of the main town. This might have originally been built in the mid-1800s. During the First World War – it was besieged by local inhabitants. Today its accessed by a flight of stairs to its south. Though, predictably, it's fenced off, you will also see a water well outside the fort.

Bait Al Rifai, on the northeast of the main town (800m south of the Ottoman Fort), is an old merchant's home – easily viewed. It has an elaborately decorated stucco-work entrance, very much influenced by North Indian Styles - and simple stained-glass windows, a Yemeni touch. Check the house on the other side of the road with its interesting interior.

Southwest of Al Rifai is **Zaylai Maritime Museum** +966507642762 SAR20 daily 16:00-20:00. It's piled high with seashells - but no information about them.

South of the main town is **Al Qessar village** (off Route 1910), with a small date palm oasis and many abandoned houses that have been partially restored. Of course, a key attraction to the island are the beaches and sea. **Dana Park**, on the beach southeast of the main town, is popular. Around the main island and **Sajid Island** to the northwest, by bridge, are attractive beaches and shallow warm seas. In the small harbour north of Dana Park, small **fibreglass fishing boats** (check regarding safety equipment & any insurance) can be hired for sightseeing. Try and negotiate the rate towards SAR200 per boat per hour - longer periods of course are possible. Opposite Dana Park, to the south) is **Qammah Island** - with the shell of the '**German Fort**'. If you are interested in **Scuba Diving** – a contact is JazanDiver@JazanDiver.net - again do research to see if their record and facilities fits your requirement. Always review safety standards with any 3rd party you choose to use, and that your own insurance covers you, as any insurance liabilities in Saudi Arabia are likely to differ from your own country's.

A **small fishing harbour** is near the ferry terminal - less than a kilometre walk. Here, boats are also available for hire. Negotiate regarding the cost etc, as above. In the north of the main island are mangroves; pink-backed Pelicans roost in them and swarm the harbour. Taking a boat from this harbour, offers proximity to the ferry, so you are less likely to miss its departure.

Harbour Farasan Islands

In the seas, you should be able to see Dolphins and both Green & Hawksbill Turtles. Birdwatchers should look for Crab Plover, Flamingos, Osprey, Saunders Little Tern, Sooty Falcon (in mid-summer), White-Eyed Gull.

There are Banks/ATMs in the main town. Here on the main west-east street is MACNA ferry office - however, if you book your return ticket in Jizan at the same time as the outward journey, there is no need to use the Farasan office.

∼

WHERE TO EAT & STAY - THERE ARE **SMALL CAFES** IN THE FARASAN TOWN centre on the principal west-east street. These come and go, but the central location makes any worthwhile looking at for breakfast. At lunch - try the **Fish Souq**. Buy a whole fish from one of the small shops selling fish and take it to a small cafe nearby to cook - (an additional charge of about SAR20 for cooking). Be clear (if possible) how you want it cooked. There are basic seats and tables outside.

Rahaf Hotel *+966173162000 in the centre of town opposite the Fish Souq. **Saraya Belqis** Apartments **+966555996562 in the town centre north of the Fish Souq. **Farasan Hotel** **+966173161166 South of Farasan Town - finally **Sasco Suite** **+966548003425 Centre of town about 700m northwest of Government Offices. **Farasan Resort** (previously Farasan Coral Resort) **+966173160000 southeast of Town overlooking Sea.

∼

GETTING TO THE FARASAN ISLANDS THE **FARASAN FERRY** LEAVES FROM Jizan at 07:00 & 15:30 (same time for the return from Farasan to Jizan – always double check timing for changes) - as a passenger arrive around 90 mins earlier (processing starts 1 hour before). Tickets are available at no cost both for passengers & vehicles from **MACNA** (Maritime Company For Navigation) (05:45-19:30 daily) +966173340227 on King Fahd Rd opposite the port in Jizan. Passports are required to make a passenger booking - and full vehicle documentation for vehicles (with specific permission from the vehicle owner to use the ferry). If taking a vehicle, be prepared to book in person, several days in advance - and arrive about 120 minutes beforehand and join the queue. There is limited parking in front of the terminal (if you do not take your car on the ferry) - or a 1500m walk from the public free car park (there is no security) next to MACNA in Jizan. In the ferry terminal there are passport & security checks. The ferries are fast and modern - with cafe & sex-segregated seating – women in front. Check all details with MACNA as changes are possible.

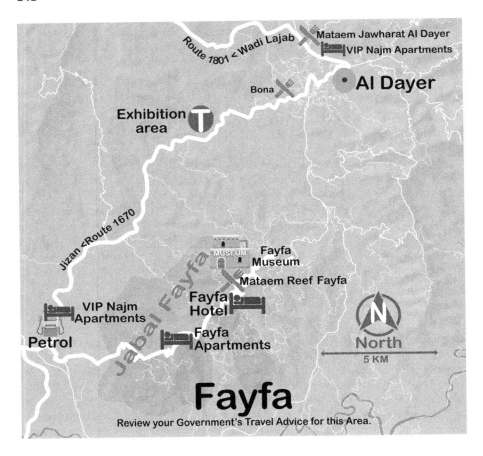

Review your Government's Travel Advice for this Area.

CHAPTER 42

JABAL FAYFA

J abal Fayfa / جبال فيفاء - GPS - 17.234605, 43.066184
What is There - **Jabal Fayfa** (Faifa, Fiyfai etc) is a remarkable mountain. With a distinct separation from its surrounds, this igneous rock massif rises to at least 1770m in its northwest, which is perhaps 1300m above the valleys - the mountain is only about 10km long. On a clear day, its peak offers extensive views including, looking south, over the Yemen border about 10km away. The surrounding mountains create a crescent from the north & Abha through the east to the south and peak at about 3,000M - it can be an incredible sight if there is no haze. Look for mini-versions of cable-cars, there are used to transport good between road and house. Search out the small **Fayfa Museum**+966501479232 Sat-Thurs 08:30-17:30 high on the slopes near the summit about 200m northwest of the local hospital. Here are cultural artefacts owned by Hussain Al Fayfa - in a building within a beautiful setting. The mountain slopes have extensive, terraced fields that cascade down from small villages on the various peaks. Small paths, many are public, meander through the farms, which are private.

Crops grown include Coffee - & fruit trees. Most months have rain, especially July-December. Temperatures in the day may range from 22-37c. Native flora includes Rosa abyssinica and Juniperus procera (on the peaks). You may see Baboon, Bruce's Green-Pigeon, Grey-headed Kingfisher, African Paradise-Flycatcher, Sunbird (Nile Valley/Palestine/Shining) & Ruppell's Weaver.

The tarmac roads are narrow and steep (driving hints Page38), with little room for passing on most roads. It's polite to park away from homes - and walk, enjoying the extraordinary scenery.

Jabal Fayfa

The attractions of the general area that includes Fayfa, Ad Dayer & Bani Malek are nature, intangible culture and scenery. Part of the culture is that the men wear garlands of fragrant flowers on their head. Simple ones may suffice for a weekend - more elaborate for weddings and Eids. Basil and Jasmin add fragrance, and Marigolds and other seasonal flowers give colour. This distinctive style is used in the area below the escarpment - from Fayfa north to Rijal Al Maa.

Fresh Coffee Beans

The small coffee farms, increasingly produce Khawlani coffee beans, a UNESCO intangible cultural heritage item. At Ad Dayer on Route 1670, 5km west of the town, is the **Open-air Exhibition Ground** for Coffee Fairs and more - with cultural displays and coffee beans for sale - see media for its random date, sometime in February or March. Jizan province is by far the largest producer of coffee beans in Saudi.

Places to Eat in & Accommodation - in the general area.

There are some small **restaurants** around Jabal Fayfa's summit. All are simple - search out **Mataem Reef Fayfa** +966532392469 (05:30-22:00) with its cream and maroon front.

As could be expected – it offers a southwestern Saudi/Yemeni cuisine. Alternatively at the '**Fayfa Hotel**' (below) there is open-air dining on its roof terrace – at a premium price, like the hotel. In Al Dayer, there are many options, particularly fast-food ones along the main road, especially at the junction of Routes 1801 & 1672. Look for **Mataem Jawharat Al Dayer** * +966558418944 (07:00-23:00) Saudi/Yemeni style rice and meat - on Route 1801 just over 2km north of the junction with Route 1672. Near the Petrol Station west of that junction, behind the Police Station on Route 1672, is **Bona***+966551614160 - 16:00-01:00 a local fast-food option with a good choice including Shawarma. There are small grocery shops in Fayfa - whose choice isn't great - but will include bottled water and snacks.

Coffee Beans from Jizan

There is **accommodation** on the mountain - priced well above comparable accommodation elsewhere. In Fayfa - **Fayfa Hotel** ***+966539176134 near the village & Police Station on the summit. **Fayfa Apartments** **+966555769936 on the road up to the summit; alternatively at the mountain's base **VIP Najm Apartments*** +966557370003 on Route 1670 near a petrol station at the suggested route up to Fayfa and in Al Dayer **Shaqaq Qimat Al Dayer*** +966555099031 on Route 1801 just north of its junction with Route 1672.

❧

GETTING THERE - A GOOD ROUTE UP TO FAYFA IS FROM ROUTE 1670 (THE Ad Dayer - Jizan road) and near an obvious turn about 19km east of Ad Dayer in a collection of roadside services - with the hotel VIP Najm Apartments (above), petrol and ATM - follow the route which has the shrubs & trees on its central divider. Other routes are less well maintained and may be washed away after heavy rains - take the same route down. The roads in the mountain are narrow, and near the village at the summit, parking is at a premium, try and park away from a person's home. A route between Jizan and Najran passes along the base of the mountain here.

CHAPTER 43
WADI LAJIB

Wadi Lajib / وادي لجب - GPS - 17.591709, 42.928367 The entrance to Wadi Lajab near **Khatwat Al Ain** village is marked by a small supermarket near the wadi's entrance. The wadi, which is initially a narrow, very deep, slot canyon, becomes a tributary to Wadi Baish, which after meandering for some 100kms through igneous mountains, feeds Wadi Baish Dam and on through Baish to the Red Sea, 20kms north of Jazan City. Along this route are small settlements, and isolated housing which are a world away from the opulence of areas in Jeddah or Riyadh.

Wadi Lajab's entrance is dramatic - its sheer cliffs towering above the rough track, with running water along the way, and a mix of trees and beautiful pink, but poisonous, oleander. In places, ferns run up the cliff face. It's possible to drive (4x4 suggested) into the wadi for around 3kms to near a small, elevated picnic location, unless heavy rains have washed the track away. The wadi splits - and through both sections are pools with small fish. Parts of the wadi look like a jungle; it's unexpected and very attractive. Walking into the wadi offers an alternative way to be awed by the scenery, and might save your vehicle from grounding on rocks. The wadi is narrow – with cliffs a couple of hundred meters high and boulders from rock falls embedded along the way. In places, the track is only wide enough for a single vehicle - a death trap when water thunders through, so avoid it when rain is forecast.

～

To get into Wadi Lajab - take Route 158, which leads off Route 1801 from Ad Dayer (Bani Malik) or Jabal Fayfa. The drive is around 60km from Ad Dayer. The road runs through fascinating countryside - and several uniformed security checkpoints. Wadi Lajab is also on a route between Jizan and Najran.

Car driving through Wadi Lajab

CHAPTER 44

THE COASTAL ROAD - HIGHWAY 5 (M55) SOUTH OF JEDDAH

A l Qunfudhah, Al Birk & Jizan are in the southern Tihamah plain. This is a potentially fertile outwash from the Hijaz Mountains. The plain stretches north past Yanbu. Despite its potential – lack of regular rain and a debilitating combination of heat, humidity and malaria has meant that, historically, it has had a low population density.

Al Qunfudhah / القنفذة - GPS - 19.123876, 41.095413 **A Brief Histo**ry - Qunfudhah was a key harbour in Mohammed Ali Pasha's conquest of the 1st Saudi State in 1814. It was governed by Tami bin Shoaib on behalf of the Al Saud at Diriyah, as he had taken the Tihamah coast for the Al Saud. The town was secured by the Egyptian forces and then retaken by Tami bin Shoaib. Early the following year, Qunfudhah was retaken by Pasha's forces. Following the late 19th century war by Italy against Ethiopia and the Italian occupation of Eritrea in 1889, the Italians were increasing their forces in the region. In 1912, an Italian fleet of 5 ships - chased an Ottoman fleet of 8 ships off Qunfudhah. Three Ottoman ships were attacked and sank, and three ran aground. It was a short part of the 1911-1912 Italian-Ottoman War.

What's There - There isn't much to see in Al Qunfudhah. The **Wadi Qanuna** east of the town has some small-scale Mango tree farming. Off the coast are shallow shoals. In town, if you wish to break the journey, there are several hotels. **Sama Beach Apartments** *are worth considering +966507007874 in the town's south off Highway 5 (M55) & southwest of Bander shopping Mall. A larger alternative **Al Azhar Palace Hotel** overlooking the sea ** +966177333770. Along King AbdulAziz Rd that runs from Highway 5 (M55), there is a selection of coffee shops & fast food, including **Al Baik** (found in most larger towns). Directly on the seafront, just south of King AbdulAziz Rd, is 'The Sailor Qadora Seafood' *** +966535529552

Getting there Al Qunfudhah is the largest town on Highway 5 (M55) between Jeddah and Jizan and, conveniently, it's about halfway - about 370km from Jeddah and 350km from Jizan.

Al Birk / البرك - GPS - 18.225177, 41.535697

What's There - The Al Birk coast is a lagoon environment with large areas of mangroves. Igneous rock hills meet the beach, adding variety. South of Al Birk, the highway is bridged over **Wadi Dhahban**. Inside the shallow wadi, cultivated Date Palms, large areas of Doum Palms and dense vegetation up the wadi attract birds. Farther along the valley, troops of Baboons (Page281) come down to feed - they use the water dam about 7km upstream and overnight in the surrounding mountains. In the centre of town, directly on Highway 55, the petrol station has a good range of places to eat.

Camels on Tihamah plain

Getting There - Using Highway 5 (M55) - Al Birk is about 500km south of Jeddah - and 230km north of Jizan. It's a tedious drive - along a flat coastal plain with the towns offering little interest or amenities. However, there are kilometres of empty beaches stretching away from the towns.

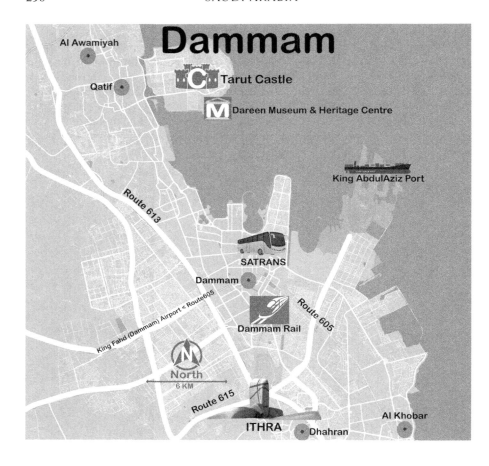

CHAPTER 45
DAMMAM, DHAHRAN AND AL KHOBAR

D ammam / الدمام Dhahran and Al Khobar - GPS - 26.456105, 50.106215 **Population** (appx) 1,386,166 **A Quick Overview Of The Geology** - Eastern Saudi Arabia is essential to the country's wealth. The first oil found in Saudi Arabia was at the Dammam Dome, a salt dome rising to less than 100m above sea level. Salt domes are a critical component of many oil fields. Over aeons, evaporating saltwater left behind vast salt basins, which were overlain by rock layers, such as limestone and other sediments, including oil. As salt is lighter than the overlaying rocks, faults in the rocks may allow a vast column of salt to rise, creating a salt dome. Oil is held in porous rock, in much the same way as water is held in a sponge. Given the right conditions with porous rocks, oil becomes concentrated by these movements into fields. Saudi Arabia's oil is associated with a series of salt domes and anticlines (dome-shaped uplifts) associated with salt basins. The basement rocks here are dated to Carboniferous time, about 320 million years ago. The rock that holds the oil is very porous - over 30% in places. Kimmeridgian age limestone (152.1-157.3 million years ago) is a crucial oil-bearing formation from the late Jurassic epoch. Overlaying them is rock of the Palaeocene 66 to 56 million years ago, lower & middle Eocene period (56-38 million) and finally from the Quaternary from 2.588 million years ago until modern times.

Coastal East Saudi Arabia is low-lying, with fine sand beaches made from lime and coral sand. Large areas of sabkha can often be found behind any coastal dunes. Sabkhas are flat areas created from evaporating water, which leaves behind a mixture of salts, gypsum, mud, and sand. When there is an increase in water saturation, these areas may become quicksand.

A BRIEF HISTORY - IN 1922, AMIR ABDULAZIZ BIN ABDULRAHMAN AL Saud met a New Zealand mining engineer, Major Frank Holmes and eventually agreed a vast oil exploration concession with him. By 1932, Holmes had defaulted on payments.

The 930,000sq km concession was then obtained by Standard Oil Company (California) (SOCAL) for 60 years in 1933, and exploration took place for oil. On 3 March 1938, oil was found near an area called Dammam. The first oil tanker was loaded on 1 May 1939 and sailed from Ras Tanura, north of Dammam. Today, Saudi Arabia's oil industry has most of its oil fields within 200kms of that original oil discovery.

The oil industry is the raison d'etre of the conurbation made up of Dammam, Dhahran and Al Khobar. Seaports developed in tandem with the oil industry. From the first jetty at Ras Tanura, the Dhahran Air Base opened to civilian transport in the 1950s, with the terminal opening in 1962. The rail line out of Dammam opened in 1951.

DHAHRAN

Dhahran / الظهران - GPS - 26.335402, 50.121009

What's There – Dhahran has one of the most rewarding places to visit in Eastern Saudi Arabia, possibly in the entire country.

ITRHA

ITHRA, King AbdulAziz Centre for World Culture www.ithra.com/ 09:00-23:00 Monday – Thursday & Saturday; 16:00-23:00 Friday closed Sunday SAR35 (per exhibition - previously SAR50 - so be prepared if it changes again) at least smart casual clothing required. Established by Saudi ARAMCO, the 90% government-owned oil & gas giant, in 2016, ITHRA focuses on culture & general civilisation. This dramatic complex was designed by the Norwegian architects Snohetta.

Interior ITHRA

Its silver cladding is intended to reflect its environment and is based on the salt dome structures common where oil is found. Designed to represent the future rising, the present spread over the ground and below ground, the past. In the evening a light show plays on the surface. ITHRA houses museum space, a library, a theatre and a cinema. The **Main Museum** focus of the four galleries is on Islamic Civilisation, the

Natural History of Arabia, Saudi Culture and Heritage & Modern Regional Art. There is a comprehensive, effective use of multi-media – in Arabic & English. A secondary **Children's Museum** has a hands-on 'Eco-lab', Islamic arts, Culture and a participatory Performing Arts unit. Illustrating the rapid cultural changes the country is currently undergoing, the cinema showcases local productions.

The building is as striking inside as outside, with the 'Great Hall' literally a highlight - the elevators up to the **Library** give an impression of scale. A small coffee shop and, separately, a Mediterranean cuisine restaurant are on-site. Within the same grounds (a 5-minute walk away) is the **Saudi ARAMCO Energy Exhibit** (same timings). Not unexpectedly, this gives an overview of oil, from its creation, extraction and use, wrapped in the history of ARAMCO. Though out of the way, this entire complex is must-see. It gives an engaging and comprehensive overview of Saudi Arabia, as it wants to be seen today. A visit will give useful background, irrespective of the purpose of your visit into Saudi Arabia. There is no public transport to this key complex, though this may change as the Dammam public bus operation only started at the end of 2022, so it may be extended to ITHRA - however, for now, use Uber.

THE COAST OF **DAMMAM** HAS EXTENSIVE AREAS OF LAND RECLAIMED FROM the sea. SAPTCO Bus Station & **Marina Mall** +966138099966 10:00-midnight Sun-Thurs Fri 14:00-midnight Sat 09:00-midnight are both on 11th St. North of them in a reclaimed peninsula is King Abdullah bin Abdulaziz Road. Along its length are a number of current and future attractions.

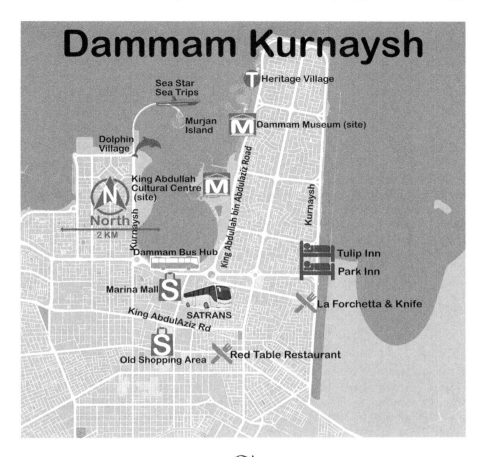

ON THE RECLAIMED PENINSULA

Heritage Village https://heritage-village.com.sa/ midday-midnight - a recreated fortification of central Saudi Arabia. Inside, it's a mix of a museum/exhibition, a Saudi-themed gift shop and a restaurant *** serving Middle East cuisine. To its south is what may open as **Dammam Regional Museum**. This museum has stalled in its construction and is awaiting completion - increased oil revenue will hopefully kick-start development. Farther south, yet another complex awaiting finishing is the **King Abdullah Cultural Centre**. In the evenings, the area of King Abdullah bin Abdulaziz Rd is busy with families having picnics - there are also several places to eat. West of this area, across the bay, are **Marjan Island** (Coral Island). This is not an island, but rather a terminus for a walk or a drive (there is limited car parking). Along the way are leisure areas – including **Dolphin Village** +966551367211 Daily 15:00-22:00 (closed Sunday) with performances by dolphins and other captured animals. On this peninsula are **Sea Star** (Dreamboats) +966558500460 Daily 13:00-21:00 SAR80 upwards for sea trips in the general Dammam area. Further west is **Water Island** +966502175217 Thurs-Sat (only) 16:00-21:00 SAR115. Here is a local water park. It's good for families, though it's not especially up-to-date.

Just over a kilometre south of Marina Mall is the original '**Old Shopping Area**' in Dammam - south of King AbdulAziz Rd. Here in the network of streets are shops selling mobile phones, cheap electronics, gold jewellery, clothing and lots more.

≈

Al Khobar

The seafront of **Al Khobar** is Prince Turki St / Kurnaysh which is also substantially in-filled, reclaimed land as with the Dammam area. The coastline has been pushed east by several hundred meters. This new land has, recently, largely been used to create parks and leisure areas. On the town side of Al Khobar, a continual stretch of shops, supermarkets, and restaurants faces the seafront. If you are travelling with children, **SCITECH** https://scitech.sa/en/on the northern Kurnaysh in Al Khobar daily from 09:00-midday 16:00-22:00 (Friday afternoon only) Adults from SAR23 - Children from SAR17.25 - it's worth visiting. The museum covers a broad range of science - in 6 themed areas - with some interactive exhibits. Less than 10km south of the Kurnaysh of Al Khobar is the **King Fahd Causeway** to Bahrain, which, as a result, is a security area.

≈

Restaurants & Accommodation - The Dammam area has a similar range of restaurants as Jeddah and Riyadh – and like them, these are generally better than elsewhere in Saudi. The **Pantry Restaurant** **+966138584338 Daily 08:00-midnight Off King Salman bin Abdulaziz Rd north Al Khobar – a broad International cuisine **Ninar Restaurant** *** http://ninar.online/ Daily – midday-midnight Junction 10th St & Makkah Al Mukarramah St Al Aqrabiyah – west Al Khobar. A bright, airy dining experience – with a modern take on Levantine food – worth searching out. **Al Hijaz Al Bukhari Restaurant** **+966501200672 Sat – Thurs 12:30-midnight Fri 13:00-midnight Junction 1st St & Prince Saad St about 300m northwest of Al Khobar Kurnaysh bus station. It has rice and meat-based food. There are a couple of other restaurants with the same name in Al Khobar – all are similar in all respects. **Red Table Restaurant** **+966532250191 Daily 07:00-midnight King Khalid Rd central Dammam – broadly a North Indian restaurant. **La Forchetta & Knife Restaurant** ***+966598090443 Daily – midday-midnight Al Ashriah St Dammam; an Italian restaurant.

Dammam's area has a good range of hotels - options include - **Holiday Al Khaleej** **+966537466444 Southwest Al Khobar King Khalid Rd. **Le Meridien** **** https://www.marriott.com Southern Kurnaysh Al Khobar. **Sofitel Al Khobar** *** https://all.accor.com/ Southern Kurnaysh Al Khobar; **The Address Palace** ***+966552555857 Abdulrahman bin Awf St; **Tulip Inn** **+966138548585/551015905 Foudalah bin Obaid St; **Park Inn** *** www.radissonhotels.com Foudalah bin Obaid St Masajah House * (was Marina

Apartments)+966500992078 Waqidi St west of 11th St. In the same area are many other similar hotels.

Also south of Al Khobar is the **Dana Beach Resort** - Page23

≈

GETTING THERE THE DAMMAM, DHAHRAN AND AL KHOBAR conurbation - along with Tarout and Qatif are served by King Fahd International Airport https://kfia.gov.sa/. This has both international arrivals from Europe, Asia and other Gulf states - as well as domestic ones from Jeddah, Riyadh and more. SATRANS coach https://satrans.com.sa/ may operate into Dammam and Al Khobar from the airport (SAPTCO used to) - along with Uber. SAR Train services www.sar.com.sa arrive from Riyadh via AlAhsa to the station south of King Fahd bin Abdulaziz Rd (use Uber for local transport).

Road connections include from Bahrain using the King Fahd Causeway (Highway 80/M50) - about 80km and allow at least 2 hours (if you already have a Saudi eVisa) to include immigration (and emigration from Bahrain) formalities, Kuwait through Route 7905/Highway95(M5), Qatar & the UAE also via Route 7905/Highway95 (M5). Oman using the Rub Al Khali desert Highway95 (M5). Riyadh has an express road, Highway 80 (M50)- around 410 km. Finally, AlAhsa is connected by Route 615 - about 150km. SATRANS coach (it was SAPTCO) has a principal long-distance coach station in Dammam south of the Kurnaysh (Corniche) on 11th St. Services are direct to AlAhsa, Riyadh (just under 7 hours) and other cities via Riyadh. SAPTCO International buses run between Dammam & Bahrain and Dammam & Abu Dhabi and other UAE cities.

There are **local bus services** in Dammam, Dhahran and Al Khobar conurbation. With a hub in Dammam on the Gulf (Khaleej) Rd just north of the main Dammam Bus Hub (the local SAPTCO bus station) and Marina Mall, and in Al Khobar west of the Kurnaysh near Al Rahmaniya Centre on Custodian of the Two Mosques Rd. The local services are limited in extent - but do include Tarout Island - but not ITHRA. A card is SAR10 to buy and needs to be loaded with money to travel - it's available on the bus. It's a tap-and-go system with a single journey SAR3.45. UBER and other app-based taxi services are available within the conurbation and AlAhsa. If travelling within Eastern Saudi Arabia area – check your own government's travel advice for the region Page22.

To the north of Al Khobar, Dammam & Dhahran are the towns of Qatif (often historically Katif correctly Al Qatif) & Tarout. Tarout is the historic port island of Qatif, and both are accessed via Route 613. North of Qatif is the area of Al Awamiyah (Page22).

CHAPTER 46
TAROUT

Tarout / تاروت - GPS - 26.569816, 50.065816 **Population** (appx) 117,646 **A Short History** - Archaeological excavations suggest occupation 7,000ya. Finds include pottery from 4500BC, statues from 2700BC, and Jemdet Nasr pottery (3100-2900BC). It was from this later period that the half-life-sized human statue, the 'Worshiping Servant' statue, was excavated in Tarout (now in National Museum Riyadh). It's probable that in the 3rd millennium, Dilmun (an east Arabian civilisation from the late 4th millennium to the mid-1st millennium) originally grew in the Tarout area. The epicentre of Dilmun seems to have shifted to Bahrain from around 2200BC - possibly as a refuge from conflict. Seleucid period (312–64 BCE) cemeteries are on the coast. An alternative name in the early & late Middle Ages for Tarout had been Darin. The current fort in the island's centre was originally built during the Portuguese period (1505-1622). Next to the fort is a 'hammam' based on a water spring. It was a centre of pearl diving in the late 19th century until the collapse of the natural pearl industry in the 1930s.

What to see –

Tarout Island is just off the east coast of Saudi Arabia near Qatif. It is a low-lying island, with a small date plantation in the north and extensive mangrove and sea grass beyond that. Access is via 3 roads from Qatif's Gulf Rd. There has been a range of archaeological finds in Tarout, including a coffin with statues for legs. Inside were the remains of a pre-teen girl who was covered in a gold mask, coins and jewellery. It's now in the National Museum in Riyadh.

In the centre of the island is **Tarout Castle** 26.569488, 50.065571. This location's human occupation may date to the Neo-lithic period, with worked flint found; certainly to 3rd MilleniumBC as Geoffrey Bibby found 'Barbar' period pottery (broadly 3,000-2,000BC) from here – a period within the Dilmun civilisation. A possible temple to the Goddess Ishtar has been excavated near here. A subsequent fort may have been built before AD1200. The current partially restored castle dates to the initial

Portuguese occupation between 1515-1521AD. Its relatively small size is determined by the hill's size. Three of the original four towers still stand. The Ottomans may have attacked the fort in 1552 and Portugal finally abandoned it in 1602 after the Persian capture of Bahrain. At the western tower is the original water spring. The island & castle were occupied by the Al Khalifa Sheikhs from Bahrain in 1834, and the Ottoman's administered the island from either AlAhsa or Basra, depending on their hold on AlAhsa, from 1871-1912. Around the castle is the old settlement with Al Dirah immediately east of the original settlement. Originally, a Date Oasis surrounded this settlement.

Tarout Castle

Dareen Museum & Heritage Centre (bin Ali Historic Home) is in the southeast of Tarout is 26.543921, 50.076521 SAR30 Sun-Thurs 09:00-12:00 16:00-20:00 +966 54 446 8286. This is a small private museum in an authentic house with a Dhow, cultural displays and photographs. To the museum's southeast are the ruins of **Mohammed bin Abdulwahab Al Fayhani Palace** (Castle), originally dated to the 16th and rebuilt by Mohammed Al Fayhani, a pearl merchant. It was initially immediately on the sea; however, a road and public park have been created on reclaimed land from the sea. Little of old Qatif survives, with Castle Sq occupying the original location of the original citadel that was the core of the town. A few old houses are to its southwest and northwest on King AbdulAziz Rd.

~

OPTIONS FOR FOOD IN TAROUT
Near the castle is -'**Tarout Castle Traditional Coffee Shop**' with a simple selection of drinks and food. **Smoke Valley Restaurant** ***+966566963351 Daily

18:00-midnight Abdullah bin Al Harith St southwest Tarout Island – an American style steak restaurant. **Amchit Restaurant** **+966538432806 Daily 16:00-midnight Al Rahma St Tarout Island. Levantine food with a modern take. **Mataem Aswar Al Deyrah** **+966591749977 Daily 11:30-23:00 Al Hassan bin Ali St Tarout Island – a mix of cuisine leaning towards Saudi.

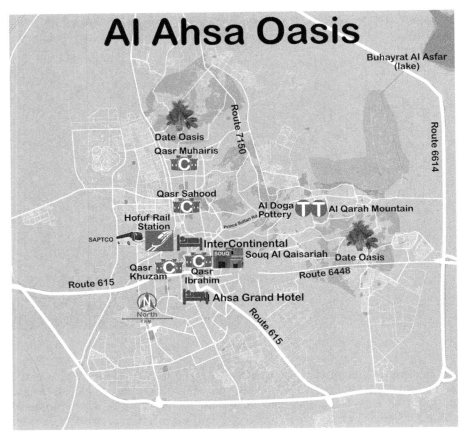

CHAPTER 47
ALAHSA

A lAhsa / الاحساء - GPS - 25.376395, 49.588944 **Population** (appx) 430,105
A Simple History - The human history of the AlAhsa oasis starts at least from 6000BC. The Neolithic settlement at Ain-Qinas has Obeid (5500-4000BC) pottery and even a pre-ceramic settlement period. From this period, the oasis has had continual settlement.

The oasis water from a near-surface aquifer was the essential element for AlAhsa's growth. However, other key elements were needed to boost the success of AlAhsa. The second element was the oasis cultivation of the Date Palm in Arabia, from around 3000BC. Phoenix dactylifera, the cultivated Date Palm, is a domesticated crop, much as wheat or maize, though wild dates were consumed in Arabia from 200,000 years ago. The date's fruit needs the heat of the desert to ripen and also regular irrigation, in AlAhsa water is supplied by the aquifer. AlAhsa was mentioned by Greek and Latin authors as the largest and richest centre of production of dates in the world. The third element in the growth of AlAhsa was the domestication of the camel, Camelus dromedarius. This animal, is only a domestic species. It's one of the key transport animals of world history, and of course, used for meat, milk, leather and so on.

Following the spread of Islam in Arabia, Al-Ahsa Oasis became the political centre of Eastern Arabia. This focus increased when Baghdad became the Abbasid capital from AD750. This capital's location increased trade up The Gulf and through eastern Arabia. The Qarmatian State (894–1067) was based in AlAhsa, once again increasing the trade into the oasis. Several local dynasties (Uyunids, Usfurids, and Jabrids) followed until 1550 - when the Ottomans occupied the area after their 1534 capture of Baghdad. It's from this time that AlAhsa's current forts started construction. In the early 1790s, the First Saudi state defeated the then rulers, the Bani Khalid. Since then, the Al Saud have been pre-eminent in the region, despite any short interruptions by armies from Egypt.

What's to Find - AlAhsa (often Al Hasa and frequently given the name of its largest town, Hofuf, where Qasr Ibrahim is located) is an increasingly sprawling urban area, which includes what is probably the largest date oasis in the world.

Souq Al Qaisariah

Souq Al Qaisariah (the name is taken from Qasr – the Arabic for a palace – referring to Qasr Ibrahim), is a renovated covered market in the Hofuf area. It has numerous small, local shops selling a wide variety of goods besides the one-way central portion of King AbdulAziz Rd. Expect the core souq's opening hours to be 09:00-midday / 16:00-22:00; individual shops will vary. Shops are aimed at the local market & include traditional men's clothing, footwear and head-dress. In origin, the souq probably dates from the early 19th with additional renovation work since, especially after a major fire in 2001. As with most leisure places in Saudi Arabia, Souq Al Qaisariah is busy with shoppers in the evenings and the weekends. During festivals, this section of King AbdulAziz Rd will probably be closed to traffic with activities and extra stalls.

Behind Souq Al Qaisariah, to the east, is **Al Rafaa district**, a jumble of older housing and more retail businesses.

Taking an anticlockwise walk around the core of Hofuf. Opposite Al Qaisariah Souq, on the other side of King AbdulAziz Rd, is a **row of shops** comparable in style, but not scale, to Al Qaisariah Souq. Behind this range of shop is an extensive area of older housing, **Al Koot**. Again, this is a mix of residential and commercial buildings.

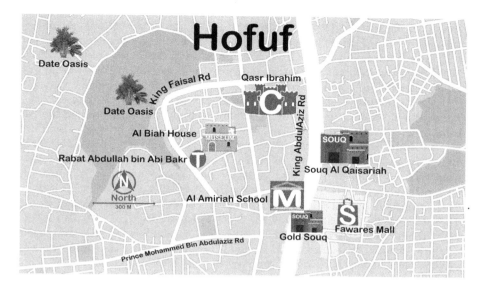

In the northern section of Al Koot is **Qasr Ibrahim** (Ibrahim Palace, previously Al Koot Fort) currently undergoing restoration it was previously open Sun-Thurs 08:00-16:00 Fri 16:00-20:00 Sat 09:00-13:00. Its far less than a kilometre walk from Al Qaisariah Souq. Qasr Ibrahim is essentially a fortified walled courtyard with bastions to allow large numbers of people to gain security in times of strife. The original is from the Ottoman period, built in about 1556. However, its establishment may date to a slightly earlier Arab construction. It was occupied by Abdulrahman bin Faisal bin Turki Al Saud (1889–1891) towards the end of his short rule. It includes a small mosque and Turkish 'hammam' while within the exterior walling are accommodation and administration rooms. A water well in the western walls completes the facilities. Occasional events have been held within the palace - when renovations are complete, look for regular events.

Saudi men Hofuf

Southwest of Qasr Ibrahim (about a 500m walk) is **Al Biah House** / Al Mullah

House Sat-Thurs 08:00-16:00 currently FOC. It was built around 1788 by Sheikh Abdulrahman Al Mullah, a judge during the First Saudi State. Its prominence arose as it was where Amir AbdulAziz bin Abdulrahman Al Saud stayed and received the local population's allegiance (Al Biah) after his occupation of the oasis in 1913. The house is a fairly typical Gulf courtyard house for the wealthy, with lime-plastered walls with some gypsum decoration. Open as a museum, there are a few artefacts to add ambience. To the west of the museum is an area of traditional housing. **Rabat Abdullah bin Abi Bakr**, is about 100m west of Al Biah House. It has irregular opening hours Built by a member of the Al Mullah family, this is an accommodation building built around 1863 for students coming to AlAhsa to study religion. The spacious rooms have been sympathetically restored. Along with Al Biah House, this is an interesting insight into housing for the wealthy in the region before the modern era.

Al Amiriyah School east of King Khalid Rd – about 4 or 500m walk southeast of Al Biah House - or 300m southwest of Al Qaisariah Souq - Tues-Weds 08:00-11:00/16:00-21:00 Thurs-Sat 16:00-00-21:00 FOC. This is the original government school in AlAhsa, now open as an occasional exhibition space cum museum. The whitewashed building is charming, with a courtyard flanked by a polylobate arched arcade. Inside, some rooms have photos and artefacts – it's worth a stroll around – especially as occasionally there are events in-house.

Al Amiriyah School,

In the far southwest, from Al Amiriyah School, is **Qasr Khuzam** (Khuzam Palace), a couple of kilometres southwest of Al Qaisariah Souq Sun-Thurs 09:00-17:00 (closed at the weekend) FOC. This is a simple, square military fort southwest of the main date oasis in the modern Al Mazrouiya district. In essence, like Qasr Ibrahim, it's also a walled enclosure with towers on each corner. It may date from Saud bin Abdulaziz bin Muhammad Al Saud (died 1814) or even as late as 1881 during the upheavals of the late 2nd Saudi State. Probably, it was used seasonally, as surrounding Bedouin tribes would congregate in AlAhsa for the date harvest. Some may have owned or rented date gardens, but all would need dates for the coming winter season. The large empty space within the fort would accommodate soldiers to deal with any disruption in the area. A substantial mosque and small accommodation for the commander are the only buildings inside.

Swinging back northeast – arriving to the south of Al Qaisariah Souq is the **Gold Souq** and a jumble of other small shops - this is to the east of King AbdulAziz Rd - typical hours of shops is the afternoon 16:00-22:00, though some will open 09:00-midday. East of the Gold Souq is a small shopping mall, **Al Fawares**, with a useful supermarket, **Al Othmaini** 07:00-01:30 Sat-Thurs on Friday 07:00-10:00/13:00-01:30.

Around 4km north of Qasr Ibrahim via King AbdulAziz Rd & Prince Abdullah Al Jalawi Rd is **Qasr Sahood**, currently its being restored. Comparable to Qasr Ibrahim, though on a smaller scale, this is a rectangular fort. It. It is possible that in origin, it dates to the rule of the Bani Khalid from 1670; however, its regular form suggests a later date, possibly under the rule of Saud bin Abdulaziz bin Muhammad Al Saud (died 1814) at the end of the First Saudi State. The wall has the typical Gulf corner towers – additionally, the longest two walls have an extra tower each. The accommodation is around the entrance wall, at the west, along with an ancient water well. Some 4km north of Qasr Sahood using King Faisal Rd is **Qasr Muhairis**, yet another fort. Possibly dating from around 1795, built by the Amir Muhairis, it is more of a fortified home than castle (the word Qasr means palace – but in Saudi, it seems to be used for any building with some importance having a government connection). It was built on a naturally elevated rock platform – perhaps to reduce the use of agricultural land. After it suffered substantial damage in 2008, Qasr Muhairis was restored, and the surrounding commercial areas were built to create a 'heritage' area.

Qasr Muhairis

Southeast of Qasr Muhairis is the main date oasis and **Al Qarah Mountain** - Daily 08:00-18:00 SAR50. It is a drive of around 17km, via King Abdullah Rd and Jubail Rd (and others) leads to 'Al Qarah Mountain'. This is a massive outcrop of limestone, whose east side is developed as a tourist attraction. Here is a small slot canyon with other attractions, including a modern Saudi interpretation of the 'Land of Civilisation' and occasional entertainment. The heavily eroded, and in places dangerous, plateau paths ascend up (around a 50-meter ascent) – these are periodically closed. **Al Doga Pottery** Daily 07:00-21:00 - on the west of Al Qarah Mountain - The entrance is enveloped by date palms. This is a small traditional pottery that uses local clays to make simple, biscuit-fired pots, including incense burners, for sale; live production on site. Other handicrafts are also available, including woven palm bowls. The pottery is worth a visit for its atmosphere, and it adds a bit more interest to the area.

About 500m southeast of Al Qarah Mountain, is a principal **irrigation channel** for the oasis on Mezawi Rd. Originally, AlAhsa has numerous natural springs over water, over 160, along with over 300 man-made wells. The use of diesel pumps has reduced the natural aquifer's pressure, so the number of springs has reduced considerably, and also water wells are failing as the underground water level drops.

To the northeast of AlAhsa are two large lake systems. Originally, these were natural aquifer-fed. Today, a mix of aquifer, residue-pumped agricultural water, and grey water fed the lakes. The largest, **Buhayrat Al Asfar** (Yellow Lake), has a variety of vegetation on its shore, with limestone and sand dunes above the water. Due to pollution, the water is unsafe. However, birds can be found, possibly Bluethroat, Clamorous Reed Warbler &

Al Qarah Mountain

Eurasian Reed Warbler, Eurasian Coot, Eurasian Marsh-Harrier, Eurasian Moorhen, Gray-headed Swamphen, Great Cormorant, Great Crested Grebe, Kentish Plover, Little Bittern, Little Egret, Little Grebe, Little Tern, Moustached Warbler, Northern Lapwing, Pied Avocet, Short-eared Owl, Slender-billed Gull, Squacco Heron, Water Rail, Whiskered Tern and if you are lucky a White-throated Kingfisher.

~

RESTAURANTS & HOTELS

Hidden inside the rear of Souq Al Qaisariah is **Al Said Restaurant*** 08:00-11:30/16:00-22:00 (closed Friday morning) - a charmingly decorated room where you can enjoy coffee and light Saudi-style meals. Just north of Souq Al Qaisariah is **Sagarmatha*** +966535684508 09:00-23:00 Al Fath St - a simple restaurant offering Nepalese/Northwest Indian food. Opposite Souq Al Qaisariah is **Ration** coffee shop +966554840140 16:00-midnight - an attractive ambience to enjoy coffee & cake - with balcony seating. Northwest of Al Amiriah School is **Green Valley*** +966502861681 08:00-22:30 - corner of King Khalid Rd & Abu Bakr Siddiq St (entrance at rear), a typical Filipino restaurant from The Gulf. The restaurant is above **Focus**. Southwest of Al Amiriah School is **Pak House Restaurant*** +966558043335 05:00-midnight Prince Mohammed bin Abdulaziz St, a good option for Pakistani cuisine. North of Fawares Mall is **Regency Family** ** +966534323278 11:00-Midnight, offering mainly Indian - but also an Indian style of Chinese food. Just west of Qasr Ibrahim is **Dar Basma*** +966563606888 west of King Khalid Rd. This offers Saudi-style food - in an attractive converted house with a small garden.

AlAhsa's hotels are not as numerous as the offering in Dammam. The lack of competition means prices for cheaper hotels are above what would be charged for a similar property in many other places. General standards in these lower-priced hotels reflect that same issue - less competition means less pressure to improve standards. **InterContinental** **** www.ihg.com Junction King Khalid Rd & Prince Talal bin Abdulaziz St in the far north of Hofuf; **Garden Plaza** ***+966558222155 Junction King Khalid Rd & Prince Talal bin Abdulaziz St.; '**Somewhere Hotel**' **** http://ksa.somewhere-hotels.com/ King Saud Rd to the north of town; **Al Koot Heritage Hotel** ***+966135822279 just south of Junction King Khali Rd & King

Faisal Rd; **Sippar Furnished Residential Units** **** www.taleen.com.sa just north of Junction King Khali Rd & King Faisal Rd; **Lily Palms Hotel** **+966135820089 south of Prince Talal bin Abdulaziz St (southwest of InterContinental); **AlAhsa Grand Hotel** ***+966135890000 Prince Faisal bin Fahd bin Abdulaziz Rd – south of city centre.

    Getting There The AlAhsa oasis at Hofuf (SAR call it Hufuf) has rail connections www.sar.com.sa with Dammam to its northeast - and Riyadh to its northwest. There is an airport, however, Dammam's airport is 140km away - and does have better connectivity. From the Dammam conurbation, AlAhsa is connected by Route 615 - about 150km - Riyadh is to the northwest, about 340kms away using Route 522 – or Highways 80 & 75. SATRANS's coach station is northwest of the Train Station. There are no local bus services - but Uber is available.

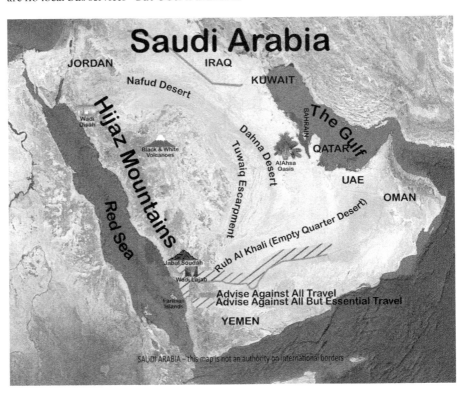

CHAPTER 48
GEOGRAPHY

The Kingdom of Saudi Arabia (often either Saudi Arabia or Saudi) occupies most of the Arabian Peninsula. The coastline is about 2,000km long on the Red Sea coast and 550km on the Arabian Gulf. In this book the Arabian Gulf is used rather than Persian Gulf, often it's just referred to as The Gulf. This choice of name is much the same as in French the English Channel is named La Manche (The Sleeve), El canal de la Mancha in Spanish, and Armelkanal in German – clearly a distinctly different term is used. Arabian Gulf or The Gulf - can refer to the body of water, and more broadly, the 5 states, Kuwait, Saudi Arabian, Bahrain, Qatar and the UAE - Oman is included when referring to the political Gulf Cooperation Council (GCC) states.

Saudi Arabia is in what the United Nations and similar organisations variously call, Western Asia; Southwest Asia; Middle East & North Africa (MENA); Middle East, Near East or simply Arabia.

With a land area of 2,149,690sq km (according to the CIA), it's one of the world's largest countries by area, just ahead of Mexico and comparable to Algeria. Saudi Arabia has a border of 4,272 km with the immediate neighbours - Jordan 731 km, Iraq 811 km, Kuwait 221 km, Qatar 87 km, UAE 457 km, Oman 658 km, and Yemen 1,307 km. The coastline is 2,640km, with a sliver of Jordan having a maritime shelf boundary (Israel is separated by Jordans Gulf of Aqaba access) along with Iran, Bahrain (connected by the causeway), Eritrea, Sudan, Egypt. There are several minor archipelagos in the Red Sea, notably the Farasan Islands in the southwest.

∾

MAPPING IN THIS BOOK MAKES NO ASSURANCE OF THE ACCURACY OF ANY border, and maps produced in Saudi Arabia are suggested for navigation and boundary reference - for border advise, your own government is the authoritative source.

Mountain escarpment Tanomah

The geography of Saudi Arabia is varied, with widespread mountain ranges in the west, the majority of the largest sand desert in the world in the south, salt flats to the east and a varied coastline on both the west and east. There are no rivers, and no natural permanent streams. Lakes are created by man, the majority are dammed valleys.

Along the western region of Saudi Arabia the Hijaz Mountains extend north from the Jordanian border to the Yemeni border in the south for over 1,600 km. The mountains are named after the Hijaz, the political & cultural region focused on Madinah, Jeddah & Makkah. Within this range in the north are the mountains of Midian and part of the Shammar Mountains. The southern part is the Sarawat Mountains. In this book, all the western mountains are called Hijaz Mountains. The mountains of western Saudi Arabia generally increase in height as they progress south. The southern areas are affected by their proximity to the Ethiopian Highlands as cloud banks and rain drift towards the east.

The geology of these mountains is extraordinarily complicated due to their formation during the creation of the Red Sea. The Red Sea is part of the rift valleys which extend from central Africa to Lebanon. These are zones where continental plates move apart; in this case, Arabia is moving away from the African and Somali plates towards the Eurasian plate at Iran. The Hijaz Mountains are often called the 'Arabian Shield' and include rock formations up to 1850-1670 Million years ago. Younger rock formations laid down over these older sedimentary rocks have, in many cases, been eroded.

More recent igneous (or crystalline) rock formations were created by the continual spreading of the Red Sea and subsequent upward movement of the igneous mantel rocks during 2 periods. An active period around 15-30 million years ago resulted in volcanos. There are also lava fields whose rock is now substantially eroded. A second period with less igneous activity from around 10 million years ago was not directly associated with the movement of the Red Sea. However, it may be the start of a new rift valley and gives many of the igneous features we see today, such as volcanos and lava fields.

To the north of the Hijaz Mountains is the Jabal Al Lawz, the north's highest peak at 2550m, towards the Jordan border northwest of Tabuk. This region includes the ochre-coloured sandstone formation of the Ordovician period 488-444 million years ago, with notable outcrops around Hegra. This is directly connected with Wadi Rum in Jordan as it's the same sandstone rock formations named Ram-Umm Sahm and Quweira. Also found here are areas of Tabuk sediments, which are fossil rich. These span the Silurian and Ordovician periods (416-488 million years ago).

In the central area of the Hijaz, Jabal Al Hadab, south of Taif, is the area's highest peak at 2,640m. This region has conglomerate rock sandstone, siltstone, limestone & volcanic rocks dating to around 655-620 million years ago. Saudi Arabia's principal gold mine at Mahd adh Dhahab is about 170kms southeast of Madinah. However, the most remarkable features are the 'Harrats', which are dramatic areas of lava flows from around 10 million years ago into historical times. One volcano, south of Madinah, was well documented, flowing in AD1256. However, the Black and White Volcanoes near Khaybar Page110 are the most spectacular. Here, Jabal AbyadhAbyadh (the White Mountain), formed from a Comendite silica-rich quartz, is the highest at 2,093 meters (though only about 400m above the surrounding general lava).

Near the southern border and overlooking Abha is Jabal Sawda, which, at around 3,000m, is almost the highest mountain in Saudi Arabia. This area around Abha has large areas of metamorphic, conglomerate and granite rocks including from 750-960 million years ago. As a result, the alluvium washed down to the coastal plain in Jizan is mineral rich and allows extensive agriculture where water resources permit.

Large valleys (called in wadis in Arabic) dissect these mountains. Two contrasting examples are Wadi Al Disah Page99 and Wadi Lajib Page247 – there are innumerable other examples.

Central and southern Saudi Arabia is dominated by great sand deserts. In the north, the An Nafud Desert of some 103,600 sq km is formed by winds predominantly from the west to the east. Sweeping south from this desert is the Ad Dahna Sands, which branches on either side of Ar Riyadh and onto the Rub Al Khali, the Empty Quarter. Though not all in Saudi Arabia – the Rub Al Khali is the largest sand desert in the world. The sand in these deserts is predominantly hard quartz grains that get their rich orange colour because they have a thin coating of iron oxide – that has rusted.

Empty Quarter Desert

Almost bisecting Saudi Arabia from the north near Buraydah south to Wadi Ad Dawasir is the 750km long Jebel Tuwaiq, an escarpment. This escarpment rises to 300m above the area to its west and slopes gently to Riyadh and other areas to the east. The rock under these deserts and Jebel Tuwaiq is Limestone from the Middle Jurassic 174 to 162.

Eastern Saudi Arabia includes the oil fields that are the basis of the economy. The Ghawar field occupies an anticline above a basement fault block dating to Carboniferous time, about 320 million years ago; Cretaceous tectonic activity, as the northeast margin of Africa began to collide with southwest Asia, enhanced the structure. Reservoir rocks are Jurassic Arab-D limestones with exceptional porosity (as much as 35% of the rock in places), about 280 feet thick and occur 6,000-7,000 feet beneath the surface. The source rock is the Jurassic Hanifa formation, a marine shelf deposit of mud and lime with as much as 5% organic material (1% to 7% is considered good oil source rock). The seal is an evaporitic package of rocks, including impermeable anhydrite. This means the oil flows easily from the source rock and is readily available in vast quantities.

Finally, The Gulf coastal area is sand formed by limestone and coal erosion and sabkha, which are low-lying areas of sand, mud and gypsum that can become waterlogged salt flats.

THE RED SEA & THE GULF

The Red Sea is unusual as it, until the creation of the Suez Canal, only had a narrow, single, natural entrance/exit - the Bab Al Mandab. It is also unique in that it has no river sources that exit into it. This creates a lack of sediment caused by natural silt entering the sea. High natural surface water temperature, up to 32c by the end of July, dropping to perhaps 19c in January, and extremely high air temperatures of around 50c create a very high evaporation and subsequent increase in the salt content. This salinity reaches 4.1% compared to the North Sea & Pacific at around 3.4% or Dead Sea at 33%. There are marked temperature differences in the surface and subsurface water, brought about by a lack of other exits and no river currents and therefore low circulation.

The Tide differences in the Red Sea are not significant, at less than a meter. Dust storms over the Red Sea deposit nutrients into otherwise relatively infertile water.

In pre-historic times, the Bab Al Mandab formed a land bridge; much earlier the sea was a dry lakebed. This has created a relatively young body of water, the narrow gap isolated from its neighbouring Arabian Sea.

The other sea on which Saudi Arabia abuts is the Arabian Gulf. The Arabian Gulf is an even younger body of water than the Red Sea, having been gradually formed from 18,000 years ago. Previously, with larger Ice Caps reducing available ocean water, the area was a river or marsh extension of the Tigris/Euphrates/Shatt Al Arab river system, which flows into the Arabian Gulf from the north. The approximate current outline of this sea was formed as recently as 4,000BC. This shallow sea has a maximum depth of less than 100m. As with the Red Sea, surface temperatures are high, and evaporation rates of up to several meters of water a year help create a relatively saline sea.

CHAPTER 49
FLORA

Though a peninsula surrounded on three sides by seas and to the north by desert, Saudi Arabia's flora is not as isolated as this would suggest. The country's flora overall needs to be studied more; however, currently, there are believed to be some 2,500 species.

Plant populations include those from the Sudano-Zambezian region (East Africa and southern Arabia), Saharo-Arabian region (North Africa and Arabia), Irano-Turanian region, East Mediterranean Region and Irano-Turanian Region (Iran and bordering Asian countries). This variety and lack of endemism can be explained by the country's location, extensive range of 16 degrees latitude, and height range from sea level to 3000m. These together create an extensive climatic range and support a variety of natural ground habitats. They include outwash plains with rich soil on the Tihamah Plain (western coast); mud flats on the southern Red Sea and Arabian Gulf coasts; steep soil-free mountain escarpments; undulating high altitude plateau; arid stone deserts; sand deserts with mobile sand dunes; rocky islands; intertidal sand islands; coastal salt flats; closed basin salt flats. In some areas, substantial man-made changes have altered these, notably the high-altitude terraced farms in the southwest and numerous date oases associated with wadi systems throughout the country.

The quintessential tree of Arabia, the **Date Palm** Phoenix dactylifera, is grown over a wide region of Saudi Arabia. Date Palms have been cultivated in The Gulf region since the Bronze Age. The date tree, in modern agriculture, is almost entirely dependent on man for water supply. This is due to low rain level and the date's need for relatively large volumes of water. Water is supplied either by man-made water canals, as in AlAhsa, or by drip feed irrigation as for the regimented lines of Date Palms southeast of Buraydah. The tree is single sex, and female flowering trees need a separate male tree for pollination. Male date trees do not produce fruit and thus 'waste' space. Therefore, an artificial ratio of around one male tree to 100 female trees is created. This results in each female tree requiring artificial pollination. After about 8 years, the tree can produce fruit. Propagation is typically done by using the natural offshoots (suckers) at the base of a tree. These are carefully cut off, their base soaked in water and planted in a hole that has been fertilised.

Date Palm Oasis

All aspects of the tree and date fruit cultivation are labour intensive; however, the fruit which ripens in mid-summer has a high value, so there is a reward. Ripe dates have a high sugar content, so bacteria or fungus do not easily damage the fruit. The date fruit can therefore be stored and used after perhaps two years. Date Palms can grow to a height of around 20 metres, living approximately 90 years, depending on the variety.

There is increasing focus on **Coffee cultivation** and marketing.

The Arabica coffee plant (Coffea arabica) is a scraggly shrub/small tree that is between 2m and 8m tall and has evergreen, shiny leaves. The flowers are white with a sweet fragrance. The Coffee plant produces red, or purple fruit. At higher elevations the flesh of the fruit is sweet – while lower down it becomes slightly bitter. Each fruit produces two green seeds, the coffee bean called 'Bunn' in Saudi. After roasting, the seeds turn brown and are ground for **Qahwa** - Arabic/Saudi style of bitter, spiced, black coffee.

Drinking coffee was known from the 15th centuryAD. It may have originated in Ethiopia or Yemen. Irrespective, its use spread from Yemen notably the port of Mocha, north through Makkah to the Levant & Turkey. From there it was traded west through the Balkans & Mediterranean and reached the European Atlantic coast by the late 17th century. Production of the plant also spread from Yemen to the to the Dutch East Indies and Americas.

In Saudi Arabia the Arabica bean is being branded Khawlani and has been recorded under UNESCO's Intangible Heritage List. The focus of production is in the southwest, around Jabal Fayfa.

Coffee Plant & Fruit

A social occasion called 'shabbah' - preparing and drinking coffee while listening to poetry and storytelling might be held. The beans are roasted on a 'al-majl', a metal pan, ground in a 'najr', a pestle & mortar, and then boiled in water in a 'Dallah', the classic Arab coffee pot. The length of boiling is often a regional preference – creating stronger or lighter taste. Spice is included, typically only cardamom - but might include, in addition, others such as saffron, clove, cinnamon, rosewater – as per taste and budget. It is a traditional beverage in Saudi Arabia. Arabic coffee is served black without sugar and without the grounds that might remain in a cup. The liquid is served in a small ceramic cup, Finjan, without a handle - in the shape of traditional western sewing thimble, except larger. A person who serves the coffee will offer additional servings until they are refused (it is polite to accept two or three). Holding the cup in the right hand and shaking it slightly horizontally indicates you do not wish more. Dates or other sweet food is often served with coffee.

The northern area of the Red Sea coast has **Mangroves**, including the south of Al-Wajh and south of Ar Rayis. To the south, beyond Jeddah are coastal areas, the coastal plain is called the Tihama, with mangroves through to the Yemen border. These mangroves are mostly Grey Mangroves Avicennia marina that may grow to 10 meters. On the Farasan Islands are stands of Avicennia marina, and at Farasan Kebir Island are Rhizophora mucronata, which may reach 20 meters high. South of Jeddah, the seas have a variety of seagrass, including the widespread Cymodoca rotunda, which grows in the intertidal zone. The southern Arabian Gulf coast also includes Avicennia marina Mangrove, with probably the best area north of Tarout.

The most abundant, non-cultivated, tree throughout Saudi is '**Acacia tortilis**' (Simr is the local Arabic) one of 17 acacia species in Saudi Arabia. It is often called the umbrella tree due to its cone shape. The small leaves have many tiny leaflets, the flowers are small, white and with an aroma that attracts bees. The resultant honey is highly prized. This Acacia is also forage for Goats and Camels and provides hardwood for humans. There are several other Acacia species, though with a scragglier appearance.

Possibly running Acacia a good second is **Ziziphus spina-christi**, locally called Sidr. They grow on the sides of wadis and hilly slopes. The flower is important for honeybees which produce Sidr honey. The small fruit, which when ripe is a nutty brown colour, is consumed by animals and used to be by people – its taste is comparable to a ripe crab-apple.

The foothills of the southern Hijaz Mountains have several Commiphora species – whose sap is often fragrant, including Commiphora myrrha, the plant that gives its name to **Myrrh**. This is a small shrubby tree with small leaves and spines, used in Egyptian embalming and a gift to Jesus.

Coastal sand dunes, created by silt swept down from Wadis, often hold substantial areas of Salvadora persica, the toothbrush bush '**Miswak**'. This natural branch (or occasionally root) is still widely used in Arabia to clean teeth, much like a modern toothbrush. The Miswak toothbrush can be found for sale in many local shops & in Al Balad's souqs.

Tamarindus indica, **Tamarind**, reaches 20m+ with a heavy canopy. Its yellow & red small flowers produce the fruit pod – with its tasty pulpy flesh. They are more common in the southwest.

South of Taif, the mountains become more wooded due to the cooler altitude and relatively high rainfall. The areas around 2,000meters and more have two varieties of **Juniper**: Juniperus procera and Juniperus phoenicea. Other high-altitude species include Olea europaea (**Olive**). Important to wildlife is the large **Fig**, Ficus sycomorus, which is both cultivated and wild. Found up to 1700m above sea, the tree fruits abundantly throughout the year. It provides ample shade from its broad branch system, which may reach 20m high and 30m in diameter.

Tamarind

Dracaena serrulata, with its grey trunk and crown

of sword-shaped leaves, is found principally on the dry desert-facing escarpment. The lack of other plants means it is often eaten by browsing livestock, especially Camels.

The **Desert Rose,** Adenium obesum, with its pink flowers and often grotesquely swollen trunk, grows in the sea-facing foothills and can reach a height of almost 2m. The sap is poisonous, and it is considered to be home to spirits.

Desert Rose

Opuntia ficus-indica (**prickly pear**) which has been introduced but is naturalised grows in regions above 1800m. The fruit can be used for several purposes and, as a result, was grown around villages. **Lavandula dentate** grows in the mountains.

Lower foothills here are home to **Aloe officinalis**, often in dense communities. The tall yellow flower spike attracts nectar-feeding insects and sunbirds. The leaf was also used for medicinal purposes.

In the coastal wadis of the Tihamah can be found **Doum palm** (Hyphaene thebaica). Visually it differs from a Date Palm by having fan-shaped leaves and often branches, rather than only a single trunk.

A type of milkweed, Calotropis procera (**Sodoms Apple**), is found throughout the country. Its purple & pale grey flowers develop into a seed-pod that contains a mass of silk-like threads. This plant however is often a sign of overgrazing, as it's a poisonous plant and remains uneaten while other vegetation is consumed by wandering livestock.

CHAPTER 50
ANIMALS

MAMMALS

Saudi Arabia has 15 carnivores, and at the top of the food chain is the **Arabian Leopard** Panthera pardus nimr. There is a centre at AlUla and the National Wildlife Research Center, east of Taif, to try and increase the population. Its local range is not well understood in Saudi Arabia. Still, it is now probably scattered in the mountains south from AlUla into the Yemen border. The world population is usually given as around 200 individuals, its wild population in Saudi Arabia is a small fraction of that total. In September 2023, an individual was filmed below the escarpment of Tanomah, Asir. A breeding program is currently underway in Saudi.

In Arabia, the leopard's preferred habitat is steep wadi and mountain escarpment, allowing it to use the advantage of height to ambush its prey. Like other Leopards, this is a solitary animal. With a large male weighing only 30kg, it is a smaller animal than in Africa. They prey on Rock Hyrax, Gazelle, Ibex and small animals. However, with rapid human encroachment into their territory, domestic animals are also possible prey.

Arabian Leopard

Loss of habitat through human development and hunting are critical issues to the ultimate survival of the Arabian Leopard in the wild.

In areas with no Leopards, the **Caracal**, Caracal caracal is the apex predator, along with the Arabian Wolf and Hyaena. Caracal males are up to 19kg, and females are much smaller - between 8-12kg. They hunt small mammals and birds. In Saudi, they probably inhabit the Hijaz Mountains and the Tuwaiq Escarpment north of Riyadh. Both sexes are medium brown - with distinctive upright ears and black hairs on the tip.

Two smaller cats are believed to inhabit Saudi Arabia. The pale-coloured **Arabian Sand Cat** inhabits parts of the Nafud Desert, Dhana Desert and isolated dune areas west of Riyadh. This nocturnal animal is usually less than 3 kilograms and has a 15 cm shoulder height. It is unlikely to be seen, especially as it often sleeps in burrows in the sand during the day. The other cat with a more uncertain range is the **Gordon's Wildcat**, Felis lybica lybica, which may be an ancestor of domestic cats and has the appearance and size of a large Tabby cat. This animal inhabits rocky plains and low-hill areas.

Caracal

Striped hyena, Hyaena hyaena sultana probably occurs in low numbers throughout Saudi Arabia, except in the empty quarter. At up to 50kg, this is the largest carnivore in Saudi Arabia. It is thought to be a scavenger in Arabia.

The **Honey Badger**, Mellivora capensis pumilio, ranges throughout Saudi Arabia, except in the deepest sand desert. At around 10kg and less than 100 cm in overall length, it is about 2/3rds of the size of its relative, the European Badger. These usually solitary animals have a broad omnivorous diet that includes honey.

There are 6 canid species in Saudi Arabia, including the **Blanford's Fox** Vulpes cana and **Rueppell's Fox** Vulpes rueppelli in areas except the Hijaz Mountains, which are less than 2kg. The **Arabian Red fox** Vulpes vulpes Arabica is larger at up to 4kg and ranges throughout Saudi Arabia, except in the deepest desert. **Fennec Fox** Vulpes zerda, though little studied, probably lives in scattered small groups in the all-sand deserts of Saudi Arabia - it is recorded in Kuwait, the Nafud and Oman. This is the smallest fox in Arabia, under 1.5kg, with a light-coloured coat.

The largest canid in Saudi Arabia is the **Arabian Wolf**, Canis lupus. Its small for a wolf at less than 20kilo and 60cms at the shoulder. This is certainly found in the southern Hijaz Mountains and may live in isolated areas and in small numbers elsewhere. They are pack animals, though usually of less than 5 animals. They feed on small animals, including domesticated ones, and carrion and will scavenge around villages.

Indian Crested Porcupine Hystrix indica is found in rocky mountainous areas of the Hijaz Mountains. Their numbers are still being determined and probably low. Though omnivorous, they are principally plant eaters.

The **Rock Hyrax** in Saudi Arabia is found throughout the Hijaz Mountains, from Jordan to Yemen, and in limited areas of the Tuwaiq Escarpment. Their preferred habitat is arid, rocky cliffs, and the animals live in groups of a male and up to 10 adult females & eat a variety of vegetation. They are a similar weight to a domestic cat and are the natural prey of larger birds of prey, Caracal and Leopard.

Hamadryas Baboon Papio hamadryas, sacred to the ancient Egyptians, inhabits the western escarpment and nearby plateau of the Hijaz Mountains. The range is south from near Madinah to beyond the Yemen border. There is a well-established population in the coastal mountains between Al Qahma and north of Al Birk on the Tihamah Plain. More recently, they have been spreading towards and into Riyadh; they are commensal with humans. These are large animals with males up to 30kg, living for up to 25 years in the wild. They live in a single male-dominated family that may have a harem of up to 8 adult females and their offspring. Several of these family groups cluster as a clan; in turn, several clans combine to form a band, and several bands may overnight in a single location, forming a troop of 700-800 individual Baboons.

The size of these animals and considerable troop numbers means that, apart from domesticated animals, this will be the most visible animal seen by visitors to the mountains they live in. Their omnivorous diet includes animals, almost of their own size, as well as fruit and plants and feed within a wide range of habitats. They need cliffs for night-time safety and an assured water source within less than 15 km of their night cliffs. Adult Hamadryas Baboons probably have no natural predators in Saudi Arabia. The male Baboon is of a comparable weight to adult male Arabian Leopards, and Baboons also have canine teeth around the same size as a Leopard, up to 3.6cm. The Baboons inhabiting areas close to human development are habituated to people; their families and individuals should be viewed cautiously. They regularly use hotel balconies as they would cliffs - windows are best locked. On the Tihamah coast, about 15 km drive (and subsequent walk or a 4x4 vehicle) southeast of Al Birk is Wadi Dhahban. The Baboons feed on the fruit of the Doum palm and use the dam's water. Near Taif, Wadi Liya & Saiysad National Park also has a dam in the north and a better one in the south next to King Fahd Ring Road – Route 281. In both of these routes, Baboons may be seen as they are near ideal natural locations for them.

Saudi Arabia would hardly seem an Arab country without the **Camel**, Camelus dromedaries, the dromedary. The word Camel comes from the Arabic جمل (Jamal, a male Camel). The word dromedary, the single-humped camel variety, from the Greek dromus, meaning race/racecourse or running, very apt in the world of Camel racing today. All living dromedaries are domesticated animals, the wild type having disappeared perhaps 2,500 years ago. This domestication started around 2,000BC, probably in southeast Arabia when the wild Camel population was declining in numbers. Though a typical colour is a mid-brown colour, it's possible for camels to have an almost white coat as with the Waddah breed, or nearly black – as with the famous Al Majaheem of the northeastern Al Murari tribe.

Male Camels can be two metres in height at the shoulder and weigh 600kg; females are perhaps 10% shorter and 30% less weight. The single hump is a fat bearing organ and as fat can release water, if used due to lack of food, it allows better survival in drought.

The Camel is a herbivore and grazes on the ground and browses bushes and trees, though nowadays, a large proportion is supplied as hay or other animal feed. As with a cow, the Camel is an even-toed ungulate and is also a ruminant, so spends much of its day either eating or ruminating! To cope with the desert climate, the body temperature can fluctuate by more than 10C and can deal with a 30% water loss; either of these changes would kill most other mammals. Camels, fortunately, can replenish water at around 20 litres a minute, helpful when finding water in a desert climate.

Al Majaheem Camels

From around four years, the Camel can breed, with a gestation period of some 15 months. Usually, single young are born, though occasional twins are also born. They can walk within 24 hours of birth and typically can expect to live for over 40 years. In some areas, a protective bag covers the udder to wean the young and allow the owner to milk the animal for his own use. Though a domesticated species, they might roam in semi-feral herds, with each individual often identified by an ownership brand. The front legs may have a rope around their ankle to prevent them from wandering too far.

The dromedary has bred with a Llama in captivity. In areas such as Iran, where their ranges overlap, dromedaries can breed naturally with the two-humped Bactrian Camel. Breeding of Bactrian and dromedary is specifically done at Turkey's Izmir province. The result is large single-humped animals, whose males compete in Camel 'wrestling' events. Historically Camels have been used for transport, milk, meat, clothing and more. It, therefore, is probably more helpful than cattle.

Today in Saudi Arabia, they are bred for the prestige they bring, especially for racing. Camels have bloodlines, as with thoroughbred horses, so that potential owners will have some idea of the quality of any young animal they buy. Camels are used for short races from about aged 18months – 24months, the prime age is around six years, and these older Camels can race at around 40kmph. Though previously children were used as jockeys for their lightweight, from the early 2000s the 'rider' has been a simple robot, with a rotating whip to encourage the animal's speed. Prizes can be hundreds of thousands of SARs and luxury cars. However, the most sought-after rewards are the prestige of owning a winning animal and the sales value of the winner, which can reach US$ 1,500,000, is an added benefit. These high prices are obtained for animals that, like thoroughbred racehorses, have a known and admired lineage. Other Camels might take part in Camel beauty contests or milking contests. Again the value of a successful animal might run to more than US$1,000,000, with the most expensive Camel ever being sold for US$ 2,720,000 in the UAE (though rumours say one has been sold for US$9,500,000). As they say, beauty is in the eye of the beholder.

A downside of all this money and prestige is that cheating might happen. In 2018 a dozen camels were banned & in 2021 40 camels were disqualified from the King Abdulaziz Camel Festival beauty pageant. The reason, they had received Botox injections and other cosmetic enhancements. Prize winners in races have their blood tested for performance drugs.

Saudi Arabia has four wild ungulates, all threatened and probably only predated by Leopard & Wolf.

The **Arabian Oryx**, Oryx leucoryx, was hunted to extinction in the wild, and captive-bred populations were reintroduced during the 1980s. Apart from zoos, in Saudi Arabia, they are found within Ibex Reserve, south of Riyadh, and in protected areas of Uruq Bani Maarid Page176. The Arabian Oryx weighs up to 90kg with a shoulder height of up to 100 cm, with the male slightly larger than the female. Both sexes have horns of up to 150 cm, which are often so straight that they give the appearance of a single unicorn-type horn in profile. The animals feed on shrubs and can obtain most of their water requirement from them.

Arabian Oryx

These two populations are within protected areas, so they have little pressure apart from occasional poaching.

The **Nubian Ibex** Capra nubiana range possibly includes all of the Hijaz Mountains, and northern areas around Hail and Tuwaiq escarpments. They inhabit steep wadis and escarpment cliffs in herds of up to 20 individuals, with males joining females to mate. Males, at up to 70kg and perhaps 80 cm shoulder height, are much heavier than females. Both sexes have horns, though the males are considerably larger with notable annual growth rings. They have a broad diet but prefer browsing shrubs. Leopards, wolves and hyenas are less of a threat than loss of habitat through human development and competition from domestic livestock, as well as hunting, which are critical issues.

The **Arabian Gazelle** Gazella arabica (also called Mountain Gazelle Gazella gazella) is found throughout much of Saudi Arabia except sand deserts and the highest mountain range. Though up to 110 cm shoulder height in the larger male, they are relatively slight with even heavier males below 25kg. Both sexes have horns, though the males are up to 3 times the length of the females. They live in semi-nomadic small groups of 4 females and young in a loose association with a male. Arabian gazelles have an extensive range of plants in their diet. In the mountains, the Gazelle, especially the young, maybe the prey of the larger carnivores. Loss of habitat through human development and competition from domestic livestock and hunting are critical issues.

Gazella marica (often under its previous name of Gazella subgutturosa), the **Arabian Sand Gazelle**, has declined markedly in numbers during recent decades, probably due to hunting. Today, few, if any, survive as a wild population. Captive-bred individuals were introduced into the Mahazat as-Sayd Protected Area and the National Wildlife Research Center in Taif. These pale brown gazelles have a greater body weight range of up to 40kg than the Arabian Gazelle, with usually only males having horns. The animals typically roam in single male-dominated groups of up to 10 animals, often within larger herds of several hundred. Females frequently give birth to twins.

~

REPTILES

As a desert country, Saudi Arabia has an abundance of reptiles. Over 100 lizards and 50 snakes are found in the country, though a casual visitor may rarely see one. They include Geckos, Agama, Chameleons, Monitors and Snakes.

Notable lizards include the large **Egyptian Spiny-tailed Lizard** (Uromastyx aegyptia) in Arabic it's a 'Dhab'. This is an Agama lizard found in plains with gravel or sand. They have a length of 70 cm with a tail of perhaps 30 cm. These are virtually vegetarian, with very occasional insects. They may lay under 30 eggs within their underground burrow. In the morning, they sunbathe to raise their body temperature, especially in winter. Large numbers of these lizards are eaten by some people in Saudi Arabia. Another interesting lizard is the **Veiled Chameleon** Chamaeleo calyptratus found from Taif south in the southern Hijaz Mountains. They grow up to 61 cm overall length, though its tail is usually coiled. This has an elongated casque on its head and a thick body, giving a heavy appearance. Living in trees and bushes, they mimic the background colour very rapidly. The body has broad stripes within the skin that can change the overall body colour, including to blue and yellow. They usually eat insects, though they occasionally eat plants. The female may lay up to 80 eggs in a sandy soil. In the northwest of Saudi Arabia, Chamaeleo chamaeleon is also found. It has a less distinct casque and range of colour changes.

Within the snakes are 2 species of cobra found in the Hijaz Mountains. **Black Desert-Cobra** Walterinnesia aegyptia is located northwest from Jeddah. **Arabian Cobra** Naja Arabica is found from the Yemen border north to almost Tabuk. Both are highly venomous and, like many snakes, live in cracks within rock. The nocturnal Black Desert-Cobra is generally a dry land snake of up to 1.7m and feeds on small animals. Arabian Cobra is a snake that likes damp areas, often in the area of permanent water.

This snake comes in various colours, including ochre and almost black. They lay around 30 eggs in a pit.

The night skies of Saudi Arabia are filled with some 24 Bat species. The **Egyptian Fruit Bat** Rousettus aegyptiacus has a 60cm wingspan, making it easily seen. This bat is found throughout much of the Hijaz Mountains, including Jeddah, and beyond to larger cities, including Riyadh. These Bats roost in colonies of up to several thousand, in caves or large abandoned buildings. At night, ripe fruit, including vital commercial crops Date, Fig, Apricot and Peach, are sought.

SEA TURTLES

Within the Red Sea and Arabian Gulf, four species of **Sea Turtle** are found:
- •Green Turtle Chelonia mydas
- •Hawksbill Turtle Eretmochelys imbricata
- •Olive Ridley Turtle Lepidochelys olivacea
- •Loggerhead Turtle Caretta caretta

However, only the **Green Turtle** and **Hawksbill Turtle** are believed to nest on Saudi Arabia's coast, and the Olive Ridley Turtle and Loggerhead turtle nest on the Yemen and Oman coasts.

Green Turtle returning to Sea after laying Eggs

The Green Turtle travels vast distances during their life; individuals who have been tagged have made a journey that must have been at least 7,000 km. Green Turtles lay eggs throughout the year, though late summer is preferred in Saudi Arabia.

Usually, the male and female turtles return to the sea of their birth to mate. Key nesting locations are the coast north of Jubail in the Arabian Gulf and along a 100km stretch of coastline north of Yanbu and the Farasan Islands in the southern Red Sea.

The mating takes place in the sea, and after several days, the female crawls into the sandy beach at night. She excavates two pits, one depression for her own body so she is hidden below the surface, and the other is a bucket-shaped hole into which the eggs are laid. Then the egg hole is filled in, and by her efforts to get out of the depression made in the sand for her body, that too is filled in. Typically, 100 eggs are laid, and from this point, they are abandoned. The female may lay several clutches over some weeks. As the animal's sex is determined by the nest's temperature, the nest closer to the cooler sea is more likely to have males, and those away from the water's cooling influence will have more females. Climate change is impacting this, resulting in more females. After around 60 days, the eggs hatch together, usually at light, and a mini volcano of hatchlings erupts through the sand. What follows is the most hazardous period of a turtle's life; the hatchlings scuttle towards the light that's hopefully reflecting off the sea, not light from a village. Waiting are predators such as foxes, seagulls, and crabs. Even after the water is reached, large fish hunt for survivors. This predation means that only 1 in 500 or less may survive. The young turtles only eat flesh; however, as they age, they become omnivorous, with the vegetation causing their fat to take a green tinge, hence the Green Turtle's name.

The Green Turtle has an eventual size carapace length of around 115 cm - and will weigh from 200kg. The animal becomes sexually mature at about 20 years of age. The females may lay eggs till they are almost 80.

Though smaller than the Green Turtle, the Hawksbill Turtle is still a substantial animal. Their shell carapace length is no more than 90 cm, and the animal weighs up to 100 kg. Their shell and plate have a serrated edge distinct from the Green Turtle. Key nesting locations are the coast near Jubail in the Arabian Gulf and the Farasan Islands in the Red Sea. They are less studied than the Green Turtle but are believed to be sexually mature at around 10 years. These animals are reef inhabitants, often seen in shallow waters near shore. Their adult diet includes sponges and a limited number of jellyfish. This diet makes their flesh toxic. Their life cycle is similar to the Green Turtle; however, they are not believed to migrate as far. The shell of the Hawksbill Turtle is still used (illegally) for decorative items.

≈

Sea Mammals

The seas are home to several large mammals.

Dugong Dugong dugon is found throughout both seas and is an entirely aquatic animal. Weighing up to 1,000 kilograms and up to 4 meters in length, these are long-lived animals of up to 70 years. It grazes on plants, principally sea grass, though other plants may be eaten. The animal may become sexually mature at 10 years. They give birth to a single calf with over 3 years between births.

Around 18 **Cetaceans** have been found in these waters. A few migrate in and out; most are infrequent; however, some are relatively common.

Pantropical Spotted Dolphin Stenella attenuata is found throughout both seas.

At up to 2.5 meters in length and around 120kg, this medium-sized dolphin lives up to 40 years and breeds from about 8 years.

Spinner Dolphin Stenella longirostris This may be the dolphin first seen at a distance as it leaps and spins out of the water. At up to 2.3 meters and 80kg, it's not a large mammal. They group with other dolphins while hunting for fish. This may be a defence from becoming prey to large sharks, orcas, and false killer whales.

Common Bottlenose Dolphin Tursiops truncatus is the dolphin often found in water parks. They are large mammals at up to 4m and 600kg and live for up to 50 years. These are group animals and, in some seas, can be in huge groups of 1,000 or more.

Indo-Pacific Bottlenose Dolphin Tursiops aduncus This used to be considered the Common Dolphin; however, at up to 3m and 220kg, it is smaller and has some differences. They are also found in pods, though their similarity to the Common Dolphin makes it challenging to distinguish.

Indo-Pacific Humpback Dolphin Sousa plumbea is commonly found near the shore and often follows large boats. This is most common south of Jeddah, though it is seen along the entire coast and in the Arabian Gulf. A medium-sized mammal at 2.5m and 140kg, this is easily identified by the hump under its dorsal fin. Generally, they do not congregate in pods. They are quite frequent in coastal waters.

Bryde's Whale Balaenoptera edeni, is a medium-sized whale at up to 15m and 2500kilos. This is very infrequently seen in either sea.

Risso's Dolphin, Grampus griseus, is occasionally seen in the Red Sea, though probably not in the Arabian Gulf. With a blunt head and up to 4m, this distinctive Dolphin usually stays in deeper water.

False Killer Whale

False Killer Whale Pseudorca crassidens is occasionally seen in small pods in the Red Sea and Arabian Gulf. This whale reaches up to 6m and might weigh 2,200kg. It hunts large fish and cooperates with other large dolphin species to hunt. They are believed to hunt small dolphins and are themselves hunted by Orca.

CHAPTER 51

BIRDS

S audi Arabia's north is included in the Palearctic region, the south is within the Afrotropical region, and it is close to the Indomalayan. This means that it has a bird population drawn from different regions. It also is on migration routes from the north of Eurasia into either Arabia or Africa.

Over a year, some 500 bird species can be seen in Saudi Arabia; some are vagrants, others are endemic or near endemic. Endemic species are Arabian Golden-winged Grosbeak (Rhynchostruthus percivali), Arabian Green Bee-eater (Merops cyanophrys). Arabian Partridge (Alectoris melanocephala),

Arabian Scops Owl (Otus pamelae), Arabian Serin (Serinus rothschildi), Arabian Waxbill (Estrilda rubibarba), Arabian Wheatear (Oenanthe lugentoides), Arabian Woodpecker (Dendrocopos dorae), Philby's Partridge (Alectoris philbyi), Yemen Linnet (Carduelis yemenensis), Yemen Serin (Serinus menachensis), Yemen Thrush (Turdus menachensis), Yemen Warbler (Sylvia buryi).

Arabian Partridge

Regional sections have some birds which can be found in them.

CHAPTER 52
HISTORY

E vidence of human activity in Saudi Arabia dates back 1.8million years, in the form of stone tools. The northwest seems an especially rich area in evidence of early humans; perhaps the 'Out of Africa' Sinai Peninsula land bridge route fed south. In AlUla, south of the town, a 200,000-year-old hand axe has been found at Qarah (Qurh) site, near the Al Mubiyat Umayyad site. Bones from Homo Sapiens have been excavated in northwest Saudi dating back 85,000 years – part of the 'Out of Africa' migration flows during the Middle Palaeolithic (300,000-30,000ya. Hints of permanent settlements include evidence of stone workings from 40,000+ years ago (Mousterian period) on the mountain's summit at Jubbah. The rock art for which Jubbah is known dates from 10,000 years ago. Historically known figures appear more recently. At Tayma in the north, two cartouches of the Pharaoh Rameses III (1186–1155BC) have been found. Major ancient civilisations included Dilmun in the late 4th – mid 1st MillenniumBC. Following his military sweep through the Lebanese Mountains and down to Dedan, the Babylonian King Nabonidus lived in Tayma for almost 10 years in the 6th centuryBC. During the 1st millenniumBC, a series of trading towns grew in Arabia, connecting the southern coast with the Mediterranean. Frankincense, Indigo and Indian Spices were crucial elements of the trade. These included Sumhuram, Shibam, Shabwa and Marib. Towns that are now in modern Saudi Arabia include Najran, Madinah, Hegra and Tabuk. The land route ended at Gaza & Alexandria.

The Nabataeans ruled in the north-west between the 1st century BC - AD106, creating the impressive rock-cut tombs at Hegra. Following the Roman occupation of Egypt in 30BC and Hegra & Petra in AD106, sea trade became more important, with ports on both sides of the Red Sea catering to the trade. The Farasan Islands had a Roman garrison around AD144. There were a range of ports on the coast in modern Saudi included Caunana/ Kentos Kome and Khor al-Humara near Qunfudhah, and Leuke Kome north of Duba. These ports were used on the trade from Southern Arabia and beyond.

In the 7th century AD, Arabia was unified under Islam, which had originated in the western Arabian cities of Makkah and Madinah. The Islamic empire rapidly expanded to Morocco – and Central Asia under the rule of Islamic caliphates and empires, including the Rashidun, Umayyad and Abbasid.

In central Arabia, the Banu Al Ukhaidhir was a dynasty that claimed descent from the Prophet Mohammed through his daughter Fatima and her son Al Hassan. They established themselves in AD867 at Al-Yamamah, near modern Riyadh. The Qarmatians from Eastern Arabia developed over a century into an Ismaili Islamic state from AD899-1077. They then became the overlords of the Banu Al Ukhaidhirs. The second Qarmatian ruler, Abu Tahir Sulayman Al Jannabi, successfully raided Makkah from Hofuf in AD930 and took the Black Stone, the rock set into the Kaaba, back; this was then returned to the Abbasid state for an annual tribute. The Abbasids eventually defeated the Qarmatians.

In the west, the Abbasid caliph granted the Tulind dynasty of Egypt rule over Hijaz in 868. Descendants of the Prophet Mohammed, called Sharifs, conquered Makkah around 967. Following the Fatimid conquest of Egypt in 969, the Sharif of Makkah, Jafar bin Muhammad al-Hasani - acknowledged the Fatimid Caliph Al Muizz as his suzerain. From this date Egypt and its rulers played an increasingly dominant role in the Hijaz. All Sharifs of Makkah descend from Jafar bin Muhammad al-Hasani. They usually acknowledged the suzerainty of the rulers of Egypt, who from 1517 were the Ottoman Sultans.

The lands of the Qarmatian state were subsumed by a local Arab dynasty, Al Uyunid, from 1078, one of the early, almost tribal, rulers of eastern Arabia. Several dynasties succeeded the Al Uyunid, notably the Bani Khalid, who were followed by the Al Saud during the period after 1727.

The origins of the modern state of Saudi Arabia lie in central Arabia and with Muhammad bin Saud (1727–1765). He allied with the religious leader Mohammad bin Abdul Wahhab, combining his military capability and Mohammad bin Abdul Wahhab's religious persuasion. This was known as the Emirate of Diriyah, or First Saudi State. The Emirate expanded – and neighbouring rulers had to pay tribute to avoid further attacks. Raids eventually reached Makkah and the Shia Muslim holy city of Karbala in Iraq – both at least nominally under Ottoman rule. Al Saud rule lasted 8 years in Makkah, and pilgrims from Ottoman lands (Cairo, Damascus and Istanbul) were prohibited from entry in 1807.

To reimpose Ottoman authority in 1807, the Ottoman Sultan instructed the new (from 1805) governor of Ottoman Egypt, Mohammed Ali Pasha, to attack the Al Saud. Mohammed Ali Pasha was yet to consolidate his grip on power in Egypt. The rapid turnover in the Ottoman Sultan's, in 1808 there had been three in little over a year, must have also influenced his attention to this venture. However, by 1811, Egyptian forces landed at Yanbu, and by January 1813, Makkah was captured. After battles across west and central Arabia, the Al Saud were defeated, and their capital, Diriyah, was destroyed in late 1818. The ruler, Abdullah bin Saud Al Saud, was brought to Istanbul and executed.

From this seemingly irrecoverable defeat, Turki bin Abdullah bin Mohammed Al Saud, grandson of the dynasty's founder, re-established power in 1824. This time in Riyadh, 18 km southeast of Diriyah. Again, territorial gains were rapidly made, and tributes were obtained from neighbouring rulers. As a power broker, Faisal bin Turki bin Abdullah Al Saud, who first took power in 1834, supported the rise of the Al Rashid dynasty in Hail from 1836. However, Faisal was opposed by a cousin and Egyptian forces, and he was exiled to Cairo in 1838. Remarkably, he returned a few years later and took power until he died in 1865. During Faisal's reign, Britain became a diplomatic and then economic supporter of the Al Saud rulers. Internecine Al Saud family feuds enabled the Al Rashid ruler, Muhammad bin Abdullah Al Rashid, to conquer Riyadh in 1891. The Al Saud family were exiled again, this time to Kuwait.

In 1902 Amir AbdulAziz bin Abdulrahman Al Saud left Kuwait and retook Riyadh with a force of 60men. Once more, subsequent territorial expansion was rapid. The tribal force, the Ikhwan, who were religiously fundamental, played a vital role in this expansion. Several battles consolidated the core Al Saud territory. By 1914, AlAhsa and Qatif on the Arabian Gulf coast were conquered. The Al Rashid were defeated, and Hail was occupied in 1921. British forces repelled a push into Jordan between 1922 and 1924. The Hijaz and southwest were gradually occupied from 1924 when, by 3 September, Taif was conquered. Makkah was taken on 5 December, and after a siege, Jeddah fell on 23 December 1925. Between 1927 & 1930, the Ikhwan appeared to throw off Al Saud command and raided into Jordan and Iraq. They were defeated after the decisive battle of Sabilla in 1929, making King AbdulAziz the undisputed ruler. Finally, the modern Kingdom of Saudi Arabia, as it is known today, results from the Treaty of Taif of June 1934, following the 1934 Saudi-Yemeni war. This confirmed Najran and Jizan as being within Saudi Arabia. It goes without saying that the name Saudi Arabia is a constant reminder of the Al Saud family's position within the country.

Oil was the ultimate key to consolidating power. Following oil discoveries in Bahrain, the Saudi area of Dhahran, 40 km northwest of the island, became a focus for oil exploration as its geology is similar. Oil in commercial quantity was found on 3 March 1938 in what is now well within the urban area of Dhahran. Export facilities were rapidly constructed, and on 1 May 1939, the first exports started from the peninsula at Ras Tanura.

Saudi Arabia has been ruled by the sons of King AbdulAziz since his death in November 1953. King Salman bin Abdulaziz has ruled since 2015.

CHAPTER 53

ISLAM

I slam is a major world monotheistic religion established during the life of the
Prophet Muhammad in Arabia in the 7th centuryAD. Muslims believe that Islam is
the final and complete word of God (Allah) to humanity and that Muhammad is the
last prophet. There are 24 earlier prophets, including Jesus & Noah. Muslims believe in
the singularity of God (Allah), angels, scriptures, prophets, judgement day and divine
decree. They do not believe that God, Jesus and the Holy Sprit are in essence the same
entity. These beliefs are expressed in the declaration of faith (shahada), the first and
most important of the five Pillars of Islam. The other four pillars are prayer (Salat),
giving a % of wealth as charitable donations (Zakat), fasting (Sawm) during the daylight
hours of Ramadhan and pilgrimage once in a lifetime to Makkah (Hajj). These pillars
are the core practices of Islam that show the submission of Muslims to the will of Allah.
Mecca is spelt Makkah in Saudi Arabia, and therefore in this book.

The history of Islam and the singularity of Allah (God) begins with Muhammad's
first revelation in Makkah around AD610. He then faced persecution and opposition
from his own tribe, the Quraysh, who worshipped idols and controlled the Kaaba, a
sacred shrine that Muslims believe was built in Makkah by Abraham (Ibrahim is the
spelling used in the Islamic world) and his son Ishmael. In AD622, Muhammad and his
followers migrated to Madinah, establishing the first Islamic community. This event,
known as the Hijra, marks the beginning of the Islamic calendar. In Madinah,
Muhammad received more revelations and consolidated his authority as a political and
religious leader. He fought several battles against the Quraysh tribe and other enemies
until he finally conquered Makkah in AD630 and destroyed idols around the Kaaba. He
died in AD632.

After Prophet Muhammad's death, his companions selected Abu Bakr
(Mohammed's father-in-law) as his successor (caliph). He faced several challenges from
rebellious tribes and people claiming to be a prophet. Abu Bakr unified Arabia under
Islam and increased the expansion of the Islamic empire. He was followed by Umar,

Uthman and Ali. These first four Caliphs are collectively known as the Rashidun/Rightly Guided Caliphs (632-661) by Sunni Muslims. However, their rule was also marked by internal conflicts and civil wars, especially regarding succession and leadership. These disputes led to the emergence of sects in Islam; the major ones are Sunni, Shia and Ibadhi. All have belief in the fact that the Prophet Mohammed is the last prophet of God, Jesus & Abraham being among earlier prophets. Sunni and Ibadhi Muslims believe that any qualified Muslim can be a caliph. In contrast, Shia Muslims believe that only descendants of Muhammad through his cousin and son-in-law Ali, and therefore also descended from Mohammed's daughter Fatima, who married Ali, can be legitimate leaders.

Within Sunni Islam, Wahhabism is a movement that follows the teachings of Muhammad bin Abd Al Wahhab, an 18th-century cleric. Wahhabism aims to purify Islam from innovations (bidah) and idolatry (shirk) by returning to the original sources of the Quran and the Sunnah. Wahhabism follows the Hanbali school of thought, founded in the 9th century, which is one of the four primary schools of Sunni Islamic jurisprudence. The Hanbali school is considered the most conservative and literalist among the Sunni schools. It relies on the Quran and the hadiths as sources of law and rejects analogical reasoning (qiyas) and consensus (ijma) as secondary sources. In Saudi Arabia the Hanbali school is the official doctrine.

The Islamic empire reached its peak under the subsequent Umayyad (661–750) and Abbasid (750 and 1258) dynasties, which principally ruled from Damascus and Baghdad, respectively. They expanded Islam to North Africa, Spain, Central Asia, India and beyond, creating a diverse and flourishing civilisation that excelled in science, art, literature, philosophy, law and trade. However, they also faced challenges from internal divisions, external invasions, political corruption, and social unrest. The vast empire gradually fragmented into smaller states and dynasties, such as the Fatimids in Egypt, the Al Moravids in Morocco, the Ghaznavids in Afghanistan and India, the Seljuks focused on Persia, and the Ottomans in Turkey.

Today, Islam is one of the largest and the fastest growing religions, primarily due to continuingly high birth rates. It has over 1.8 billion followers who belong to various branches, schools, movements, and traditions within Islam.

Practically all Saudi Nationals will profess absolutely the belief in all the appropriate tenants of Islam.

CHAPTER 54
GLOSSARY

Thank you for buying this Saudi guide
"Saudi Arabia: Travel Guide (Not Including Makkah)"
If you found it useful, please leave a review.
with the retailer you purchased it from
As we are not a big publisher
it will help us know what we need to improve
and more importantly, let others know if it's right for them compared to other Saudi
guides.
THANK YOU 🙏
Ibn Al Hamra

There are feminine endings to masculine nouns in Arabic, typically with an 'a' at the end of the word – however the meaning would usually be clear with the usual masculine word. There are, however, nouns whose only ending is always feminine – such as car 'sayaara'. Other words would never, currently, have a feminine ending, such as Imam.

Abu - father

Ain - spring of water. In non-Gulf states, it only refers to an eye, which it can also do in The Gulf

Al Wudu - ablution ritual washing before prayer as prescribed by the Quran.

Amir/Emir - Has several meanings – Prince, Governor, Military commander. It can also be used as a man's name. There is a feminine version Amira – Princess, etc. In Saudi it is the Prince version that will typically be meant. The style "His/Her Royal Highness" is used by sons & daughters of King AbdulAziz and his patrilineal grandchildren – and presumably other generations. King Faisal's family might use Al Faisal Al Saud. Cadet Al Saud branches, including Al Kabir, Al Jiluwi, Al Thunayan, Al Mishari and Al Farhan, use His/Her Highness. Elsewhere in The Gulf, the head of state in Kuwait & Qatar use the title, Amir. The King of Bahrain previously used Amir as his title. Though in The Gulf, Amir is the usual English spelling – Emirate is used for the airline and state governed by an Amir.

Bab - gate, door, entrance etc

Bahr - sea

Bait - house

Bani - tribal prefix meaning 'sons (children) of xyz' in Arabic.

Bedouin - desert nomads

Bin - (also ibn) son

Bint - daughter

Broast – a restaurant offering Kentucky style chicken.

Bustan - garden

Caliph - A religious/political person who claims succession to the Prophet Mohammed. Examples include the first four Islamic rulers after the Prophet Mohammed, the Fatimids, and Ottomans.

Dhow - generic term for any traditional Arab wooden boat

Eid - religious holiday

Hadith - collection of records from the Prophet Muhammad's lifetime.

Hajj – a religious obligation, if possible, of pilgrimage to Makkah during the lifetime of a Muslim. There are number restrictions, the largest number was 3.2 million in 2013.

Hajji - It is a common honorific for a person who has completed the Hajj. Within Saudi Arabia, this may have a lower prestige than it will in other, more distant, Islamic populations.

Imam - It is a leadership position associated with Islam. In Saudi Arabia, it was the honorific used by the Al Saud ruler in the 19th/18th century, indicating their religious authority. Today, it is used for the leader of the mid-day Friday prayers. Most (all) of these leaders will be appointed or approved by the government. The most prominent appointment by the government is the Imam of the Masjid Al Haram in Makkah. There may be several Imams at this mosque at any one time – they also may be a Sheikh. Currently, all have appropriate PhDs. Usually referred to as His Excellency. Elsewhere, historically, it is also used for specific descendants of the son-in-law of the Prophet Mohammed, Ali bin Abi Talib.

Jabal - mountain

Jinn - a spirit attested to exist in the Quran.

Juzor/Jazirah - islands/island

Kabir - big

Malik – King - The rulers of Saudi Arabia have carried the title King since 1926 after the conquest of the previous Kingdom of the Hijaz. Since 23 September 1932, they have had the sole title - King of Saudi Arabia. The honorific is "The Custodian of the Two Holy Mosques" (in Makkah and Madinah). When referring, 'Your/His Majesty' is used. The word King (Malik) is from the root associated with absolute ownership & possession. The feminine is Malika and like sheikh and sheikha these names might be a person's forename.

Mihrab - the prayer niche in a mosque, which shows the direction of Makkah for prayer.

Mina - port

Minbar - pulpit in a mosque

Mufti - Specifically, this is a person who might issue religious opinions, for example, the Grand Mufti of Egypt, a government appointee. Usually referred to as His Excellency. It is more broadly used as an honorific for a religious person.

Qadi/Qadhi - A legal judge. Appointed by the government. Usually referred to as His Excellency.

Qahwa - Arabic coffee, see Page276

Ramadhan - Muslim month of fasting (Page6)

Sharia - Islamic law, according to the Quran and the Hadith – this is the foundation of law in Saudi Arabia

Sharif - In Saudi Arabia's history – this will generally refer to the rulers in the Hijaz. There were several families, each of whom might have ruled a particular town, Yanbu, Madinah, etc– all descended from the Prophet Mohammed's grandson, Hassan bin Ali. The Sharif of Makkah was pre-eminent and usually had the support of the external power, Fatimids, Ottomans, and even the British. A Sayyid refers to the descendants of another grandson, Hussain bin Ali. There is an exception in Oman, where it is exclusively used by members of the ruling family. Sayyid also simply means Mister.

Sharm - a ships anchorage. Today many of these have become leisure areas such as Sharm El Sheikh in Egypt.

Shatti - beach

Sheikh - In Saudi Arabia, a sheikh is a chief of a tribe, accepted by that tribe and the government. Typically, they are from within a hereditary family. There may be other members of the family also using the honorific. With larger tribes, the principal Sheikh will have considerable regional & national importance and might be called His Excellency. In some other Gulf Staes – a sheikh is only a member of the ruling family. The feminine ending gives sheikha. Both sheikh and sheikha are used as personal first names in many countries.

Shia - a branch of Islam, theoretically believing a hereditary principle of leadership from the son-in-law of the Prophet Mohammed, Ali bin Ab Talib

Souq - any place for shopping. In modern days with large shopping malls, the word souq is almost invariably used to mean a street area with places to shop or an ancient, covered, bazar.

Sultan - head of state in a Muslim country, referred to as His Majesty. As with many other titles the masculine & feminine endings (sultana) are used for personal names.

Sunni – a branch of Islam theoretically believing that the finest Muslim should be the leader. In Saudi Arabia, the Sunni Ḥanbali school of thought, founded by Aḥmad bin Ḥanbal (8th centuryAD), is followed.

Sura - chapter of the Quran

Umm - mother.

Umrah – a voluntary pilgrimage to Makkah. It is comparable to the Hajj in terms of what is involved and is most commonly undertaken, during Ramadhan or the months immediately before. It however may be taken at any time.

Wadi - natural watercourse, some are short, at only a few kilometres, others long as the Wadi Al Nile, it might be shallow or a deep valley or canyon.

Wazir - A government minister. Usually referred to as His/Her Excellency. The feminine is wazira.

Brief phrases that are easy to remember

GREETINGS

As-salaam alaykum, meaning literally 'May peace be upon you.
Hello, welcome — marhaba, ahlan
Goodbye — maa as-salaama the phrase As-salaam 'alaykum can be used if needed
Some other words to use
Yes — aiwa, naam
No — laa
Please — min fadlak
Thank — youshukran
Thank you very much — shukran jazeelan
You're welcome — afwan
Sorry, excuse me — muta assif, afwan,
Hurry up, let's go — yallah
Is it possible? May I? — mumkin?
My name is — ana ismee ...
What is your name? — min ismak?
I don't understand — ana maa afham
Where are you from? — min wayn inta?

ARABIC NUMERALS

1 ١ (Wahid)
2 ٢ (Ithnan)
3 ٣ (Thalathah)
4 ٤ (Arbaah)
5 ٥ (Khamsah)
6 ٦ (Sittah)
7 ٧ (Sabah)
8 ٨ (Thamaniyah)
9 ٩ (Tisah)
10 ١٠ (Asharah)
20 ٢٠ (Ishrun)
30 ٣٠ (Thalathun)
40 ٤٠ (Arbaun)
50 ٥٠ (Khamsun)
60 ٦٠ (Sittun)
70 ٧٠ (Sabun)
80 ٨٠ (Thamanun)
90 ٩٠ (Tisun)
100 ١٠٠ (Miah)
110 ١١٠ (Miah wa asharah)

120 ١٢٠ (Miah wa ishrun)

INDEX

Index.

Printed in Great Britain
by Amazon

46293420R00185